DATA STORES,
DATA WAREHOUSING,
AND THE
ZACHMAN
FRAMEWORK

OTHER McGRAW-HILL BOOKS OF INTEREST

To order or receive additional information on these or any other McGraw-Hill titles, please call 1-800-822-8158 in the United States. In other countries, contact your local McGraw-Hill representative.   **WM16XXA**

Data Stores, Data Warehousing, and the Zachman Framework
Managing Enterprise Knowledge

W. H. Inmon

John A. Zachman

Jonathan G. Geiger

McGraw-Hill
New York   San Francisco   Washington, D.C.
Auckland   Bogotá   Caracas   Lisbon   London
Madrid   Mexico City   Milan   Montreal
New Delhi   San Juan   Singapore   Sydney
Tokyo   Toronto

Library of Congress Cataloging-in-Publication Data

Inmon, William H.
　　Data stores, data warehousing, and the Zachman Framework : managing
enterprise knowledge / W. H. Inmon, John A. Zachman, Jonathan G. Geiger.
　　　　p.　　cm.
　　Includes biographical references and index.
　　ISBN 0-07-031429-2
　　1. Database management.　2. Management information systems.　I.
Zachman, John A.　II. Geiger, Jonathan G.　III. Title.
　QA76.9.D315376　1997
　005.74'068—dc21　　　　　　　　　　　　　　　　　　　　97-1276
　　　　　　　　　　　　　　　　　　　　　　　　　　　　　　CIP

McGraw-Hill

A Division of The **McGraw·Hill** *Companies*

1 2 3 4 5 6 7 8 9 0　FGR/FGR　9 0 2 1 0 9 8 7

ISBN 0-07-031429-2

The sponsoring editor for this book was John Wyzalek, the editing supervisor was Caroline R. Levine, and the production supervisor was Claire Stanley.
This book was set in Vendome by Priscilla Beer of McGraw-Hill's Professional Book Group composition unit.

Printed and bound by Quebcor/Fairfield.

McGraw-Hill books are available at special quantity discounts to use as premi-
ums and sales promotions, or for use in corporate training programs. For more
information, please write to the Director of Special Sales, McGraw-Hill, 11 West
19th Street, New York, NY 10011. Or contact your local bookstore.

 This book is printed on recycled, acid-free paper containing
a minimum of 50% recycled de-inked fiber.

CONTENTS

V

Contents

PART THREE   APPLICATIONS

Contents

Contents

FOREWORD

John Zachman is the foremost expert on comprehensive architectures for Information Technology. His profound work, culminating in the Zachman Framework, has been the cornerstone for many IT departments struggling with the difficult problems of building, integrating, and maintaining their complex systems.

For years, John spoke to individual companies, in seminars and conferences the world over, educating and entertaining us with his brilliance. And for years, people have begged him to write "the book" on the Zachman Framework. I am so very pleased to say that—at long last—the book has indeed been written.

The integration of John's framework with Bill Inmon's important work in data warehousing and operational data stores is an unbeatable combination. Their ideas mesh perfectly giving all of us the ideal roadmap to build our operational systems and strategic decision support systems. Now we have the complete architecture from which to build sustainable systems.

Finally, it is the practical experiences from Jonathan Geiger that provide us with the real-world advice on implementing the Framework. His pragmatic additions to the book reflect the many data warehouses and operational systems he has built using the Zachman Framework and Inmon methodology. His recommendations are of the highest quality.

I hope that you find this book to be as useful as I do. It is, without a doubt, one of the most important books published for IT professionals everywhere. Thank you, John, Bill, and Jonathan, for providing us with such a valuable addition to our IT libraries!

—CLAUDIA IMHOFF
PRESIDENT AND FOUNDER
INTELLIGENT SOLUTIONS, INC.

PREFACE

Data . . . Information . . . Knowledge. There is a difference.

As companies prepare to move into the twenty-first century, data and information alone will not suffice. Knowledge will be one of the distinguishing assets of successful corporations. Data simply reflects details found throughout a company, and information provides meaning to the data. Knowledge entails the synthesis of information to provide a corporate entity with an improved awareness and understanding of itself, its human and other resources, and its business environment. Armed with this wisdom, companies will be better prepared to compete in an ever-changing global economy.

The data warehouse, operational data store, and client/server systems have been instrumental in helping companies obtain, manage, and leverage data, transforming it into valuable information. These concepts have been made possible through the integration of advances in database management systems, programming and data access languages, computer hardware and software, and communications facilities. These technologies, by themselves, do not yield the right information . . . at the right time . . . at the right place . . . in the right form. To achieve that end, to consistently convert information into knowledge, companies need to adopt an architected approach.

The state of computer utilization evolved with changes in technology. Companies adopted more powerful computers, computer terminals, client/server tools, database management systems, and the like, to improve productivity and to process data into information. With this technology-driven approach, companies moved through three generations of an evolving computer environment. The Formation Generation introduced the computer to the commercial sector. Recognizing its value, companies expended great sums of money on additional computers and support personnel and facilities, leading to a Proliferation Generation. Money alone did not overcome the unsatiable demand for computer applications. As the backlog grew, business units took matters into their own hands and built their own systems. The Dispersion Generation is typified by widespread use of computers throughout the company without a focused effort directed toward managing them.

Clearly, a better approach is needed. That approach, the Unification

Generation, requires a shift in management emphasis. Companies must shift from managing the computer and the associated technologies to managing the environment within which the computers operate and to managing data as a corporate resource. With this shift, the vast amount of bits and bytes contained in a company's computers can be transformed from data into information, and from information into knowledge.

The Zachman Framework provides the foundation for architecting such an environment. Developed by observing work performed in other disciplines, the Framework addresses all aspects of the Enterprise as a whole and of the Enterprise as viewed by the information technology organization. An architecture such as the one provided by the Framework is required to satisfy modern needs. This architecture enables companies to evolve from their legacy system environment into one which employs data warehouses, operational data stores, and client/server technology to meet their changing needs in a competitive environment.

This book is divided into three Parts. In Part One, the importance of architecture is stressed, and the evolution of the computer environment is traced through the four generations. This review of history points out why some of the approaches of the past have failed, and how an architected environment can help.

Part Two describes the Zachman Framework and demonstrates its role in transforming the traditional *data administration* and *information resource management* role into a *knowledge management* role. The transformation is illustrated by describing the application of the Framework as a generic thinking tool for improving understanding and for making better decisions about designing and managing change for any complex object. In this context, the complex object may be a product, the enterprise itself, the architecture of the enterprise, or the knowledge base of the enterprise.

After describing the Zachman Framework and its transformation role, the Framework is applied directly to develop a strategy and methodology for building and managing data warehouses. Within these chapters, concrete examples of guiding principles and model components are developed. The foundation laid through the Framework enables companies to extend their data warehouse as a means for building an architected knowledge management environment.

Part Three applies the first parts. First, the Framework-based methodology is used to develop a data warehouse. The value of the architected approach is then demonstrated as the complexity of the data warehouse increases, and as the information gained from its development is used to build an operational data store. The Framework is then used to help define the metadata needs. Chapter 11 portrays the data warehouse and operational data as a means to an end. Using the Framework, these serve as a foundation to help companies migrate to an architected environment which supports processes and systems that are engineered to meet the challenges posed by the dynamic business environment.

The book is designed primarily for managers who are interested in improving the management of complex technological environments. It emphasizes the criticality of an architecture-based approach and provides a conceptual description of the Zachman Framework as the basis for gaining greater business value from information systems and electronic databases. Parts Two and Three are also aimed at the practitioner. After developing a Framework-based strategy and methodology in Chaps. 5 and 6, respectively, the value of the Framework is applied toward building a data warehouse and an operational data store, migrating systems to a new environment, and supporting reengineering efforts and total quality management. This book explains key concepts and their importance and provides information to assist practitioners in understanding the critical steps in the process.

There are many people who have contributed directly and indirectly to this effort. The authors wish to acknowledge particularly the following individuals for their contributions:

- Jim Ashbrook, Prism Solutions
- Arnie Barnett, Barnett Data Systems
- Genevieve Blair
- Jeff Colen, Club Runner
- Larry English, Information Impact International
- Lowell Fryman, Intelligent Solutions
- Tom Hokel, Framework Software
- Sam Holcman, Pinnacle Systems
- David Houssian, Utility Partners
- Claudia Imhoff, Intelligent Solutions
- John Ladley, META Group
- Sue Osterfelt, NationsBank
- Ron Ross, *Database Newsletter*
- Phil Seeger, Florida Power & Light
- Ron Shelby, American Express

- Ben Stern, Israel Electric
- Bill Wallace, Cambridge Technologies
- J. D. Welch, DataWing Consulting Services
- Ed Young, D2K

The number of companies which are using the Zachman Framework is continuously increasing. In 1995, the Zachman Institute for Framework Advancement (ZIFA) in Pinkney, Michigan was formed to provide a forum for companies to build on each others' successes in applying the Framework. Over 100 people attended the first ZIFA conference in June 1996. The energy level of the participants was exhilarating. The message was clear: Architecture is not an option—it is a mandate for companies which want to survive and thrive in the twenty-first century. Additional information about the Framework and its application can be obtained by contacting the Institute directly through the Internet at www.zifa.com.

—W. H. INMON
JOHN A. ZACHMAN
JONATHAN G. GEIGER

DATA STORES, DATA WAREHOUSING, AND THE ZACHMAN FRAMEWORK

PART 1

The Need
for an
Architecture

1

A Look at History with a View to the Future

One of the keys to success for modern corporations is access to the right information at the right time at the right place in the right form. Figure 1-1 illustrates the four generations of computer evolution. The current third-generation computer environment is often failing to provide the level of data access needed by modern competitive companies. Within the third generation, companies have succeeded in transforming data into information, but the quest for knowledge remains elusive. The lessons learned through an analysis of the first three generations help define the framework for a fourth generation for companies who want to thrive—not just survive—in the twenty-first century.

Figure 1-1
Four Generations of
Computer Evolution.

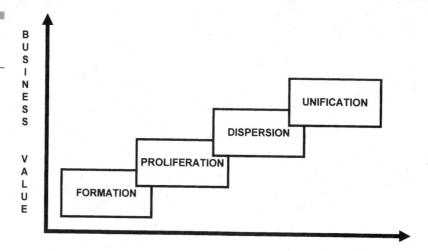

This chapter traces the progression through the first three generations which evolved with technology. Throughout this evolution, companies were provided with often-ignored signals about the importance of pursuing an architectural approach. Chapter 2 deals with the fourth generation, which must be management driven. It explains the importance of the architectural approach and how the combination of knowledge and technology can help companies gain or keep a competitive advantage.

Four Generations

During the first generation of the computer environment (1950s to early 1970s), the computer was introduced and was used primarily to improve the efficiency of selected tasks using tools and techniques which today would be considered primitive. Companies got a taste of what the computer could do, but their appetites were left unsatisfied, despite significant expenditures for new technologies.

In the second generation (1960s to 1980s), application of the computer within business proliferated, and business people were able to interact with the computer through terminals to improve both efficiency and effectiveness. The computer was doing more, but the appetites of users were even bigger and the backlog of unsatisfied requests grew. Users throughout the company began exercising different options to satisfy their demands.

In the current third-generation environment (1980s to 1990s), computer components are being dispersed throughout corporations, and the business community is encountering numerous challenges as it strives to gain the benefits which can be provided. Attempts to satisfy the growing appetite for information are often not effectively managed, resulting in increased costs and redundancy without the desired productivity improvements or data access. Left unchecked, the resulting chaos could eventually cripple the enterprise.

In the fourth generation, which is being pursued by progressive companies, the corporate information resources are unified from a business perspective and dispersed from a physical and technological perspective. In this architected environment, the redundancy is managed, and knowledge is obtained by successfully providing the required information when, where, and how it is needed.

Formation

Computers were first developed for military purposes during World War II, with their commercial introduction coming in the early 1950s. Early application systems were developed primarily to improve the efficiency of operational processes, thereby enabling companies to reduce operating expenses by either reducing staffing levels or increasing the volume of work performed by existing personnel. Examples of typical systems developed during this period are shown in Fig. 1-2.

The builders of these early systems faced numerous limitations, the foremost of which was that this was virgin territory. The technology was, by today's standards, primitive; the programming languages were

Figure 1-2
Application Systems during Formation.

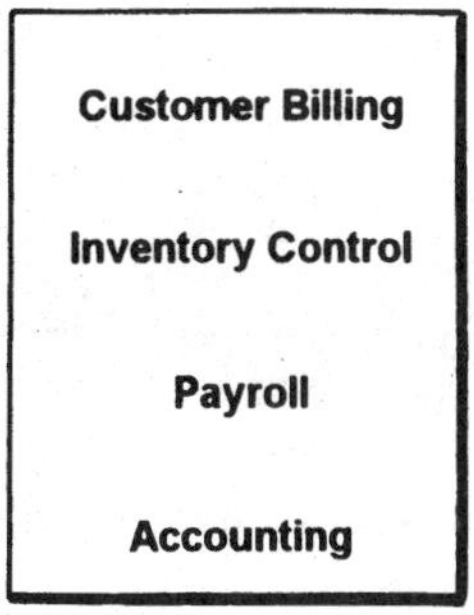

| Customer Billing |
| Inventory Control |
| Payroll |
| Accounting |

in the process of being created; and there was no accepted, established discipline for either developing computer systems or for using the computer.

The focus during the first generation was on harnessing data in its most primitive form.

Computer Technology

The first computer built in the United States was the Electronic Numeric Integrator and Computer (ENIAC), which was developed during the early 1940s by John V. Mauchly and J. Presper Eckert. While the ENIAC was not practical for commercial purposes, its inventors firmly believed in the commercial viability of computers and were largely responsible for the development of the UNIVAC computer which was delivered to the United States Bureau of the Census in June 1951. Enthusiasm for the UNIVAC was lukewarm, until, in the 1952 presidential election, its practical application for processing data was demonstrated when it accurately projected the electoral college results less than an hour after the polls closed.

During the early years of computing, the computer was technically very complex and required that all operations be performed within a physically interconnected, environmentally controlled area. The power of the computer was largely controlled by the specialists in charge of the computer operation.

Data Management

Database management systems were virtually nonexistent during the early days of computing. Corporate data was stored in the form of master files, and these master files were stored first on cards and then on magnetic tape. A major limitation of these data storage devices was that they needed to be traversed sequentially. To select a particular record of data required either knowing its location (e.g., fifth record) or knowing a sufficient portion of its content (e.g., record type identifier and employee number) to uniquely identify it. Without a database management system to locate data through other means, adding data usually required the creation of a new set of records. The subsequent development of index-based access methods and database management systems enhanced companies' abilities to manage electronic data.

Programming Languages

During most of the 1950s, programming of computers was done using either machine languages (frequently called first generation) or assembly languages (frequently called second generation). Commonly used third-generation languages such as FORTRAN and COBOL were developed in the late 1950s and early 1960s. FORTRAN (FORmula TRANslator) was developed by a team led by John Backus. This language was aimed at the engineering and scientific community, and one of its primary objectives was to improve programmer productivity. COBOL (COmmon Business Oriented Language) was developed to help the rest of the business community to use the computer. One of its primary objectives was standardization, with a major design consideration being that COBOL programs developed on one computer should be able to operate on another computer.

In a sense, Grace Hopper, who led the COBOL development team, should be credited for introducing the concept of architecture into the programming arena.

Methodology

During the early days of commercial computer use, formal methodologies were virtually nonexistent. Computer-related work was considered to be new, and analogies to other disciplines were not prevalent. Eventually, a group of methodologies commonly called *waterfall* evolved. These methodologies typically consisted of a phase in which the requirements were defined, followed by specifications, followed by development, followed by implementation, followed by maintenance. (See Fig. 1-3.)

The term waterfall was derived from the formal handoffs which took place at the end of each phase. The resulting systems development life cycle brought some discipline to systems development. Largely due to technological limitations, strict adherence to the defined life cycle resulted in very lengthy development cycles which did not meet the needs of

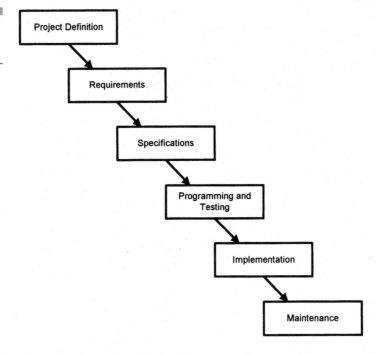

Figure 1-3
Waterfall Methodology.

the impatient business users. As a result, shortcuts were often taken, and with these shortcuts, any hope of an architected foundation to information management dissipated.

Assessment

Businesses got a taste of the power of the computer, but with it came a taste of the potential problems. In the resultant systems environment each system controlled its own data. (See Fig. 1-4.)

The complexity of the computer and the programming languages required people with specialized skills to develop and operate the systems, leading to the birth of the data-processing department. The very name of the department—*data* processing—served to describe and sometimes limit the focus of the early applications.

Almost from the start, the data-processing department was doomed to failure.

- Development cycles were very long.
- Response times could be measured in days.

Figure 1-4
Systems Environment
during Formation.

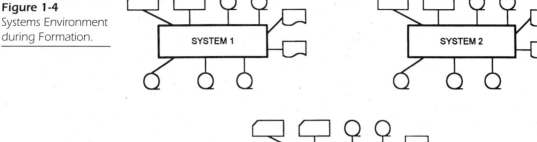

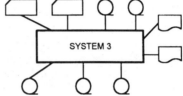

- Business needs were not met in a timely manner.
- Expenditures for data processing were constantly growing.

While many of the factors contributing to the problems were outside the control of the data-processing department, its management did not communicate effectively with corporate management.

From a business perspective, a potentially powerful tool existed, but the people responsible for applying it to benefit the company were generally unresponsive.

Top management's frustration began to grow, and with it came an attempt to solve the problem by spending money on it. (See Fig. 1-5.)

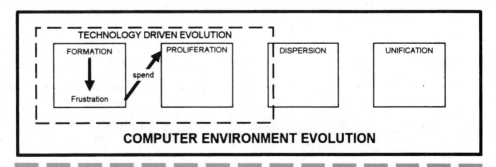

Figure 1-5 Transition to Proliferation.

Proliferation

While there is no clear line of demarcation between the first- and second-generation information environments, the second-generation environment can be characterized by the widespread proliferation of computer applications. Business applications began to address more than just the efficiency of the work; they provided functionality which added to the value of the tasks performed. Systems which focused on efficiency migrated to ones which focused on effectiveness and work management. (See Fig. 1-6.)

The change in focus marked the recognition of the value of information over data.

The shift in emphasis and value was made possible by the emergence and adoption of database management systems, scientific techniques for application development which emphasized an engineering approach and active participation of the business users' programming standards, increased levels of power within the mainframe computer, and the advent of the computer terminal.

Computer Technology

Computer technology evolved very quickly. The advent of the computer terminal was perhaps the most significant innovation from the business user's perspective. No longer was everything on the computer performed behind closed doors; no longer would it take days to get an answer from the computer. Business people could actually interact with computers and provide customers with answers while talking to the customers. (See Fig. 1-7.)

Figure 1-6
Application Systems
during Proliferation.

Figure 1-7
Computer Terminal
Use.

A more subtle impact of the computer terminal was the inherent shift in control from the people operating the computer to the people programming and using it. Programs and transactions were now executed when the people at the terminals issued the appropriate commands.

The transfer of control presented new challenges to the management of the computer resources.

During the early 1990s Michael Hammer and James Champy emphasized the role of technology as an enabler in helping companies to reengineer themselves. The computer terminal was such a technology. Some companies resisted the move to computer terminals unless concrete productivity improvements could be shown. Progressive companies which recognized the potential of this innovation for improving customer service and embraced the new technology had a distinct advantage over the more cautious companies.

Data Management

The emergence of database management systems provided companies with the opportunity to more effectively separate program logic from data handling logic. The database management system itself contained facilities to manage the physical location of the data within the database. The programmer no longer needed to be concerned with this information and could be shielded from most changes within the physical database that did not impact the specific data being sought.

This is analogous to a filing system in which the clerk would need to know which file cabinet and which drawer contained the desired document, but within the drawer, the position of the document did not need to be known to retrieve it. It differs from the previous methods of storing and retrieving data, in which the location within the drawer also had to be known.

While others existed, two major database topologies were widely adopted—the hierarchical structure and the relational structure. Within the hierarchical structure, the organization of the data permits a reasonable degree of reusability. The data is arranged in a treelike fashion, with the root segment being analogous to the trunk of the tree. Access to a specific set of data (e.g., information about an employee named Jim Jones) was direct. Access to the desired data element (e.g., job classification in 1970) required traversing through the base hierarchy or a modification of it. In the hierarchical structure, the database is analogous to the file cabinet, the segment corresponds to the drawer, and the field or element is equivalent to the document.

The relational structure, on the other hand, presents data as a series of matrices called tables. The columns identify the different data elements, while the rows represent the data records. Tables could be related to each other through the use of common fields as keys. With this structure, appropriate sets of data could be grouped and indexed so that not only was access to the major grouping direct, access to the subgroup was also direct. In the relational structure, the database is analogous to the file cabinet, the table corresponds to the drawer, and the intersection of a row and a column is equivalent to the document.

While database management systems in general facilitated the separation of the physical data handling logic from the processing logic, relational database management concepts enabled the practical implementation of many aspects of a comprehensive data resource management program.

Tools were becoming available to manage information as a resource, but few companies took effective action to govern this valuable asset.

Programming Languages

With the advent of third-generation programming languages, the programming task itself became much easier. While numerous languages existed, COBOL quickly became a standard for business applications. Consistent with the standardization philosophy of COBOL itself, techniques for structuring the COBOL programs evolved. The structured programming techniques facilitated both the design of the initial program and its subsequent maintenance. The structure of the COBOL language provided for separating functions through the use of separate divisions for program identification, environment description, data definition, and process declaration. This structure, combined with the facilities inherent in the database management systems, provided the foundation for creating programs and program modules which could be reused.

The programming languages and database management systems supported architectural concepts such as separation of components, but these were often violated in practice.

Methodology

As companies became more and more dependent on computers for their operational and management activities, they searched for better ways to ensure that the systems performed the required tasks accurately. Data processing is not the first discipline to take a raw material and create a product. (See Fig. 1-8.)

In other, more mature disciplines, an engineering approach was employed—both to develop the process and to apply the process. Within the computer industry, numerous techniques to address portions of the process of developing systems were created, and many fit within the

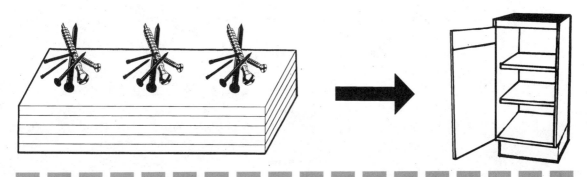

Figure 1-8 Product Creation Disciplines.

Figure 1-9
Information
Engineering Frame-
work.

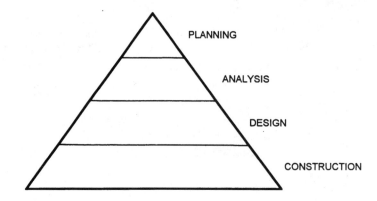

framework of *information engineering.* Information engineering provides a set of interlocking techniques which build on business, data, and process models to provide a comprehensive storehouse for creating and maintaining information systems. Its four major steps, as shown in Fig. 1-9, are:

- *Planning.* To define the scope of the problem or opportunity
- *Analysis.* To define what the solution needs to do
- *Design.* To specify how the solution will be developed
- *Construction.* To actually build the solution

The Information Engineering Framework brought with it the required discipline and a hope that an engineering approach would be used for application systems development. Computer-aided system engineering (CASE) tools evolved to support the systems development activities. To varying degrees, they enforced the consistency of different steps in the development processes. Expectations of the CASE tools were often inflated, and when organizations discovered the discipline which was needed for their effective application, they were often abandoned.

Repositories and data dictionaries, which stored information about the system and its development activities, also evolved. Data dictionaries focused on storing and providing limited information about the databases and their contents. Repositories provided a broader focus. These tools encompassed other artifacts which were defined by the common methodologies as being important. With the advent of *active repositories,* the tools absorbed a capability of being a control point for managing changes to the systems and databases.

Proper execution of the planning, analysis, and design steps reduced the life cycle cost of a system, but impatient users wanted results faster.

The pressure to produce systems quickly often prevailed, and shortcuts were taken. The impacts of these shortcuts sometimes actually lengthened the development process. The more significant impacts, however, frequently did not manifest themselves until after the system was implemented. These impacts included the inability of the system to meet the true business needs, its inflexibility to react to business changes in a timely fashion, and its incompatibility with other systems. Information engineering's emphasis on data and process also failed to adequately fully recognize other dimensions of the system, such as location, people, time, and motivation.

The emphasis on data and process, combined with the shortcuts taken during analysis, often combined to yield systems which met the stated needs but not the real business needs.

Assessment

The computer was integrated into the business. Few activities within a large corporation had no dependence on the computer during the 1970s and 1980s. But most of the problems of the first-generation business systems did not go away, and some became even more critical.

Instead of the islands of automation of the first-generation computer environment, companies now had to contend with a myriad of interconnected systems, employing multiple technologies, a variety of programming languages and database management systems, and incomplete or inaccurate documentation of the environment and its components. Some systems were created simply to provide interfaces to move data from one application to another. Three of the systems in Fig. 1-10 do just that—they have no direct interaction with the people who either provide or receive information.

Because of the complexity of the environment, a concentration of skilled people was still needed and the data-processing department continued. The business community continued to expect more and more from the computer as it saw the extent to which the computer could be used to improve both efficiency and effectiveness. In addition, because of the widespread business use of computers, college curriculums for engineering, business, and other fields, frequently included computer courses, thereby raising the computer literacy of the business community.

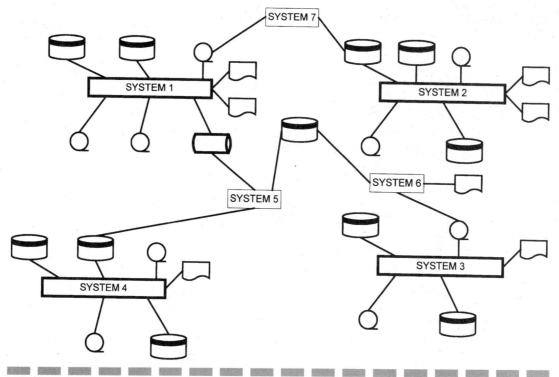

Figure 1-10　*Systems Environment during Proliferation.*

The perils of proceeding without an architecture were becoming visible. Many tools were in place:

■ Terminals provided people with the ability to better control their use of the computer. The use of the terminals removed a major barrier in terms of access to the computer and also increased the visibility of errors and processing delays.

■ Data storage devices provided the needed flexibility. The combination of disks and database management systems improved companies' abilities to both store and access data.

■ Database management systems, along with repositories and CASE tools provided the ability to manage data as a resource. With these tools, companies could catalog their data and could manage its acquisition, maintenance, use, and disposition.

■ Programming languages and techniques supported reuse of components through the segregation of the program components and the use of program modules.

- Methodologies and tools provided the means to implement well-designed systems for companies which recognized the benefits of adhering to them.

but

- Similar data was often entered multiple times into multiple systems, and complex interfaces were created to attempt to keep this data in sync.
- The required management structures were not effectively implemented to manage data as a resource and to reuse system components effectively.
- System maintenance resources grew dramatically and were consuming ever increasing portions of the people and computer capacity which would otherwise be available for new applications.
- Business needs were not being met in a timely manner.

Tools were becoming available for business users to perform simple tasks, and the level of frustration with the responsiveness of the data-processing department grew. The value of information over data was recognized, but the funding for major systems development projects was still largely dependent on a traditional cost-savings analysis. The new systems did provide some information, but the focus was on information about past events rather than on information to support strategic decisions.

The data-processing department continued to be frequently viewed as a department which was crucial to the business of the company but which did not understand that business. The business community began to use its available tools to satisfy its thirst for information, sometimes bypassing the data-processing department in the transition to Dispersion. (See Fig. 1-11.)

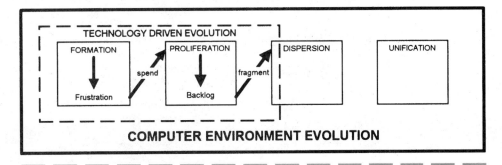

Figure 1-11   Transition to Dispersion.

Dispersion

The third-generation computer environment can be characterized by the explosive growth in the number of options available for meeting the almost insatiable need for information and by the dispersion of these options throughout the company. From an application perspective, the creation of systems to help improve efficiency and effectiveness continued, but new opportunities for harnessing the power of the computer were also being addressed. The most notable new applications were in the areas of workflow management and decision support. (See Fig. 1-12.)

Information was increasingly being recognized as a valuable strategic resource.

As was the case when moving to second-generation application systems, many companies attempted to move to third-generation application systems by building upon the existing systems. While this was an expedient solution, it frequently resulted in situations in which systems were forced to perform tasks for which they were not designed. There was no underlying architecture to support the new functions, and the related problems further frustrated the business community. This is analogous to putting a motor on a bicycle instead of getting a moped or motorcycle. The bicycle can be modified to accept the motor, but use of the motor increases vibrations, changes the balance of the bicycle, and places additional stress on the frame and the steering and braking mechanisms. Like the existing systems, there is no underlying architecture to support the new power source for propulsion. Forcing the bicycle to accept the new feature without addressing constraints which are inherent in its design increases the risk of accidents and results in higher maintenance costs.

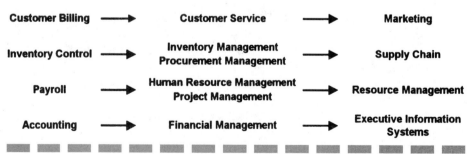

Figure 1-12 Application Systems during Dispersion.

Processing and data-management power was brought to the desk top. Graphical programming languages emerged, significantly simplifying program semantics. The frustration of the business people was unleashed, and various business departments frequently used the new tools to perform tasks previously delegated to the centralized data-processing department. The uncontrolled use of these tools by disparate business departments made it very difficult, and sometimes impossible, to enforce adoption of a set of standards which would facilitate integration. The short-term rewards were perceived to be too great.

Computer Technology

The pace of innovation in computer technology accelerated. The emergence of the client/server environment provided companies with a wealth of new options for satisfying information processing needs. In a client/server environment, end users interact with a *client* device, typically a workstation, and work is performed at the *server* device(s), typically a minicomputer or mainframe computer. (In some cases, the same device may serve as both a client and a server.) Various combinations are available to perform information processing activities.

Just as the advent of the computer terminal opened the doors to the mainframe computer, the workstation opened the doors to end-user computing and provided a means to eliminate the mainframe computer in many cases. No longer was the mainframe perceived to be a prerequisite for information processing; no longer was the business unit completely dependent on the information management professional for developing computer applications.

Business people could not only interact with the computers to operate systems, they had the power to create the systems.

These additional capabilities provided needed flexibility for meeting customer demands. For example, instead of being limited by the capabilities of the rigid systems of the past, business users could develop needed applications to provide improved customer service. (Fig. 1-13.)

Data and Object Management

The direct-access storage device remained as the primary storage device for data. Improvements were made in its access speed, density, and relia-

Figure 1-13
Improved Customer
Service.

bility, and other devices for archiving data were developed, but that technological concept has proven to be quite adequate for storing and retrieving data.

Relational database management systems dominated most of the information processing during third-generation business application systems. The prevailing database management systems were oriented toward databases residing on a single server. For full implementation of a client/server environment, the database management systems needed to effectively handle databases residing on multiple computers.

Object-oriented programming emerged to provide a better way for computerized processes to emulate business events. With the emergence of object-oriented development, object-oriented database management systems also emerged. Within the context of object orientation, these databases expanded upon the relational platform to capture the entire object in a manageable form.

More companies recognized the importance of managing data as a resource during this generation, and data administration groups were formed.

Fully functional data administration groups were rare, but some headway was made in managing data as a raw material in the production of information.

Programming Languages

In the third-generation business systems environment, both the programming language interface and its nature changed. Instead of being driven by an English-like semantic interface, this generation of programming languages uses graphical interfaces extensively.

In addition to powerful programming languages which used the graphical interfaces, another set of tools, aimed specifically at accessing data, also emerged. With these tools, access to data was facilitated through point-and-click operations on views of the database tables.

The introduction of object-oriented programming brought with it a fundamental change in the building blocks of the programs. Programs written using conventional techniques were typically driven by either processes or data. With object-oriented technologies, the programs are driven by business events. The object-oriented languages were well-suited for building the workflow-oriented application systems introduced during the Dispersion Generation, and companies sometimes introduced these languages for that reason.

Object-oriented technology was built around the concept of small, reusable objects which encapsulate a business process (method) with the data it uses. As Fig. 1-14 shows, communications between objects is handled with messages. The encapsulation of the methods and data into a single substance results in a loss of the individual identity of each. Since the process and data could each change independently, a change in either requires a redefinition of the object.

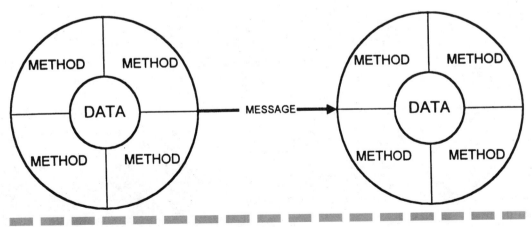

Figure 1-14 Communications between Objects.

Object-oriented programming often delivered on the promise of reuse for technical features such as screen design, including radial buttons and drop-down menus. The promise of reuse proved to be elusive in the business arena where it has the greatest benefit. Companies did not achieve the desired levels of reuse for some of the same reasons that reuse benefits were not attained with modular COBOL programming techniques. The technology changed, but the foundation needed to effectively apply that technology—the explicit definition of the business processes and data and their transformation into electronic representations—did not.

Without an architected and disciplined approach to object-oriented programming which explicitly defines the business and technical models the objects represent and recognizes the implications of merging activities with data, the promise of reuse will not be fully attained.

Methodology

Extensions of the Information Engineering Framework dominated traditional systems development. Extensions such as Rapid Application Development and Prototyping were implemented to deal with the growing desire to see results faster. Joint Application Development (JAD) was introduced to gain better involvement of the business people with the design of the systems. These extensions, for the most part, did not change the foundation of information engineering—they took advantage of the latest technology to advance the cause of information engineering. Success with these techniques required discipline. A prototype developed to demonstrate the final product was just a prototype. Instead of using the prototype to shorten or clarify the requirements definition activities as intended, the prototype was sometimes inappropriately used as the foundation for the final system.

A wealth of CASE and repository tools were also introduced to improve development productivity. Companies looking for a quick payback on the first project using the new tools frequently failed to realize the desired results. Companies which recognized that the results will appear in subsequent projects or later in the life cycle, and applied the necessary discipline, received them.

In 1987, the Zachman Framework for Information System Architecture, which provides a significantly improved perspective for developing systems, was introduced. This framework was derived based on observations of similar types of activities in other disciplines. It recognizes that an architected approach is essential for systems development to succeed, that different views of information are needed for different purposes, and that all aspects of the information are needed for a complete view.

The Zachman Framework expands on the dimensions emphasized by information engineering to encompass all six interrogatories with equal emphasis.

Assessment

With the advent of the third-generation business systems environment, several things began to improve. Not all the problems, however, went away, and some actually got worse. Instead of the islands of automation of the first generation and the networks of centrally managed systems of the second generation, the maze of systems became even more complex, with the added dimension of geographical dispersion and technological incompatibility. (See Fig. 1-15.)

The role of the data-processing department began to shift. During the second generation, its externally viewed emphasis was on developing and operating the business application systems, since the technology changes were managed within this framework. In the third generation, the technology changes had a broader, corporate view, as people throughout the company became involved in developing and operating systems. The role of the central group evolved into one which more visibly managed the technological environment and which developed only some of the systems. Along with the changing role, the name of the department also changed to the information systems, information services, information technology, or information management department.

To compound the problem, a new set of departments—information systems groups within business units—was born. These information systems departments focused on the systems which could be built quickly using the new tools. With an emphasis toward quick delivery, they often left the large systems to the information technology department. In their zeal to satisfy their constituency, they, too, failed to adequately undertake an architected approach to their activities. (See Fig. 1-16.)

Even though more and more was being done with the computer, the business appetite was insatiable. With increased access to information about technology, business departments were prone to experiment or to request opinions from the information technology department. The

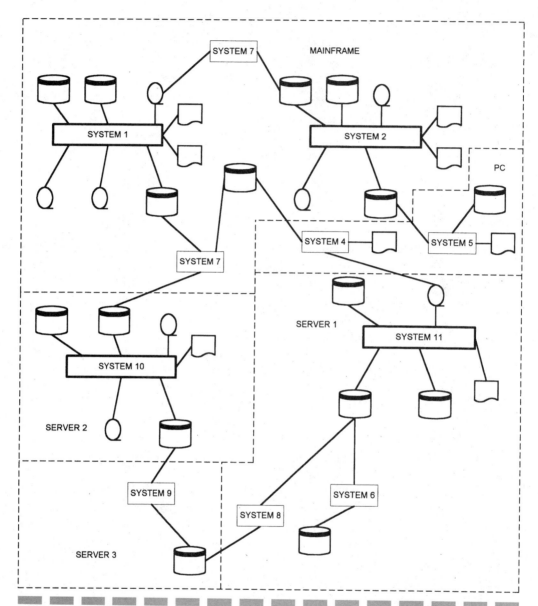

Figure 1-15 *Systems Environment during Dispersion.*

information technology department, meanwhile, was struggling to maintain the existing technology and to monitor developments which would
lead to further improvements in the company's environment while maintaining the necessary degree of connectivity and compatibility. Respect
for parts of the information technology department (typically not the sys-

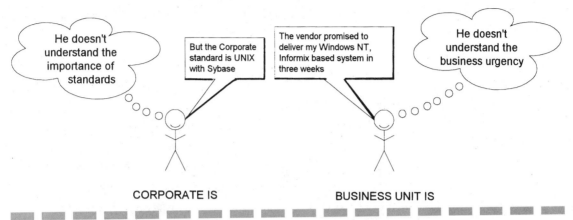

Figure 1-16   Business Unit Information Systems: Rebellious or Responsive?

tems development section) grew as people understood more about the complexity of the environment. This department, however, was still frequently bypassed if a business department felt it could get results faster through independent action.

More tools were in place:

- Client/server technology provided people with the increased ability to control their use of the computer and with a perception of independence.
- Data-storage devices continued to provide the needed flexibility. Their speed contributed to achieving subsecond response time for on-line transaction processing systems.
- Database management systems were being enhanced to address data residing at multiple locations.
- Object-oriented techniques promised improved productivity and high levels of reuse.
- Information engineering tools to provide results faster were introduced.

but

- The systems development backlog for multidepartmental systems was growing. Systems groups within the business units were tackling the smaller information-oriented applications, leaving the large complex ones for the information technology department.

- Environment maintenance was getting out of control. The business unit systems groups brought in additional tools and technologies to help them meet their constituencies' needs.

- System maintenance was getting out of control, as companies continued to force systems to perform functions which were not inherent in their designs.

- Data redundancy problems continued, with many occurrences of people taking data from reports of one system and manually entering them into a spreadsheet of another system.

- Data integrity problems got worse due to independent activities.

- The promise of reuse with object-oriented programming became elusive, as companies failed to invest in the required infrastructure.

- Business needs were still not being met in a timely manner, and opportunities enabled by the new technologies were not fully exploited.

Instead of helping the company, the disintegration of the systems brought with it the potential for disintegrating the enterprise itself.

A management-driven approach was needed to unify the computer environment so that the information being gathered could be transformed once again to create knowledge. (See Fig. 1-17.)

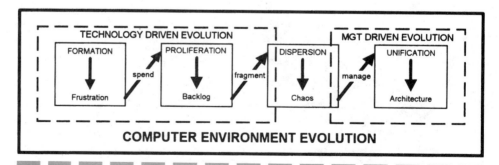

Figure 1-17   Transition to Unification

Summary

Throughout the first four decades of the computer environment, companies certainly received significant benefits from their technology deployment. Along with these benefits also came numerous problems. Many of the problems arose because the evolution of applications was technology-driven. Companies jumped on each new technology with fervor in an attempt to gain an improvement in productivity.

For companies to survive and thrive in the twenty-first century, they must employ a management-driven approach. This approach recognizes that the technology is an enabler, but that a discipline, such as that provided by the architectural construct of the Zachman Framework, is needed to gain maximum value from the available technology. Chapter 2 expands on the necessity of the architecture and its role in helping companies in the Unification Generation.

2

Satisfying Modern Information Needs

The problems can be fixed, but without the discipline inherent in the concepts of architecture, companies risk making the problems even worse. Investments in legacy systems continue to grow, and new technologies are pursued without addressing the fundamental problems. This chapter explains the importance of architecture and its critical role in helping companies move to the next generation of the computer environment in which information can be transformed into knowledge.

The Unification Generation is the environment in which competitive companies should operate. Companies operating in this mode unify the management of their information resources from a business perspective while dispersing them from a physical and technological perspective. In this architected environment, the redundancy is managed; the needed information is available when, where, and how it is needed; and knowledge is produced.

The Unification Generation described in the latter part of this chapter is attainable. Reaching it requires a disciplined, architected approach. Part 2 of the book describes the Zachman Framework which helps to apply architectural concepts in managing the information assets of a company.

Need for an Architecture

To understand the need for an architecture, the first step is to define it—so, what is an architecture? *Architecture* is a word that takes on a different context and meaning in the eyes of every beholder. Trying to define and articulate what architecture is and is not is like trying to describe the sky and the heavens. The description and definition of architecture as it relates to information systems is no easier than it is for any other discipline. And yet architecture is very real and very important to the world of data, information, and process.

One way to understand architecture is to understand what architecture does. Consider a road builder who does not understand architecture. One day the road builder grades and paves a fine road. Cars soon start to travel down the road. However, the flow of traffic is interrupted when the road must be dug up in order to place a power line below the road. Traffic resumes when the power line is in place. The next week traffic is disrupted again when the road must be tunneled under in order to place a sewer beneath the road, a few hundred feet from where the power line was placed. Drivers are disgruntled but wait through the construction period. Traffic returns to normal only to be interrupted once again by the tearing up of the road in order to place a water main beneath the road. Once again the traffic on the road is disrupted. At such time as the water main is in place, the surface of the road is so disheveled and broken that the entire road needs to be repaved, and traffic is yet again disrupted.

Architecture would have told the road developer that before the road was initially graded and paved certain major constructions must be done. Architecture would have told the road developer that there was a proper order in which things should be developed. Not developing in the proper order is wasteful.

A second perspective of architecture is that architecture defines a universally recognizable pattern. A Greek column is as recognizable in Greece as it is in England and Spain. Whether the Greek column was

Figure 2-1
What Is Architecture?

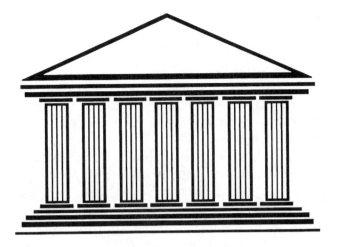

designed and built 1000 years ago or whether the Greek column is part of a new office building, it is still recognizably a Greek column. Universal recognizability then is another dimension of architecture. Figure 2-1 suggests the universal recognizability of architecture.

Information Systems Architecture

The information systems that have evolved in the corporate world have grown into a very recognizable architecture. That progression will be described.

In the very early days of information systems technology, systems were built in order to facilitate repetition. Repetitive manual activities were automated. As discussed earlier, these repetitive early systems typically centered around accounting functions, such as accounts payable and accounts receivable. The early information systems were built on sequentially oriented technology such as magnetic tape and paper tape.

The volume of data and the limitations of accessing data sequentially soon led to the need to manage data differently. The technology that appeared was called *direct-access storage*, or *disk storage*, and soon allowed systems to be written so that data could be directly accessed. At the same time, computers grew in size and power. Networks began to spring up, and soon a whole new style of computing—on-line transaction processing—was possible.

With the advent of on-line transaction processing the technician was positioned at the very heart of the business. Airline reservation systems, bank teller processing, manufacturing on-line systems, and the like soon became a reality. The use of information systems automation was far more sophisticated and much closer to the heart of the business than in the day of repetitive processing.

With the sophistication of on-line processing and the ability to get at the heart of business interactions, the size, cost, and complexity of systems began to spiral. At the same time, the strategic importance of the computer rose sharply.

The success of on-line processing led to a massive profusion of applications. These applications reflected the business requirements of the day and age of their construction. Soon data began to be collected as a by-product of all the on-line business application processing that was being done. The on-line systems primarily helped business interactions at the clerical level. With the explosive growth of volumes of data came the realization that much more could be done with the data than merely feeding the on-line systems that addressed the clerical needs of the corporation. There arose the desire to use data strategically. Figure 2-2 reflects the general progression of systems that has been described.

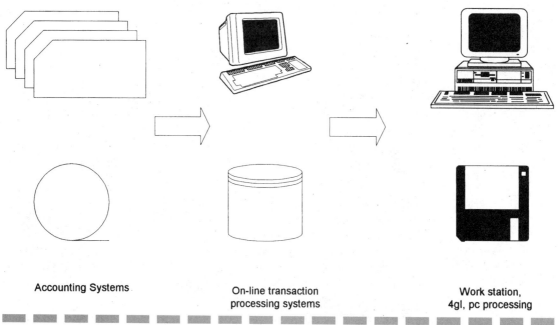

Accounting Systems

On-line transaction processing systems

Work station, 4gl, pc processing

Figure 2-2   The Progression of Processing.

The desire for strategic information was fed by technology such as the personal computer (PC) (or the larger, more sophisticated version of the personal computer called the workstation). Other technological advances in the evolution of information systems architecture included fourth-generation languages (4gl) and spreadsheets. With 4gl technology and with spreadsheets, individual analysts could with ease and flexibility manipulate their numbers to achieve analytical results. The decision-support-system (DSS) analysts turned their tools against the on-line systems in search of data. By now the on-line systems had grown and aged to the point that they were called *legacy* systems. The free-form mixture of analytical tools in the on-line systems environment produced an environment called the *spider web* environment, as seen in Fig. 2-3.

The spider web environment was an anomalous, heterogeneous collection of systems and data where many purposes were met all at once and in one place. While the spider web environment represented the ultimate in expediency and autonomy of processing, it was essentially unstable. The instability of the spider web environment was a result of many deficiencies, including

- The lack of consistency of results achieved in analyzing data from the spider web environment
- The difficulty in getting results from the spider web environment in any case
- The lack of integration of data in the spider web
- The lack of historical data in the spider web environment
- The lack of metadata in the spider web environment, and so forth

The woeful and obvious inadequacies of the spider web environment led to the creation of an architectural structure called a data warehouse.

The data warehouse is an integrated, historical collection of both summary and detailed data that is fed by the spider web environment. (See Fig. 2-4.) The data warehouse served to give DSS processing a foundation. With the data warehouse, the end-user analyst could at long last do the analysis that enabled management to make important strategic decisions. The feeding of the data warehouse from the spider web environment had the effect of shrinking the size and complexity of the spider web environment. Its architecture directly addressed the deficiencies noted above.

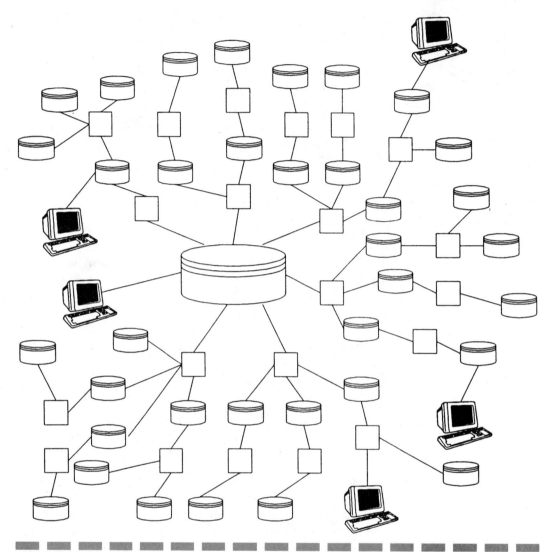

Figure 2-3 Spider Web Architecture.

Data Warehouse Architecture. As an integrated, subject-oriented collection of data, the data warehouse brings together common information from various sources. As a nonvolatile, time-variant collection of data, the data warehouse provides a stable source of information gathered over a period of time. The supporting metadata provides a road map into its contents. Thus, a business analyst can use the data warehouse to discover what current and historical information is available on

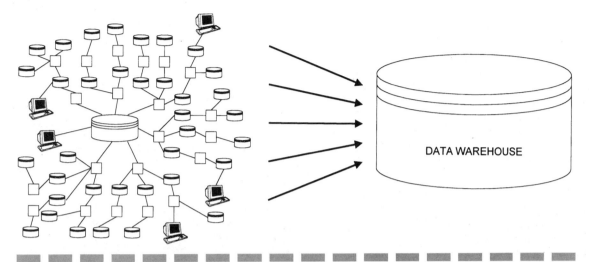

Figure 2-4 Progression from Legacy Systems to the Data Warehouse.

a particular subject and then to obtain it based on business data retrieval needs, without being confined to limitations of individual systems which were built to improve the efficiency or effectiveness of business processes. (See Fig. 2-5.)

The structure of the data warehouse typically includes three major levels of information: granular data, archived data, summary data, and metadata to support them. The granular, or detailed, data represents the lowest level of detail which resides in the data warehouse. It is important to note that since the data warehouse is oriented toward decision support, the granular level within the warehouse is often not the same as that in the operational system. Granular-level data should typically be retained on-line for only a year or two. It may be transferred to another medium for archival purposes, to support drill-down analysis at some future date.

The data warehouse gets much of its strength from the summaries it contains, and most direct access of the data warehouse is at this level. These summaries contain groupings of data elements which are commonly used together. The philosophy in creating the summary views is to provide end users with the ability to get to the data they need quickly and easily. It is very common for summarized data to be retained for years, and possibly decades. Within the concept of the summaries, various levels existed, including lightly summarized and highly summarized data.

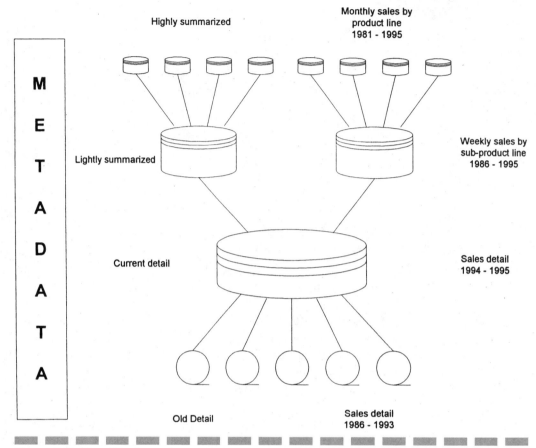

Figure 2-5   Data Warehouse Structure.

But the data warehouse failed to address integration in the operational, clerical environment. Put another way, for all the advantages of the data warehouse, the data warehouse did little or nothing for the clerical community making day-to-day, up-to-the-second decisions. A further refinement of the data warehouse was the operational data store (ODS), as seen in Fig. 2-6.

The ODS was, in essence, the data warehouse in the operational environment. The ODS served the day-to-day clerical community in an on-line integrated mode. The ODS was used for an entirely different kind of decision making from the data warehouse. Like the data warehouse before it, the ODS shrank the spider web environment as it was populated and used.

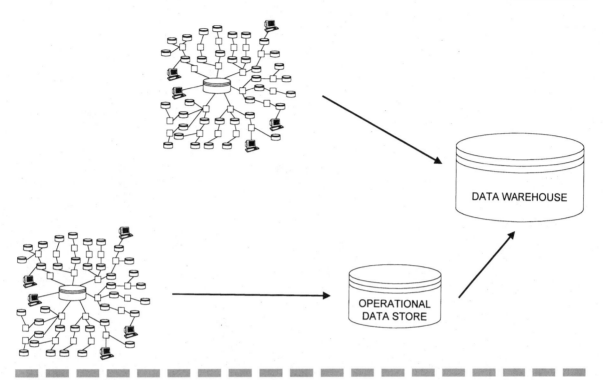

Figure 2-6 *From the Data Warehouse Emerged the ODS.*

At about the same time that the ODS was becoming a recognized and common architectural entity, the data warehouse began to sprout limbs. These limbs were departmentalized to suit the decision-making needs of various departments such as marketing, finance, sales, and accounting. These sprouts from the detailed data found in the data warehouse were called *datamarts,* as seen in Fig. 2-7.

A datamart is a collection of data suited to serve the analytical needs of a limited group of people. Typically the datamart contains data that is refined from the detailed data of the data warehouse. This latter point is worth repeating—the datamart is refined from detailed data of the data warehouse. Otherwise, it becomes an extract (of an extract of an extract...) which simply applies a new technology without applying the needed architecture. (See Fig. 2-8.)

Without the data warehouse as a source, the datamart risks being just another component in the spider web.

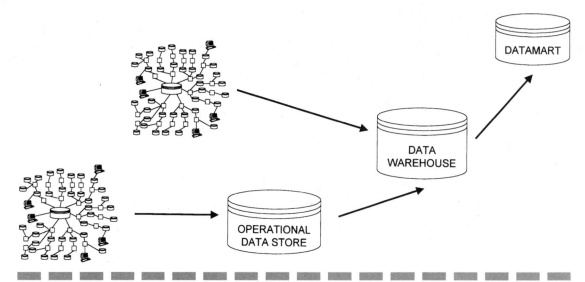

Figure 2-7   Emergence of the Datamart.

Figure 2-8
Unarchitected
Datamart.

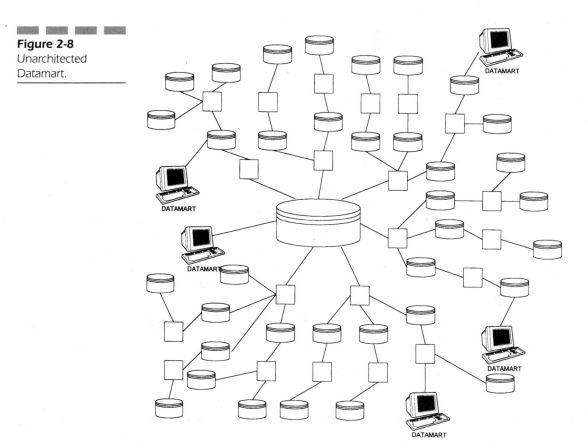

Zachman Framework

The Zachman Framework was formally published in 1987 to describe an architecture for capturing the artifacts of the information systems. This framework is described in Part 2 of the book and is applied toward improving the computer environment in Part 3. One of the major applications of the Zachman Framework, described in Chap. 11, is to help companies in migrating from legacy systems.

Migration of Legacy Systems

Each component of modern systems architecture evolved as a result of some powerful need.

- The data warehouse evolved from the legacy systems environment because of the demand for effective informational processing by the end-user community.
- The ODS evolved from the legacy systems environment and the data warehouse because of the need for operational integration.
- The datamart evolved from the detailed data of the data warehouse as a result of the need for customization of departmental informational processing and the need for decentralization.

Throughout the different phases of the evolution of information systems architecture, the evolution has been moved along by one or more pressing needs. In some cases the need was economic. Other needs were fueled by technology and business. Oftentimes the needs worked in tandem. And in every case the needs were real and powerful—so powerful that migration to the architected information systems environment is inevitable.

The question is not whether an organization will migrate to the architected information systems environment but how soon and how gracefully the migration will occur.

Taken as a whole, the evolution of information systems architecture has produced a very recognizable and very predictable migration away from legacy information systems. From a simple foundation of applications to a sophisticated world of operational processing, informational processing, and departmental informational processing the appearance of each of the architectural components has produced an order and discipline to information processing. Architecture has acted as a vehicle to move from chaos and cacophony to order and structure.

Influencing Factors

One of the interesting aspects of the migration to the architected environment from the legacy systems environment is that the age and complexity of a company greatly influence the rate at which the migration occurs. Figure 2-9 shows a grid in which the age of information systems and the complexity of those systems are divided. There are four quadrants in the grid in Fig. 2-9. One quadrant is for young and simple information systems. There is a quadrant for older and simple information systems. Another quadrant is for young and complex information systems. And finally there is a quadrant for older and complex information systems. Organizations whose information systems fall into the young and simple quadrant are not subject to the forces of migration to any great extent. These organizations can make do with basic applications.

Organizations whose information systems are either complex and young or old and simple are subject to the forces of migration to a much greater extent. These organizations feel the stress to migrate fairly strongly. And organizations whose systems are old and complex are the most susceptible to the forces of migration. There is tremendous motivation to migrate information systems in this environment.

However, age and complexity are not the only mitigating factors in moving an organization down the path of migration. Another mitigating factor is that of the size (measured in terms of volume of data and number of transactions executed) of systems. The larger the legacy information systems environment, the more difficult it is to migrate the system. Conversely, the smaller the information systems environment, the easier it is to migrate the system.

Figure 2-9
Information Systems
Migration Grid.

	simple	complex
young	Migration not mandatory	Subject to forces of migration
old	Subject to forces of migration	Highly motivated to migrate systems

The migration to the modern information systems architecture is not something that is accomplished sequentially or all at once. The migration is accomplished in many small steps. First a data warehouse is built. Then a datamart is built on top of the data warehouse. Next the legacy environment is shrunk in proportion to the data that has been removed from it. Soon another part of the warehouse is populated, and the cycle begins anew. The achievement of the architected environment is not sudden and is not dramatic. It is more like the dew falling silently on a mountain meadow in the summer. Suddenly and silently at dawn, it is just there. Section 3 of the book explains how the Zachman Framework supports this migration.

The migration from the legacy systems to the architected information systems has been witness to and a participant in the change in the politics of automation. In the very earliest days, there was a computer department. The early computer department was in charge of everything that related to computers. But as the demand for information swelled with the growth of the jungle of the legacy systems environment, new technology appeared which placed a great deal of power in the hands of the end user. Spreadsheets, 4gl technology, and personal computers all were affordable and controllable. The end users soon began to take their own destiny in hand. The first reaction of being free from the shackles of the computer department was one of exhilaration. But as the end users pushed further into technology and as the systems being produced by them became complex, they began to run into the barriers that constrained the computer department. Small end-user legacy environments began to spring up. As time passed the end user recognized the need for discipline and structure.

Role of Technology

The migration to the architected information systems environment has been fueled in no small part by advances in technology. It is simply the truth to state that the migration would have never occurred had the world been forced to operate on early technologies. As a good example of growth in technologies, consider the technologies required for the storage of data.

The first storage technologies were card-based. Cards could store only a small amount of data, could not be reused, wore easily, were difficult to manipulate, and had to be kept in a physical sequence. Next came the paper tapes which could store more data. Paper tapes were followed by

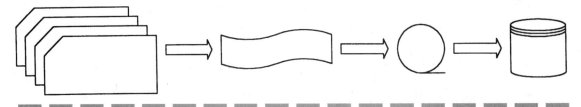

Figure 2-10   Storage Technology Evolution.

magnetic tapes. Magnetic tapes could store data much more densely and were not limited to many of the physical limitations of cards. But the oxide on magnetic tapes was not terribly stable, and magnetic tapes required records of data to be stored sequentially. Direct-access storage soon followed magnetic tapes and with them data could be accessed directly. (See Fig. 2-10.)

In today's world, on-line memory stores volumes of data that once were on cards and tape. And silos of tapes dwarf the amount of data that once appeared to present a challenge. Because of the increase in the speed and volume of magnetic storage and the decrease in the unit cost of storage, the economics and the potency of applications increased dramatically. The advances in storage technology allowed the migration to the architected information systems environment to occur. Had there been no technological advances, there would have been a very different migration of information systems.

Unification

The Unification Generation of the computer environment reflects on the value of the architected environment and applies the discipline needed to realize its benefits. If the third generation computer environment is characterized by the chaos resulting from the explosive growth in the number of available options for meeting the company's information management needs and their dispersion throughout the company, the fourth generation is characterized by the tranquillity provided through the implementation of an architected environment. The architected environment provides a framework for better understanding the environment and the roles which each of the components can play in helping the corporation.

Business applications continue to address efficiency and effectiveness, though the emphasis is increasingly on addressing opportunities.

Within the architected environment, the systems orientation of the past yields to an orientation of transactions and objects which represent business events and to data which is used to support them and to information to make decisions. The concept of behemoth systems development projects which take years to complete gives way to smaller, more manageable efforts which build on existing components and assemble them to create the needed systems. The design philosophy of the data warehouse is extended to serve as the cornerstone for the architected environment.

The data warehouse remains as a subject-oriented, integrated, time-variant, read-only collection of data organized for strategic decision support. It is fed by the ODS which is a subject-oriented, integrated collection of current and near-current data organized for operational activity and tactical decision support. The ODS is in turn fed by reengineered systems which are composed of reusable components. To ensure that people understand the information which they are getting, the whole structure is supported by an accessible, comprehensive directory of the data, systems, and other components.

The irony of the ODS concept becomes very apparent in the architected environment. Unlike the data warehouse, which addresses information retrieval, the ODS addresses operational activities. The ODS, which is essential in today's environment, might not have even been necessary, except in extremely high volume transaction processing environments, had systems been properly architected in the first place. This is why the ODS is so effective as a medium for helping companies migrate from their operational systems, as described in Chap. 11.

The processing and data management power which was transmitted to the desk top is becoming more powerful, and graphical programming languages and associated development techniques are maturing.

The major change taking place is not in the technology itself but in the way companies are applying it to help them succeed.

Computer Technology

For Unification to succeed, tools are needed to manage a distributed environment. Some of these tools exist today, and others are evolving.

These tools need to provide companies with the ability of operating the distributed systems environment as though it were contained within one complex. Functions provided by these tools include performance management, software distribution, and security. The beauty of the architected environment is that it helps companies select and employ the applicable tools when they become available.

During the third generation computer environment, the need for improved connectivity among the various components of the distributed environment was recognized. Increasing emphasis was placed on standards which would be vendor- and platform-independent, so that applications and databases could easily migrate to the platform and environment which is best suited for them with a minimal amount of work.

Tools to manage the distributed environment continue to evolve. By employing an architected approach, companies are better equipped to deploy these tools.

Data and Object Management

While the relational structure remains as a dominant structure for data storage, and the object structure evolves further, two specialized database management systems aimed specifically at data warehouses are evolving. One of these retains the relational structure but incorporates features which provide improved performance for read-only applications. These features include special indices to facilitate data retrieval and reductions in the logging functions which are not needed in a read-only environment. Another characteristic is the inclusion of features to improve performance for data warehouses which employ a star schema in their design.

Star Schema.   The star schema design recognizes that the data patterns for decision support related to some business processes have a distinct pattern. (See Fig. 2-11.) This pattern is characterized by the existence of a large number (millions) of records of data about a business activity, supported by relatively small reference tables. For example, a retail company with many stores will have millions (or tens of millions) of point-of-sale transactions. Each transaction may take place at a different date and time, at a different store, be for a different product, and be made by a different salesperson.

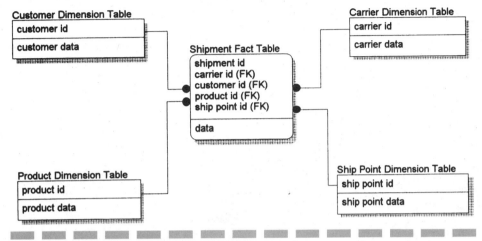

Figure 2-11　Star Schema.Configuring WINS.

There are two distinct sets of information which yield two very different characteristics in the tables which represent them. The detailed transaction table, often referred to as a fact table in the star schema, is typically very long and very narrow. It is long because the number of records is huge; it is narrow because the information in each record is typically a set of numeric facts such as quantities, measurements, and monetary values. On the other hand, the retail company probably has a relatively small number of stores (hundreds or thousands), salespeople (thousands or tens of thousands), and products (tens of thousands). Some numeric information is maintained about these dimensions, but much of the information, such as name and description, is textual. Hence these tables are typically short and fat.

Multidimensional Databases.　The second structure used for data warehouses recognizes that business analysts often want different views of the same data. (See Fig. 2-12.) These multidimensional databases facilitate accessing these views and provide significant performance and usability improvements for their intended niche. Very often, the multidimensional databases are used to support a star schema. The business analyst using these tools would be provided with a matrixlike view of the data and the ability to quickly change each axis and its level of detail, as well as the data quantities presented in the body of the matrix. (See Fig. 2-13.)

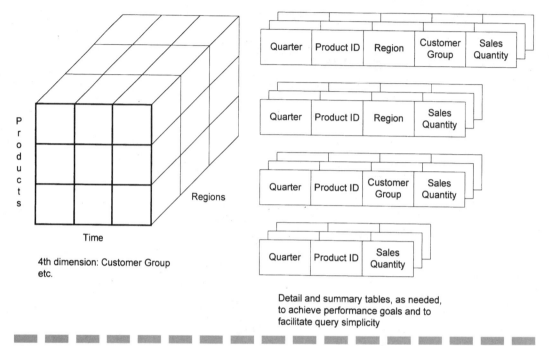

Detail and summary tables, as needed,
to achieve performance goals and to
facilitate query simplicity

Figure 2-12   Multidimensional Database.

Figure 2-13
Multidimensional
Query Dialog.

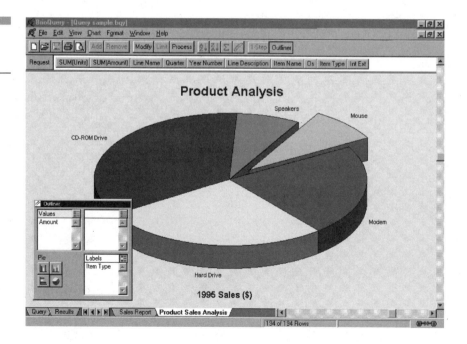

Distributed Data Management. The sophistication of the database management systems deserves attention, too. During the previous generations, the database management systems operated very well at an individual node; they did not operate well across the distributed network. Additional advances are still needed to fully attain an environment in which the data location can be transparent to the person using the data; however, enough is known about the subject for companies to plan for that environment.

During Unification, information is treated as a corporate resource, and information resource management (IRM) becomes a reality.

Through IRM, data and object redundancy is controlled (not necessarily eliminated) and directories of metadata to help people locate data, objects, queries, etc., are implemented. The implementation of data management concepts also makes possible the development of the architected data warehouse and operational data store. Both the data warehouse and the operational data store are based on a subject-oriented organization of the company's data.

Programming Languages

The graphical programming languages developed during the 1980s continue to proliferate. The sophistication of these tools simplifies some of the analysis tasks, as they enable the system to be developed as it is programmed. This provides business users with the ability of seeing the potential results, rather than trying to decipher them from voluminous requirements documents.

As the tools evolve, logic is built into the tools themselves to anticipate the upcoming development steps. In that respect, the tools become intuitive and help developers walk through the process of building applications. Even though the tools facilitate and appear to merge the development steps, the objectives of each step of the development process still need to be addressed.

With the advent of the data warehouse and other data stores, data-access tools for retrieving information also evolved. These tools were typically designed for business analysts and managers and require only a rudimentary knowledge of information technology to be used.

With the aid of metadata and intermediate tools, managers and analysts can be shielded from the physical environment

so that they can access the needed data using business terms and business-oriented groupings of data.

Methodology

The methodologies are the primary contributors to the architected environment. Companies migrating to the Unification Generation recognize that information is a valuable resource and are managing it as such.

By applying methodologies linked to architectures such as the Zachman Framework, businesses can gain the necessary control over the distributed computer environment, while taking advantage of the technological capabilities for quickly providing business functionality.

Assessment

In the architected environment, the role of the information management organization shifts from one which manages the technologies to one which manages the environment and forms partnerships throughout the company to help the firm succeed. As can be seen in Fig. 2-14, the systems environment itself is better architected. Many of the problems of the previous generation of business systems tend to dissipate, and the architectural approach helps companies deal with new ones as they emerge.

In 1979, Richard Nolan identified six stages of data-processing growth. (See Fig. 2-15.) The technology and management tools have progressed significantly since then, but much of what Mr. Nolan said still holds true today.

To a large extent, the migration through the first three generations was facilitated by technological developments. Movement into the fourth generation, the Unification Generation, requires the same management shift Mr. Nolan called for in migrating to his fifth (Data Administration) and sixth (Maturity) stages. It requires recognition of the value of information as a resource to be managed, and it also requires recognition of the enabling technologies which can help companies to cost-effectively manage these resources. The implications of moving to that level of information management are significant, as described in subsequent chapters.

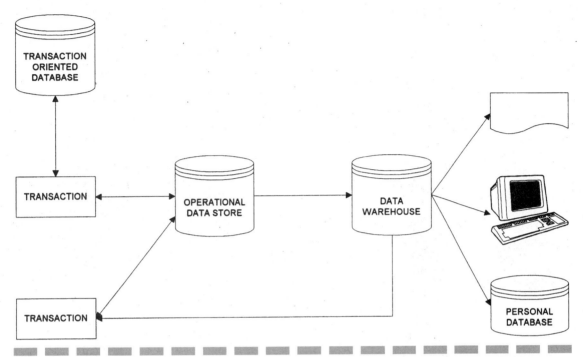

Figure 2-14 *Architected Environment during Unification. (Reprinted by permission of Harvard Business Review. An exhibit from "Managing the Crises in Data Processing," by Richard L. Nolan, March/April 1979. Copyright 1979 by the President and Fellows of Harvard College. All rights reserved.)*

Summary

Since the computer was first introduced into the commercial environment in the 1950s, technology, data storage media, database management systems, programming languages, and methodologies have evolved significantly. (See Fig. 2-16.)

Modern corporations depend on information. That information must be dependable and must be available at the right time, at the right place, and in the right form. To thrive in the twenty-first century, companies must evolve into the Unification Generation computer environment. This new generation is founded on an architectural framework and builds upon the technology, programming languages, database management systems, data storage devices, and methodologies which have evolved during the last 40 years. The architected environment is represented by the Zachman Framework which was developed by

GROWTH PROCESS	STAGE I INITIATION	STAGE II CONTAGION	STAGE III INTEGRATION	STAGE IV INTEGRATION	STAGE V DATA ADMIN.	STAGE VI MATURITY
APPLICATIONS PORTFOLIO	Functional cost reduction applications	Proliferation	Upgrade documentation and restructure existing applications	Retrofitting existing applications using database technology	Organization and integration of applications	Application integration mirroring information flows
DP ORGANIZATION	Specialization for technological learning	User-oriented programmers	Middle management	Establish computer utility and user account teams	Data administration	Data resource management
DP PLANNING & CONTROL	Lax	More lax	Formalized planning and control	Shared data and common systems	Shared data and common systems	Data resource strategic planning
USER AWARENESS	Hands off	Superficially enthusiastic	Arbitrarily held accountable	Accountability learning	Effectively accountable	Acceptance of joint user and data-processing accountability

Figure 2-15 Six Stages of Data Processing Growth.

	FORMATION	PROLIFERATION	DISPERSION	UNIFICATION
TECHNOLOGY	Complex Expensive components Physically interconnected	Complex Expensive components Remote terminals	Complex Inexpensive components Distributed servers	Complex Inexpensive components Distributed servers
DATA MANAGEMENT	Punched cards Magnetic tape	Magnetic tape Magnetic disc	Magnetic tape Magnetic disc Optical disc	Magnetic tape Magnetic disc Optical disc
	Sequential	Hierarchical Networked Relational	Hierarchical Relational Object	Relational Object Multidimensional
PROGRAMMED LANGUAGES	Machine language Assembler	Assembler Procedural	Procedural Graphical	Graphical Intuitive Retrieval
METHODS	Emerging Waterfall	Information engineering CASE	Expedited information engineering CASE driven Repositories	Architected approaches with tool support Repositories Object-oriented methodlogies
BUSINESS APPLICATION SYSTEMS	Complex, inflexible Data and process integration Redundant data entry Redundant data storage	Complex, inexpensive Significant data and process integration Some redundant data entry Some redundant data storage Complex interfaces	Complex, flexible Some redundant data storage Very complex Interfacers Object-oriented Decision support	Very flexible Managed data storage redundancy Reusable components Data driven for decision support Data and object driven for operational support
STAFF GROUP	Small Specialized Centralized	Large Specialized Centralized with limited decentralization	Large Specialized Centralized and decentralized	Medium Specialized Partnerships

Figure 2-16 Evolution.

observing the discipline required in fields such as construction and manufacturing.

Richard Nolan described this environment as Stage VI: Maturity. In this environment, applications emulate the business, information is readily available to support decisions, and partnerships are formed to manage the company's information resources.

According to Alvin Toffler, knowledge will become the central resource of the advanced economy, and because it reduces the need for other resources, its value will soar.[1] Data warehousing concepts, supported by the technological advances which led to the client/server environment and by architectural constructs such as the Zachman Framework, can prepare organizations to tap their inner banks of knowledge to improve their competitive positions in the twenty-first century.

---

[1]Alvin Toffler, *Power Shift,* New York: Bantam Books, 1990, p. 91.

PART 2

Architectural Framework

CHAPTER 3

The Zachman Framework

A tree house can be built without formal plans, but a 50-story office building cannot be created without an integrated set of standards for planning, building, using, and maintaining it. A paper airplane can be made with little forethought, but a jet airplane cannot be created without an integrated set of standards for planning, building, using, and maintaining it. Similarly, while a spreadsheet application may be developed spontaneously, a complex system cannot be created without a set of integrated standards for planning, building, using, and maintaining it. (See Fig. 3-1.) The Zachman Framework for Information Systems Architecture provides a means of ensuring that standards for creating the information environment exist and that they are appropriately integrated.

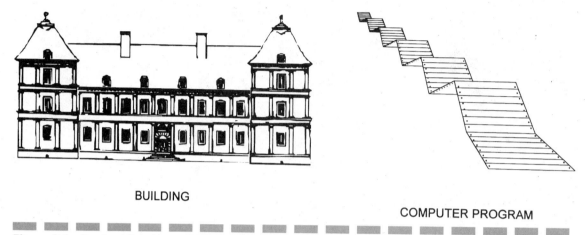

BUILDING

COMPUTER PROGRAM

Figure 3-1   Products Requiring a Disciplined Approach.

The Zachman Framework evolved through observations of the way work was planned and performed in disciplines which have existed for centuries. It is based on the philosophy that the same fundamental concepts exist within the information environment and that applying them can provide systems and other products with the same lasting power and reliability of buildings and quality machinery.

This chapter provides an overview of the Zachman Framework and its components. The description provides a basis for applying the Framework for defining the Knowledge Management function, for developing data warehouses and operational data stores, and for migrating to an improved environment. Those topics are discussed in subsequent chapters.

Zachman Framework Overview

The Zachman Framework recognizes that computer systems must relate to the business world. In the business world, people have different perspectives or roles, depending on their need for and use of information. The needs at each perspective can be expressed by understanding each of a series of dimensions or abstractions. A thorough understanding of these needs helps to build a system which can meet them.

Perspectives

There are five basic roles that people play in the creation of a product.

- The planner is concerned with positioning the product in the context of its environment, including specifying its scope.

- The owner is interested in the business deliverable and how it will be used.

- The designer works with the specifications for the product to ensure that it will, in fact, fulfill the owner's expectations.

- The builder manages the process of assembling and fabricating the components in production of the product.

- The subcontractor fabricates out-of-context (and hence reusable) components which meet the builder's specifications.

The Zachman Framework provides a means of sequentially viewing product development from each of these views. (See Fig. 3-2.)

Dimensions

A good detective strives to answer six basic questions in solving a mystery. Similarly, in developing a building, a piece of machinery, or a system, the dimensions or abstractions covered by these questions must be addressed. (See Fig. 3-3.)

Therefore, each perspective must address

- The entities or things (what?)

- The activities (how?)

- The places (where?)

- The people (who?)

- The timing (when?)

- The motivations (why?)

The Zachman Framework represents the perspectives and dimensions in the form of a matrix, with the perspectives representing the rows and the dimensions representing the columns. Figure 3-4 shows the Framework as a matrix, with the system-related products of the dimensions and perspectives shown at the bottom and right, respectively.

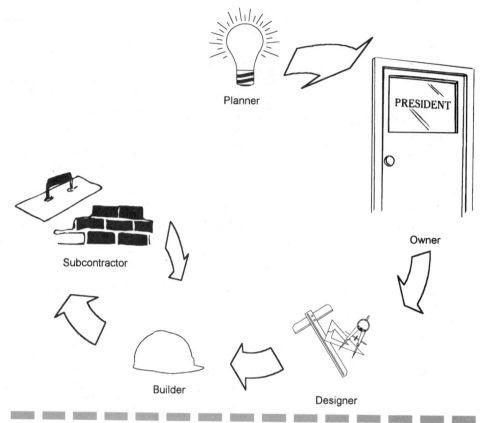

Figure 3-2 Zachman Framework Perspectives.

The Zachman Framework supports, and does not conflict with, commonly adopted techniques used throughout the information management industry. Information system plans, entity relationship diagrams, decomposition charts, data flow diagrams and the like all fit within the context of the Framework.

The Zachman Framework places each of the techniques, its objectives, and its artifacts in context with the others to provide a complete picture of the product, the enterprise, or the opportunity being addressed.

While there are exceptions, particularly with object-oriented techniques, each technique typically addresses a single cell (or intersection point of a row and a column) or several cells within the Framework.

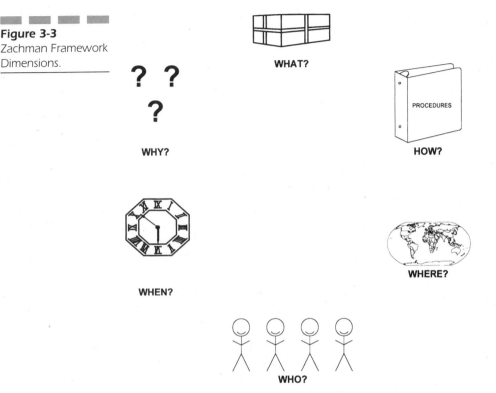

Figure 3-3
Zachman Framework
Dimensions.

WHAT?

WHY?

PROCEDURES

HOW?

WHEN?

WHERE?

WHO?

The data flow diagram, for example, primarily addresses the designer's view of the processes of the system. Hence, it is applicable in the cell representing the third row (Designer perspective) and the column representing the dimension of Function (or how). Data stores represented in the data flow diagram are actually representative of information from the Entities dimension.

On the surface, objects appear to contain characteristics of two columns—Entities and Activities. Peeling off the surface and looking at the details, however, reveals that some characteristics of the objects such as the methods fit into the Activities column, while other characteristics, such as instances, fit well in the Entities column. Looking deeper reveals that objects exhibit characteristics from each of the six columns of the Framework. They have structure, behavior, locations, presentation, sequence, and rules. Even though these are encapsulated in a single deliverable, individual treatment of each of the six dimensions increases the potential for achieving business reuse.

	ENTITIES	ACTIVITIES	LOCATIONS	PEOPLE	TIMES	MOTIVA- TIONS	
PLANNER							SCOPE
OWNER							ENTERPRISE MODEL
BUILDER							SYSTEM MODEL
DESIGNER							TECHNICAL MODEL
SUBCON- TRACTOR							COMPO- NENTS
	DATA	FUNCTION	NETWORK	ORGANI- ZATION	SCHEDULE	STRATEGY	

Figure 3-4 Zachman Framework.

Perspectives—Rows of the Zachman Framework

The rows of the Zachman Framework represent the different perspectives which may be used to view a business, a situation, an opportunity, or a system. (See Fig. 3-5.) Unlike the columns (which are described in the next section) the rows have a definite order, and movement from one row to another is more than merely the addition of detail. The view represented by each perspective is described in the sections which follow.

Figure 3-5
Zachman Framework
Perspectives.

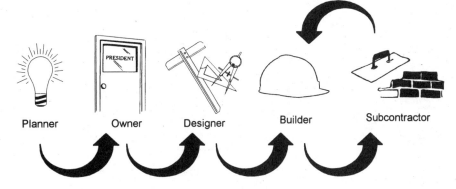

| Planner | Owner | Designer | Builder | Subcontractor |

Planner's Perspective

Planners think about things which could be built to improve the business and then convey information to help others create them. Planners are often visionaries or dreamers and therefore operate under very few constraints other than the external environment, including the marketplace, and regulatory controls. Since their objective is to provide something to help the business, they do, however, need to be cognizant of limitations imposed by regulations, the customer requirements, and the need to be financially responsible.

From a planning perspective, a young couple needing a starter home may want a mansion, but their economic situation may dictate something less grand. Similarly, the planner in a new company may want a system which assimilates data from all the competitors instantaneously but may be constrained by regulations dealing with privacy and nondisclosure, as well as by the cost of such a system. A viable solution in that situation may be a set of reference books or compact discs with last year's information on activities within the industry, with minimal or no system support. (See Fig. 3-6.)

Effective planners focus their efforts on defining the scope of a project by identifying the major components of the desired product and by addressing its financial viability (costs and benefits). Identification of the major components is typically limited to lists of things, activities, locations, people, events, and goals related to the proposed product.

To plan a house for someone, the architects obtain some basic information so that they can propose something realistic and hopefully be engaged to perform the next set of activities. Some of the information obtained relates to the constraints, and other information relates to the

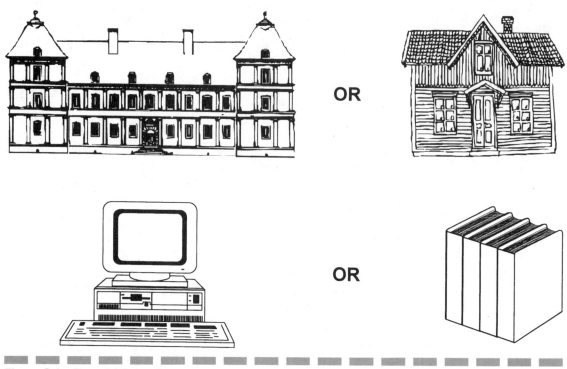

Figure 3-6   Financial Constraints.

description of the house. Constraint information includes items such as budget, neighborhood (which may indicate additional constraints due to deed restrictions), and lot size. Descriptive information addresses the six dimensions.

Similarly, to plan a system, the planners generate or obtain some basic information so that they can propose something realistic and hopefully be funded to perform the next set of activities. Some of the information obtained relates to the constraints, and other information relates to the description of the system. Constraint information includes items such as budget and legal restrictions which may impact the storage and access of information concerning people. Descriptive information addresses the six dimensions.

Planning culminates with the definition of the scope of the product, be it a house or a system, within the applicable constraints. Typically the product of this activity is in the form of a proposal which identifies the parameters of the product, provides information relative to the constraints (e.g., costs and benefits), and requests permission to proceed.

Care must be taken to keep the view at a high level. Too much detail is typically unnecessary at this stage, and, since the techniques applied at this stage are those which pertain to planning (not design), misleading results may appear.

The planning perspective is typically addressed in the first phase of a project. In this phase additional project-related work is also performed. This work includes development of the plan and staffing. Consideration of the Framework as it pertains to the total project can also help in developing the plan and in identifying the skills needed to complete the project.

The most critical scope decision that has to be made, particularly in the domain of information systems is "What is the broadest possible scope we will ever have to support?" That is, What is the broadest definition of *enterprise* for scope definition. Once this is determined, if a system that is less than the broadest possible scope is implemented, its integration with existing systems and with future systems needs to be addressed to ensure that the appropriate level of integration is preserved. Using a building analogy, the strength of the foundation determines the maximum number of stories which can be built. Even if fewer stories are built initially, all supporting structures need to take the eventual height of the building into consideration. Otherwise, the integrity of the final building, built to the level supported by the foundation but having an improperly designed supporting structure, is in jeopardy.

Owner's Perspective

Owners are the people who want practical products which can be built within the planning constraints governing them. The definition of practicality is up to the owner, and the definition imposed creates the next level of governing constraints. If the product being built is a house, the owner imposes constraints dealing with the style and use of the house so that the architect can design one which meets the owner's needs. (See Fig. 3-7.) If the product is a system, the owner imposes constraints dealing with its use and applicable policies, so that the analyst can design one which meets the owner's needs. For example, the owner would dictate requirements with respect to data update capabilities (e.g., on-line versus batch) and data retrieval flexibility (e.g., standard reports versus ad hoc queries, and security).

The prospective owners of a house provide information on the activities for which the house will be used, the flow desired within the house,

Figure 3-7 Usage and Style Constraints.

the occupants (e.g., adults, children, pets), etc. Similarly, the business owners of a proposed system define the business relationships of the entities,
the activities addressed by the system, the places the system may be used,
the types of people who will be using it, etc. Hence, the analysis related
to the owner's view culminates with the business model, which
describes the business as it will exist when the system is completed. (See
Fig. 3-8.) As with the preceding view, this description, to be complete,
must address all six dimensions.

Designer's Perspective

Designers are people who understand the product from both the business perspective and the technical perspective. They transform the real-

Figure 3-8
Owner's View.

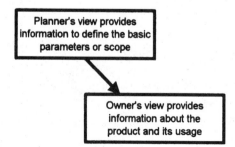

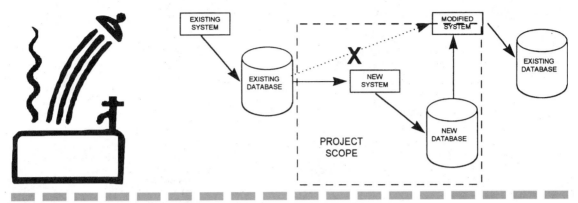

Figure 3-9 Environmental Constraints.

world description of the product into specifications of the product so that it can be built. A home owner, for example, may be concerned about the location of outlets and their capacity relative to the equipment which will be plugged into them. The designer reflects this need in the electrical plan which specifies circuit breakers, wire sizes, wiring paths, etc. Similarly, a systems designer needs to specify the information in the employee record in the computer based on the business needs related to employees.

In addition to the constraints which were considered in the owner's view, designers need to heed the operational environment and laws of physics. (See Fig. 3-9.) In developing the plumbing plan for a house, for example, the designer must ensure that the drain outlet is lower than the drain. In developing the system, the designer must be aware of the interactions of the new system with existing systems.

The design related to the designer's view culminates with a set of specifications which describe in technical terms what must be built to meet the usage needs defined by the owner, within the basic parameters declared by the planner. (See Fig. 3-10.) As with the preceding views, this description, to be complete, must address all six dimensions.

Builder's Perspective

Builders are the people who construct or assemble the final product. Their view requires instructions concerning the materials, specifications for the components being built by subcontractors, and information concerning the sequence of events for building the product. For example,

Figure 3-10
Designer's View.

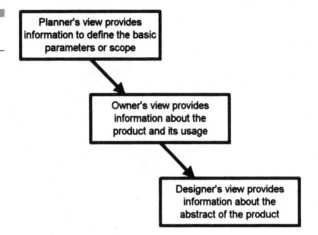

for the plumbing to work as designed, the drainage pipes must be capable of carrying water [e.g., made of galvanized steel or polyvinyl chloride (PVC)] and must be installed before the foundation is laid. If a standard assembly is used to connect a sink to a wall bib, then the distances must be such that the component fits.

The builder is also subject to constraints. Some of these relate to the building equipment available (e.g., lifting capacity of a crane), and others relate to state-of-the-art building techniques (which may require installing the supporting walls before the trusses are laid). For a system to be built, the technological environment (communications facilities and devices available to end users) dictates the access tools and performance which may be available. (See Fig. 3-11.)

The work related to the builder's view culminates a plan for building the product according to the specifications previously defined to meet the usage needs defined by the owner within the parameters declared by the planner. (See Fig. 3-12.) As with the preceding views, this description, to be complete, must address all six dimensions.

Subcontractor's Perspective

Subcontractors are specialists who build specific parts of a product. The subcontractor's view is a set of detailed plans for the component being built, independent of the entire product. The subcontractor's view lends itself to the potential for manufacturing a reusable component (e.g., door, window assembly, object, data base) which can be used in multiple

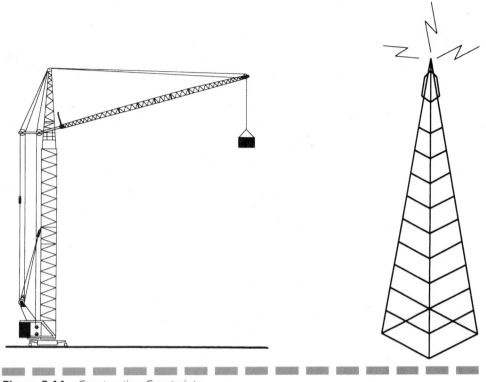

Figure 3-11 Construction Constraints.

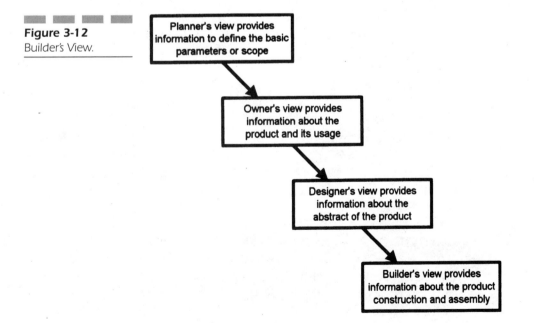

Figure 3-12
Builder's View.

Planner's view provides information to define the basic parameters or scope

Owner's view provides information about the product and its usage

Designer's view provides information about the abstract of the product

Builder's view provides information about the product construction and assembly

Figure 3-13
Implementation Constraints.

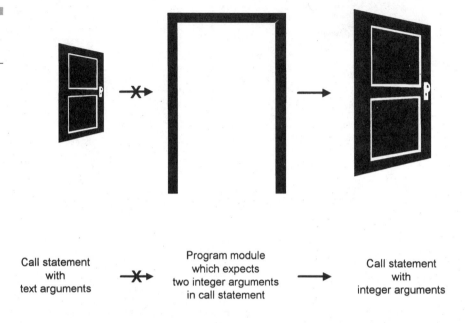

| Call statement with text arguments | | Program module which expects two integer arguments in call statement | | Call statement with integer arguments |

products. In addition to the builder's set of constraints, the subcontractor is also subject to implementation constraints. In the case of the door or window assembly, the subcontractor is constrained by the opening size. In the case of a system, the programmer is constrained by the arguments which can be passed between the module being built and the one calling it. (See Fig. 3-13.)

The design related to the subcontractor's view culminates with specifications and instructions for fabricating a component to be inserted into the final product within the implementation constraints imposed by the builder, who abides by the specifications the designer devised to meet the business needs defined by the owner, within the parameters set by the planner. (See Fig. 3-14.) As with the preceding view, this description, to be complete, must address all six dimensions.

Summary of Perspectives

Five perspectives exist to fully define a product. Each of these perspectives serves a different purpose, is dependent on its predecessors, provides a different product, and is subject to different constraints. (See Fig. 3-15.)

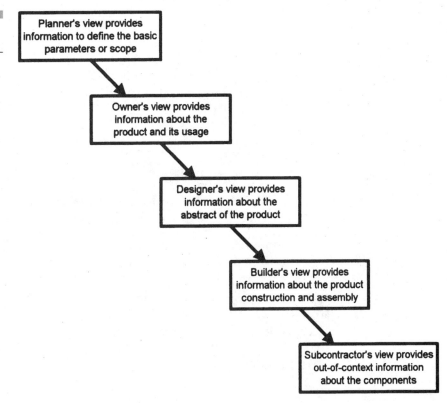

Figure 3-14
Subcontractor's View.

PERSPECTIVE	PURPOSE	PRODUCT	CONSTRAINT[1]
PLANNER	Define scope	Scope definition	Financial and regulatory
OWNER	Describe real-world product	Business model	Policy and usage
DESIGNER	Describe abstract product	System model	Environmental and physics
BUILDER	Describe product construction and assembly	Technology model	Construction and technological state of the art and available equipment
SUBCONTRACTOR	Describe component construction	Out-of-context models	Implementation and integration

[1] Constraints are additive

Figure 3-15 Characteristics of Perspectives.

The sequential nature of the Zachman Framework is similar to common methodologies, but the Framework enhances an understanding of the risks created by working at one perspective without completely addressing the preceding ones. It is possible to write a program or create a database without a thorough analysis and design. The probability of the program or database truly meeting the business needs, however, increases dramatically if the steps on which it depends are completed first. Paying attention to these dependencies can significantly reduce the amount of rework and can provide a quality, maintainable system which meets the true business needs.

Recognition of the subcontractor's role in the Zachman Framework is critical for building a reuse environment.

Methodologies based on information engineering frequently combine the builder's and subcontractor's perspectives into "Construction." That merger implicitly assumes that everything needs to be constructed; the separation in the Framework emphasizes that some things are constructed and others are assembled. (See Fig. 3-16.)

Proponents of object-oriented programming stress reuse as one of its major benefits. For reuse to come to fruition, the object-oriented methodologies need to keep the roles separate.

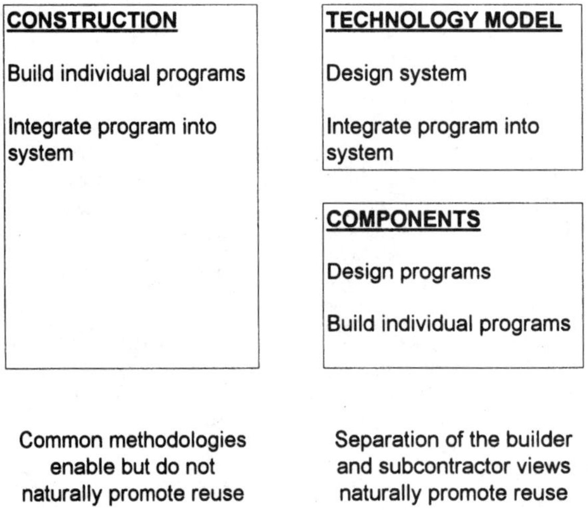

Figure 3-16
Reuse Is Promoted.

CONSTRUCTION	TECHNOLOGY MODEL
Build individual programs	Design system
Integrate program into system	Integrate program into system

	COMPONENTS
	Design programs
	Build individual programs

Common methodologies enable but do not naturally promote reuse

Separation of the builder and subcontractor views naturally promote reuse

Dimensions—Columns of the Zachman Framework

The columns of the Zachman Framework represent the different dimensions which apply to each perspective of the business, situation, opportunity, or system. The abstraction provided by the columns permits a focus on each dimension while keeping the others constant. The interactions with the other dimensions can then be addressed at the appropriate time. Unlike the rows, which must be traversed successively, the columns have no inherent order, priority, or importance. Each column represents a unique abstraction of the whole, and all six columns are necessary to portray each view in its entirety. (See Fig. 3-17.)

Entities (What?)

One of the columns is Entities (things of interest). In considering a house, entities are the physical items which are assembled, built, or needed to produce the house. In building a system, Entities are the data, databases, object classes, and business items which these represent.

The representation of the Entities varies at each stage of the development of a system, just as they do at each stage of building a house. From a planning perspective, the architect determines the types and numbers of rooms, that is, the roles the objects play in the natural composition of the product. The subcontractor, on the other hand, focuses on the technical composition of components such as the doors or windows which are to be acquired or fabricated within the builder's specifications. With a system, the planner identifies the things of interest to the business which must be addressed by the system, while the builder concentrates on the databases that will represent these things. (See Fig. 3-18.) While this is one of the most visible dimensions in information engineer-

Figure 3-17
Zachman Framework Dimensions.

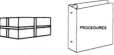

WHAT?   HOW?   WHERE?   WHO?   WHEN?   WHY?

Figure 3-18
Perspectives of Entities.

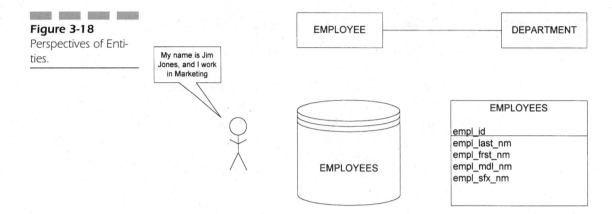

ing—based methodologies, it is no more important than any of the other five dimensions.

Activities (How?)

Another column in the Framework is Activities. In considering a house, activities are the things people expect to do in the house such as live, sleep, eat, entertain, sew, and play. In building a system, activities are the functions and processes which need to be supported. The representation of the activities varies at each stage of the development of a system, just as they do at each stage of building a house. The planner needs to identify the major functions or processes which the system must perform, typically in the form of a list. During planning, the prospective home owners should indicate that they plan to do some woodworking. The specific woodworking activities have a different impact during design, as the electrical circuitry specifications are determined at that time. In building systems, the planner identifies the business activities which must be supported. The interactions of the computerized processes to support them is determined in the designer's perspective. (See Fig. 3-19.)

While this is the second dominant dimension in information engineering—based methodologies, it is no more important than any of the other five dimensions, either.

Figure 3-19
Perspectives of Activities.

Locations (Where?)

The third column is Locations (places of interest). In considering a house, locations are where items are placed, such as the rooms relative to each other within the house as well as the location of the house itself within the lot available. In building a system, locations are where components of the system (e.g., application server, database server) may reside or be used.

The representation of the locations at each stage of the development of a system varies, just as it does at each stage of building a house. The planner simply needs to know the pertinent business locations. The owner needs to know about their connectivity, and the designer needs to translate that need into a description of the physical environment which provides the needed connections, protocols, speed, reliability, etc. (See Fig. 3-20.)

When the original information engineering—based methodologies were developed, remote computing was not common, and, hence, the locations of the end users were not a major focus. As remote computing grew, development teams became somewhat concerned with network traffic, but connectivity issues were typically under the jurisdiction of another group and hence were still not stressed in the development process.

Providing appropriate emphasis to location is recognized as essential for implementing systems in a client/server environment. By carefully considering location from each perspective as the system is developed, a better-architected solution can be developed. As visible as this dimen-

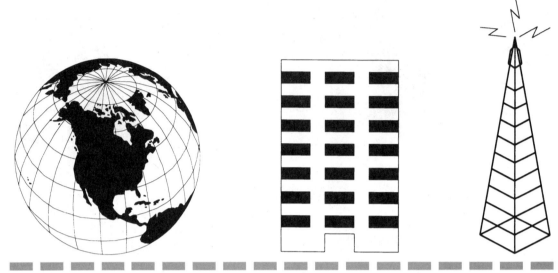

Figure 3-20 Perspectives of Locations.

sion is with client/server applications, it remains, however, no less or more important than the other five dimensions.

People (Who?)

Another of the columns is People (individuals and organizations of interest). In considering a house, the people are the residents (both humans and pets) of the house and others who may visit. In building a system, the people are the organizations, departments, and individuals who directly, and indirectly, interact with the system as well as the workflow and interfaces, or presentations.

The representation of the people varies at each stage of the development of a system, just as it does at each stage of building a house. The planner needs to know the pertinent organizations. The owner needs to know more about the organization of the departments to identify the people or sections who perform the work which the system will address. The subcontractor is concerned with the physical interaction and screens and addresses items such as security. (See Fig. 3-21.)

Failure to focus on the people perspective can easily lead to development of systems which do not adequately consider the skills or orienta-

Figure 3-21   *Perspectives of People.*

tions of those involved. For example, a marketing analyst may be willing to deal with transactions and screens full of data, but an executive may prefer to have an alert system which automatically sends messages when certain conditions exist or a screen with a few buttons which execute the programs needed to display information in graphical or pictorial form.

Times (When?)

Another column is Time (when things occur). In considering a house, time is the sequence of events involved. In building a system, time is the key events and their dependencies.

The representation of the time varies at each stage of the development of a system, just as it does at each stage of building a house. The planner needs to know what events are pertinent. The owner defines the business interaction and interdependency of the events, and the designer translates that into the system interactions, interfaces, and job sequences. (See Fig. 3-22.)

Traditional information engineering focuses on processes and data. Timing is considered but typically only as it relates to these two dimensions. Object-oriented techniques are driven by business events and therefore consider this dimension more naturally. In object-oriented development, just as in any other development, however, care must be taken not to consider this dimension as being any more or any less important than any of the others.

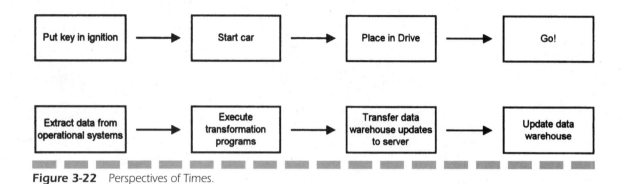

Figure 3-22 Perspectives of Times.

Motivations (Why?)

The last column is Motivations (reasons and rules). In considering a house, motivations are the reasons the house is needed. More important-ly, they are the foundation from which the rules to be followed in its design and construction are derived. Similarly, in building a system, motivations are the reasons the system is needed, from which the tangi-ble and intangible benefits of the new system are derived. More signifi-cantly, it is from the motivations that the rules or constraints for its design and operation are derived.

The representation of motivations varies at each stage of the devel-opment of a system, just as it does at each stage of building a house. The planner focuses on the environmental constraints and opportuni-ties, while the owner defines the business objectives and strategies. (See Fig. 3-23.)

If motivations are ignored, the result may be a system which is very efficient in addressing the wrong objective. This dimension deserves the same attention as the other five.

Summary of Dimensions

Each of the six dimensions is needed to fully define a particular per-spective of a product. (See Fig. 3-24.) Each serves a different purpose, and no single dimension is more or less important than any other.

Figure 3-23
Perspectives of Motivations.

BUSINESS VIEW

We will provide
superior
customer service

- Improve responsiveness to customer queries
- Reduce number of complaints
- Know more about each customer

The equal importance of each dimension dictates that all six dimensions need to be addressed to derive a complete perspective. Practicality may dictate a particular sequence for addressing the dimensions, and a particular step in systems development may dictate an emphasis on a particular dimension. Just as omission of a precedent perspective adds risk to a project, inadequate consideration of a dimension reduces the

Figure 3-24
Properties of Dimensions.

DIMENSION	QUESTION ADDRESSED	SAMPLE PRODUCT IN HOUSE CONSTRUCTION	SAMPLE PRODUCT IN SYSTEMS DEVELOPMENT
ENTITIES	What?	House, room	Employee, department
ACTIVITIES	How?	Play, eat, sew	Hire employee, promote employee
LOCATIONS	Where?	Placement on lot, relationships of rooms to each other	Headquarters, district office
PEOPLE	Who?	Occupants, guest, pets	Human Resources Department, Recruiter
TIME	When?	Construction sequence	During interview, each January
MOTIVATIONS	Why?	Accommodate growing family, reduce lawn maintenance	Ensure adequate staffing levels, ensure adequately skilled staff

Figure 3-25
Zachman Framework Rules.

Dimension Importance	Each of the six dimensions is of equal importance
Dimension Simplicity	Each of the six dimensions has a simple, basic model
Dimension Uniqueness	Each of the six dimensions has a unique basic model
Perspective Uniqueness	Each perspective represents a distinct, unique view
Cell Uniqueness	Each meta entity appears in only one cell
Dimension Necessity	All six dimensions are needed to fully represent each perspective
Logic Recursiveness	The Framework concept is recursive with respect to versions and decomposition

chances of success. The important thing to remember is that each of the six dimensions is unique, that all six are equally important, and that all six are needed to fully represent each perspective. The rules which follow expand on the Framework attributes. (See Fig. 3-25.)

Rules of the Zachman Framework

The Zachman Framework provides a systematic approach for creating a product—from conception through completion. Like any other systematic approach, the Framework has a set of rules which are needed to preserve its integrity.

Dimension Importance

Within the Zachman Framework, all dimensions are of equal importance. (See Fig. 3-26.) Their order of appearance as columns has no significance with respect to their importance or priority. The order within the published Zachman Framework merely reflects concessions to the matrix format. The Framework, if represented in a graphical form, may appear as a hexagon, with all dimensions interconnected. (See Fig. 3-27.)

This concept represents a departure from common methodologies which are built upon the information engineering foundation. Information engineering emphasizes processes and data. Some proponents pro-

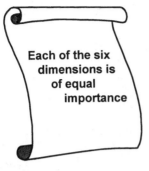

Figure 3-26
Rule 1.

Each of the six
dimensions is
of equal
importance

mote process as the most important dimension and are process-driven in their approach to systems, with the data being treated as a secondary item (and other dimensions frequently ignored completely). Others promote data as the most important item. With the advent of object-oriented programming, a group of people is now promoting objects (which combine process and data with an event trigger) as the answer. None of these addresses the full picture.

Data is no more important than process, and process is no more important than data. Similarly, neither supersedes motivation, time, people, or location. Focusing on data and process while ignoring motivation during planning, for example, may result in a fantastic system which

Figure 3-27
Dimension Equality.

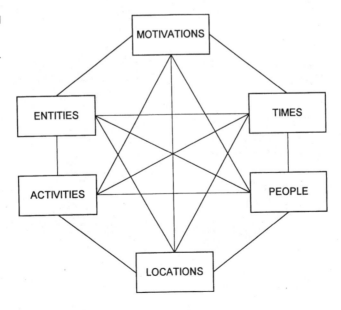

does not address the business need. In planning a house, the architect needs to understand the reasons that people want the new house. If the architect ignores identification of a motivation of lawn maintenance reduction, he or she may design an elaborate landscape scheme and totally miss one of the new occupant's primary motivations for moving. Similarly, planning a system for a company wanting to merely survive is different than planning a system for a company which wants to become the leading edge in a particular niche.

Building a system for a company which is located in a single building is very different than building a system for a multinational concern. If the planner fails to consider business expansion plans which may impact the locations of interest, the resulting system will miss the mark when the company attempts to apply the system to operate seamlessly at multiple locations.

Practicality (or methodologies) may dictate a sequence for addressing the dimensions, and the sequence may differ from project to project and, within a project, from perspective to perspective. The sequence selected should reflect a conscious decision for the case at hand and should not be based solely on a generic methodology constraint. The suboptimization of any particular dimension may also sometimes be justified, but when a dimension is suboptimized, that fact should be recognized so that the increased project risk is consciously accepted.

Dimension Simplicity

Each dimension represents an abstraction of the complete picture to help focus attention to a particular aspect of the situation. (See Fig 3-28.) The abstractions correspond to the six basic interrogatives of what?,

Figure 3-28
Rule 2.

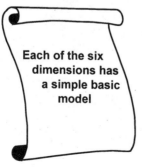

Each of the six dimensions has a simple basic model

Figure 3-29
Dimension
Metamodels.

DIMENSION	ENTITY	CONNECTION	METAMODEL
ENTITIES	Entity	Relationship	Entity - Relationship - Entity
ACTIVITIES	Function	Argument	Function - Argument - Function
LOCATIONS	Node	Link	Node - Link - Node
PEOPLE	Agent	Work	Agent - Work - Agent
TIMES	Time	Cycle	Time - Cycle - Time
MOTIVATIONS	Ends	Means	Ends - Means - Ends

Figure 3-29
Dimension
Metamodels.

how?, where?, who?, when?, and why? Answers to these questions provide information on entities (or things), activities (or functions and processes), locations, people, times, and motivations. For building a product, the answers must also include the connections or interactions among these. For example, within the Entities dimension, the relationships among the entities is important. A visible example of this is the entity relationship diagram, which is developed to provide the designer's perspective of entities. Similar requirements exist in each of the other dimensions. (See Fig. 3-29.)

The basic model for each dimension is valid for all perspectives of that dimension. The representation of the entity or connection will vary among perspectives, as each perspective represents a transformation from the previous one and each is subject to different constraints.

Dimension Uniqueness

The Zachman Framework is a classification scheme, and for any classification scheme to be valid, there can be no ambiguity in the classifications. (See Fig. 3-30.) Each metamodel defined in the previous sections,

Figure 3-30
Rule 3.

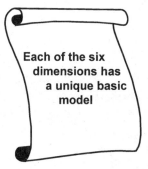

Each of the six
dimensions has
a unique basic
model

therefore, can only be applicable to a particular dimension. Nodes and links, for example, apply to all cells within the Locations dimension, but do not apply to any other cells. The nodes may interact with agents, but the agents themselves are only represented in the Peoples dimension. The interactions between the nodes and the agents are reflective of the interactions among the six dimensions, all of which are needed to fully represent each perspective.

Perspective Uniqueness

Another aspect of eliminating ambiguity in the classification scheme within the Zachman Framework is the uniqueness of each perspective. (See Fig. 3-31.) Each perspective deals with the product in a particular way. This topic was dealt with extensively in a previous section. The differences among the perspectives are driven by the constraints, and the cumulative nature of these constraints dictates the sequence of the perspectives. Figure 3-32 summarizes the characteristics of the perspectives.

Cell Uniqueness

The third rule addresses the unique metamodel of each dimension (or column) within the Zachman Framework, and the fourth rule addresses the unique view each perspective (or row) provides. Logically, then, the cells, which represent the intersections of the columns and rows, must each be unique. (See Fig. 3-33.) The uniqueness of the cell is represented by the metaentities it contains. (See Fig. 3-34.)

Figure 3-31
Rule 4.

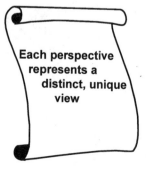

Each perspective represents a distinct, unique view

■■ ■■ ■■ ■■
Figure 3-32
Characteristics of Per-
spectives.

PERSPECTIVE	PURPOSE	PRODUCT	SAMPLE PRODUCT IN ENTITIES DIMENSION	CONSTRAINT*
PLANNER	Define scope	Scope definition	List of things important to the business	Financial and regulatory
OWNER	Describe real-world product	Business model	Business entities and their relationships	Policy and usage
DESIGNER	Describe abstract product	System model	Data entities and their relationships	Environmental and physics
BUILDER	Describe product construction and assembly	Technology model	Data bases	Construction and technological state of the art and available equipment
SUB-CONTRACTOR	Describe component construction	Out-of-context models	Data definition descriptions	Implementation and integration

* Constraints are additive

Since each cell contains unique metaentities, it follows that the connections between metaentities are also unique to each cell. Additionally, since each cell deals with a unique dimension of a unique perspective, the graphical representation and applicable techniques are also unique to each cell. (See Fig. 3-35.[1])

There are still some unknowns about the graphical semantics for some of the cells, just as there are unknowns about some of the chemicals which could fit into cells in the chemical periodic table.

■■ ■■ ■■ ■■
Figure 3-33
Rule 5.

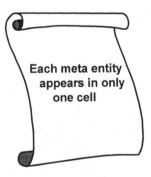

Each meta entity
appears in only
one cell

---

[1]Framework Software, Inc.; P.O. Box 3415; Redondo Beach, CA 90277;(310) 374-8076.

	ENTITIES	ACTIVITIES	LOCATIONS	PEOPLE	TIMES	MOTIVA-TIONS
PLANNER	Class of business thing	Class of business process	Major business location	Major organization unit	Major business event	Major business goal
OWNER	Business entity	Business process	Business location	Organization unit	Business event	Business objective
DESIGNER	Data entity	Application Function	Node function	Role	System event	Criterion
BUILDER	Segment or row	Computer function	System software	User	Execute	Condition
SUB-CONTRACTOR	Field	Language statement	Address	Identity	Interrupt	Subcondition

Figure 3-34   Zachman Framework Metaentities.

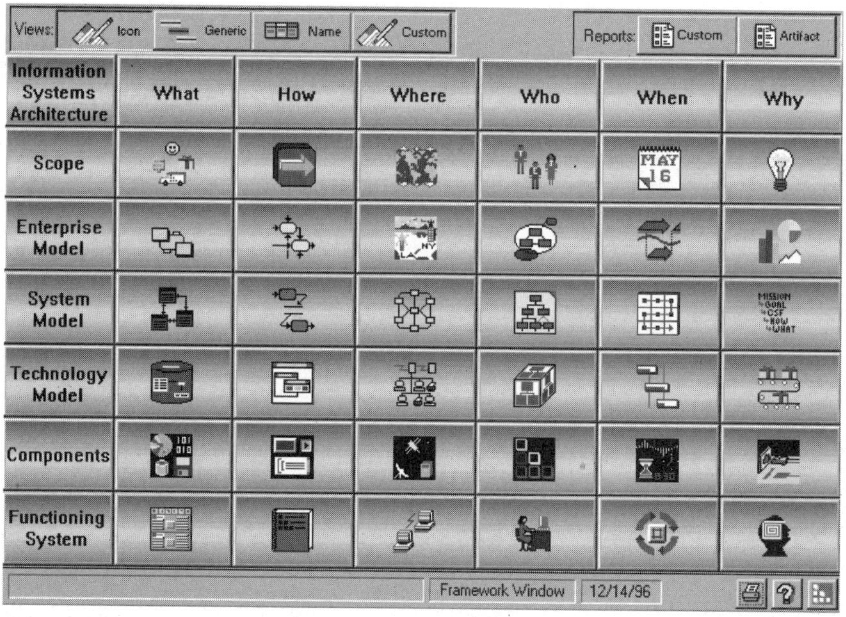

Figure 3-35
Zachman Framework
Graphical Represen-
tations.

Most methodologies consist of techniques which are performed at particular times in the systems development life cycle. Placement of these techniques within the context of the Zachman Framework can be extremely useful. Techniques, which at their elemental level address multiple perspectives should be avoided, since they are unlikely to recognize the constraint differences among the perspectives. Techniques which are repeated at multiple steps of the life cycle should be examined carefully to determine their proper applicability within the context of the Framework. Some techniques in existing methodologies also address multiple dimensions. These techniques should also be carefully examined to ensure that each dimension is addressed by a subset of the technique applicable to it and that the technique does not inadvertently diminish the weight of any of the dimensions.

Chemical Periodic Table Analogy.   The classification scheme of the Zachman Framework is analogous to the classification scheme of the chemical periodic table. The Zachman Framework scheme uses dimensions (columns) and perspectives (rows) to classify unique metaentities and their connections. The periodic table uses groups of elements with similar chemical properties (columns) and periods (rows) to classify chemicals. When the periodic table was first introduced, a number of the cells were empty. Scientists had not yet discovered the elements which fit into these cells, but that did not diminish the value or validity of the classification scheme. The periodic table structure facilitated the search for new elements, and when discovered, the new elements fit into an appropriate cell within the table. (See Fig. 3-36.)

Similarly, the state of the art for systems development has not advanced to the point that complete information is known about every cell. This does not diminish the value of the Framework. By identifying the need for certain constructs, the Zachman Framework may promote research to improve the state of the art of systems development.

Dimension Necessity

Dimensions provide an abstraction of an entire view, aimed at addressing a particular interrogative. The dimension which deals with things addresses the items which are important to the business and the items' derivatives. It does not deal with people, locations, etc. To get a complete model for a perspective, all six dimensions need to be developed, and

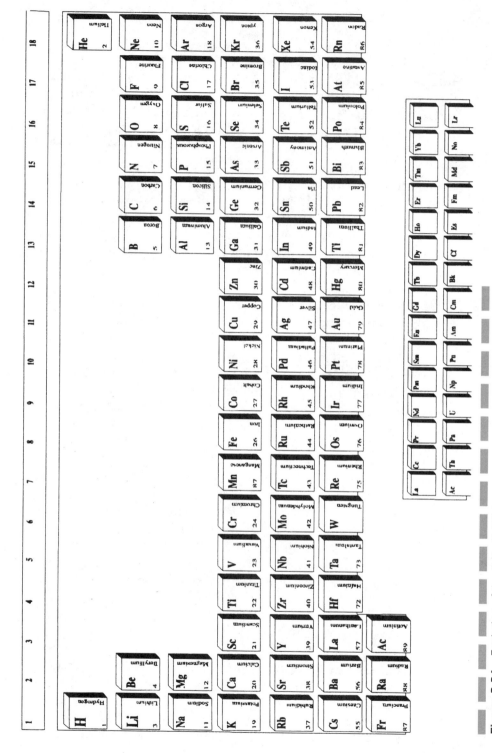

Figure 3-36 Evolution of the Periodic Table.

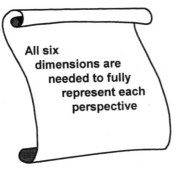

Figure 3-37
Rule 6.

All six
dimensions are
needed to fully
represent each
perspective

the connections among them must also be addressed. (See Fig. 3-37.) By connecting the cells within a perspective it is recognized that each cell is an abstraction but that there is also a dependence among the abstractions. In the Owner perspective, for example, if the Activities dimension deals with hiring and promoting, then the Things dimension must include items such as employees and job classifications, the Times dimension must include the business events which would lead to the activities being invoked, and so on. (See Fig. 3-38.) The implications of not addressing all the dimensions at each level are more fully described in conjunction with the information about the first rule.

Logic Recursiveness

The Zachman Framework supports two types of recursiveness. (See Fig. 3-39.) The Zachman Framework can be used to provide the architectural context for building any product. It can be used to build a house, a plane, a car, a system, a process, or any other tangible or intangible item. It is also applicable for defining a function or process, as described in Chap. 4 which uses the Zachman Framework for managing enterprise knowledge.

ENTITIES	ACTIVITIES	LOCATIONS	PEOPLE	TIMES	MOTIVATIONS
Employee	Hire	Human Resources Office	Recruiters	End of new candidate evaluation	Fill job opening

Figure 3-38 Six Dimensions for Employment.

Figure 3-39
Rule 7.

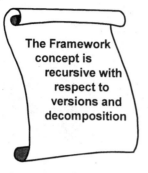

The Framework concept is recursive with respect to versions and decomposition

Version Recursiveness. The Framework is recursive with respect to versions. This aspect of recursiveness permits the Framework to be used to describe an existing system, as well as variants of potential replacement systems. If a husband and wife want to build a house, the information in the Planner and Owner perspectives of the man may differ from that of the woman. Appropriate cells of the Framework can be used to represent each of the views, permitting quick recognition of areas of agreement and better identification of the differences. After the differences are resolved, a third version, which will become the basis of the remaining perspectives, can be created.

Using the Framework can help focus attention to those areas which change, while addressing the other areas only to the extent needed to confirm that they are unaffected. The confirmation step is analogous to developing the information for the new system by using a reusable component (contents of a cell for the existing system). In Chap. 7, the Zachman Framework is used to develop a simple data warehouse. Chapter 8 uses the recursiveness property to expand the data warehouse, Chap. 9 applies it toward the development of an operational data store, and Chap. 11 builds on these further to replace legacy systems and help companies improve their business processes.

The cells which are likely to encounter changes differ, depending on the change being introduced. If the change is being introduced to account for an organizational change, the greatest impact is likely to be in the Peoples dimension, with some impact possibly felt in the Locations dimension and the Subcontractor perspective of the Things and Activities dimensions. If the change is being introduced to account for the addition of a step in processing a new customer, the primary impact is likely to be in the Activities and Times dimensions, with impacts in the other cells dependent on the effects of the change and likely to be in

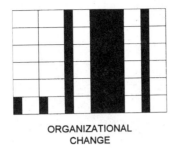

Figure 3-40
Cells Impacted by
System Changes.

ORGANIZATIONAL
CHANGE

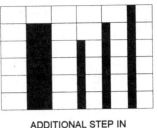

ADDITIONAL STEP IN
EXISTING PROCESS

the lower-level perspectives. Regardless of which perspective of each dimension is first impacted, all dependent perspectives could be impacted. (See Fig. 3-40.)

Decomposition Recursiveness. The Zachman Framework is recursive with respect to decomposition. This aspect of recursiveness takes several forms. In the selection of a set of repository and CASE tools, for example, the Owner perspective of the product (e.g., repository or CASE tool) changes based on who is represented in the Owner row. Each owner's view can be decomposed into a full framework to represent the architecture required to complete that view. To the repository manufacturer, the repository itself is the product, and the owner in that environment defines the business model for the repository. To the repository customer, the business model of interest is the metamodel portrayed by the repository. To the information systems customer, the business model of interest is the metadata which is stored in the repository. (See Fig. 3-41.)

A variant of this form of recursiveness pertains to the breadth of the customer of a system. An executive's list of major activities may be very broad. A department head's list may provide more focus, and the potential customer of the system may have a narrower focus. Each of these could be considered to be a subset of the other. (See Fig 3-42.) The recur-

Figure 3-41
Decomposition
Recursiveness—
Owner Views.

OWNER	PRODUCT OF INTEREST
Repository manufacturer	Repository itself
Repository customer	Metamodel represented in the repository
System user	Metadata stored within the metamodel in the repository

EXECUTIVE'S VIEW	DEPARTMENT HEAD'S VIEW	SYSTEM USER'S VIEW
Sales	Recruiting	Identifying skills needed
Marketing	Hiring	Developing courses
Staffing	Placing	Training instructors
Procurement	**Developing**	Training employees
etc.	Firing	Monitoring attendance
	etc.	etc.

Figure 3-42 *Decomposition Recursiveness—Granularity.*

siveness of these views is very different from the transformation between perspectives. The recursiveness essentially changes the level of granularity; the transformations are needed to address different constraints.

Summary

The Zachman Framework provides an architectural context for building any product or process. It accomplishes this through a classification scheme which ensures that all 30 aspects of the product's life cycle receive the appropriate attention. The 30 aspects occupy cells within a matrix pictorial of the Framework. In this matrix, the rows represent different perspectives of the product and the columns represent its dimensions.

The classification scheme of the Zachman Framework is analogous to that of the chemical periodic table. Just as the schema of the periodic table helps scientists understand the known elements and anticipate characteristics of the unknown ones, the Zachman Framework helps systems professionals understand the role of each aspect of the systems life cycle, even though some of these are not yet fully developed. The schema may help systems professionals further develop those which need it.

The Zachman Framework classification scheme abides by seven basic rules. (See Fig. 3-43.) These rules ensure that there is no ambiguity concerning the applicable perspective, dimension, or their intersection point.

Figure 3-43 Zach-
man Framework
Rules.

Dimension Importance

Dimension Simplicity

Dimension Uniqueness

Perspective Uniqueness

Cell Uniqueness

Dimension Necessity

Logic Recursiveness

**The Zachman Framework differs from traditional method-
ologies in that it is, in actuality, not a methodology. It is a
classification scheme for the deliverables from a methodology.**

As a classification scheme, it therefore places equal priority and
importance on the descriptive representations for each of the six dimensions of a product as well as each of its five distinct perspectives. It is
not inconsistent with prevailing techniques or methodologies, as the
deliverables from any technique or methodology can be mapped against
the cells. In this sense, the Framework is very helpful for positioning any
technique or methodology to understand what it is attempting to
accomplish, as well as what it is not addressing.

The use of the Framework for defining enterprise knowledge management is explored in Chap. 4. Chapters 7 and 8 further apply the Framework in the contexts of developing a data warehouse. Chapter 11 portrays
the role of the Framework in extending the data warehouse to become a
means for achieving a better-managed information environment.

CHAPTER 4

A Framework for Managing Enterprise Knowledge

The first section of the book traced the evolution of information management, pointing out the value of moving to an architected environment. Chapter 3 described the Zachman Framework, its structure, and the rules governing its structure and demonstrated its flexibility with respect to its application. It can be applied equally well to tangible products such as airplanes, buildings, and systems and to intangible objects such as enterprises.

It is helpful to first describe the utility of the Framework as a generic thinking tool for improving understanding and for making better decisions about designing and managing change for any complex object. Because the Framework is universally applicable, there are several objects within an enterprise for which it can be beneficially employed. Four of these are particularly interesting when it comes to managing the enterprise knowledge:

- ■ The Product Framework

- ■ The Enterprise Framework (that is, the framework that embodies the process of designing, building, distributing, etc., the product or service of the enterprise)

- ■ The Enterprise Engineering Framework (that is, the Framework that embodies the process of designing, building, distributing, etc., the enterprise itself, as differentiated from the product or service)

- ■ The Repository Framework (that is, the Framework that embodies the generic process of designing, building, distributing, etc., the models of any complex object)

The majority of this chapter is devoted to defining these four Framework applications, describing their relationships, and using them as a context for defining knowledge management.

Observations about the Framework

The Zachman Framework is a classification scheme for design artifacts, that is, descriptive representations, of any complex object. The utility of such a classification scheme is to enable focused concentration on selected aspects of the object without losing a sense of the contextual, or holistic, perspective. In designing and building complex objects, there are simply too many details and relationships to consider simultaneously. Isolating single variables and making design decisions out of context, however, results in suboptimization, with all its attendant costs and dissipation of energy. Restoring the integrity of the whole, or retrofitting the suboptimized components of the resultant object, such that the object might be used for the purpose originally intended, could well be financially prohibitive. This is the condition in which many companies find themselves after about 50 years of building automated systems out of context.

A typical company has a large inventory of current systems (sometimes called stovepipe systems, or legacy systems). These systems were often built out of context and were designed to meet a specific, sometimes narrow, set of functional requirements. They were not truly integrated into the company's application suite, and they communicated with other systems through complex interfaces. (See Fig. 4-1.) Their ability to meet the company's current and future needs tends to be extremely

Figure 4-1
Legacy Systems.

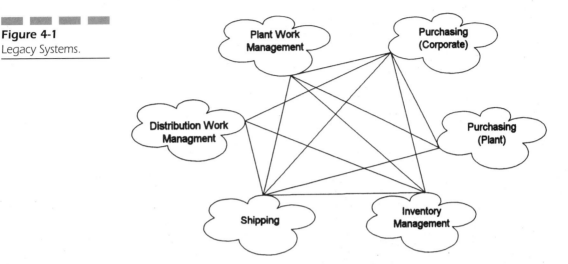

limited. Further, these systems consume enormous amounts of resources for maintenance and support and are far too costly to replace en masse. The word *legacy* has a negative connotation, implying the systems are kind of an albatross, a penalty to be paid for the mistakes of the past.

A balance between the holistic contextual view and the pragmatic implementation view can be facilitated by a framework that has the characteristics of any good classification scheme. (See Fig. 4-2.) These classification schemes allow for abstractions intended to

- Simplify for understanding and communication
- Clearly focus on independent variables for analytical purposes
- Maintain a disciplined awareness of contextual relationships that are significant for preserving the integrity of the object

It makes little difference whether the object is physical, like a product, or conceptual, like a company or other enterprise. The challenges are the same.

Figure 4-2
Framework Facilitates
Focus.

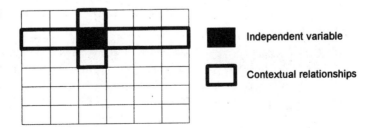

How do you design and build an object piece by piece such that it achieves its purpose without dissipating its value and raising its cost by optimizing the pieces and suboptimizing the object?

In every company there are several objects, including the enterprise itself, that are sufficiently complex and inherently critical to the organization's purpose that they warrant applying Zachman Framework concepts and formally producing the relevant descriptive representations.

The Product Framework

Each of a company's product is one such object, especially if it is a complex engineering product such as an airplane, a building, or a computer system. The Framework logic itself was derived from observing the descriptive representations of such complex products. While studying the manufacturing discipline, it became clear that the descriptive representations for the product were depicting different views of the product. Some represented the owner's perspective, some the designer's, and some the builder's. The descriptions also focused on different aspects. Some focused on the material, some on the function, and some on the geometry. It was fairly straightforward to see that there was a relationship between the perspectives and the foci (or abstractions). The Framework logic was simply a statement of the obvious, a logical structure for classifying the descriptive representations that are relevant for the object (or subject) of interest.

Figure 4-3 contains names of examples of complex product design artifacts for the first three Framework columns from which the Framework logic was initially observed. These describe the tangible aspects of the product.

It was only after the Framework logic was articulated initially that it became apparent that there were descriptive representations of the intangible aspects of the product as well. The representations of the intangible aspects of the product are manifest in the other three columns of the Zachman Framework, which, from a product perspective, are descriptive of the product operation (people and workflow), product timing cycles (event sequence/cycle, i.e., relative time as opposed to absolute time), and design objectives and strategies (values and tradeoff decisions).

In general, there is far less formalization of the intangible aspects of the product (the other three columns) than the tangible aspects. This is

Figure 4-3
Descriptive Represen-
tations for a Product.

PRODUCT FRAMEWORK

	MATERIAL	FUNCTION	GEOMETRY
CONTEXT	Mission Definition / Concepts Package		
OWNER	Work Breakdown Structure	Functional Specifications	Scale Drawings / Mock-ups
DESIGNER	Engineering BOM (As Designed)	Product Physics (Theoretical)	Engineering Drawings
BUILDER	Mfg. Eng. BOM (As Planned)	Function Design (Practical)	Engineering Drawings
OUT-OF-CONTEXT	Parts List (As Built)	Function (Actual)	Assembly & Fabrication Drawings
PRODUCT	Delivered Product		

Figure 4-3
Descriptive Representations for a Product.

not to say that the models (design artifacts) of the intangible aspects of the product do not exist. In fact, they do exist, but in many cases they remain implicit rather than being made explicit. That is, the cost and time required to make them explicit is perceived to be greater than the risk incurred from making assumptions about them. As described in Chap. 3, recognizing the existence of all six columns enables conscious strategy decisions concerning the models that can be left implicit versus those that must be made explicit. These are areas in which assumptions can be made without undue risk. On the other hand, when a significantly increased investment up front is considered inexpensive relative to the cost of rectifying the erroneous assumptions of implicit descriptions discovered after the fact, it is advisable to define the models explicitly.

Every organization which produces a product has an implicit or explicit Product or Service Framework. As the degree of complexity increases, the likelihood is that many, if not most, of the design artifacts are explicitly defined. For the remainder of this chapter, only the first three columns of design artifacts are discussed and/or illustrated, purely for the purpose of simplification in presenting the important concepts.

With the advent of computers, automation, as it has been applied to the Product Framework models, has resulted in shop floor control systems from the column-A (material) models, embedded systems deriving from column-B (function) models, and computer-aided engineering and

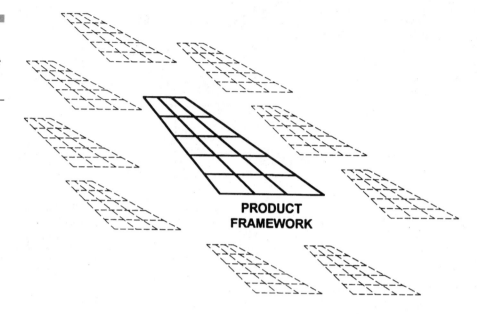

design systems deriving from column-C (geometry) models. These application implementations tended to fall within the purview of the engineering and manufacturing organizations or their production equivalents in the service-oriented enterprises.

As a matter of fact, the enterprise may use a number of complex objects that merit a framework of design artifacts in their own right. However, if the enterprise is not *producing* and/or *changing* the objects but merely *using* them, its needs for information about the objects could be satisfied simply through object attributes. That is, only a producing enterprise is likely to realize sufficient business value to warrant expending the resources necessary to create and maintain the comprehensive set of design artifacts required for production and change management for the product. Figure 4-4 attempts to convey the implicit nature of the design artifacts of objects that are merely used as opposed to the explicit nature of the design artifacts of the product that is being produced and maintained.

The Enterprise Framework

The realization that the framework logic for products (owner, designer, builder; material, function, geometry; etc.) could be applied to enterprises (or organizations or companies) was a significant breakthrough for purposes of enterprise design and change management because all the lessons learned in the older disciplines that produced physical products could be directly employed for conceptual products, such as the enterprises themselves. The Zachman Framework, as it has been discussed in Chap. 3, describes the six columns or dimensions of design artifacts, or models, that are relevant for enterprises.

Relationship to Product Framework

The Enterprise Framework has a definitive relationship with the Product Framework. To illustrate the relationship between the two sets of framework models, consider a hypothetical instance of a business process model (row 2, column B of the Enterprise Framework) as depicted in Fig. 4-5.

Figure 4-5 is an example of a very high level model of a generic product development and production business process, showing no input or output relationships between the subprocesses. It demonstrates that the logical deliverables of these subprocesses in the Enterprise business process model are actually the design artifacts of the Product Framework. That is, since the end objective of the product development

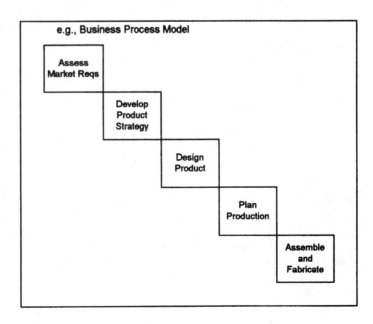

Figure 4-5
Enterprise Business Process Model Sample.

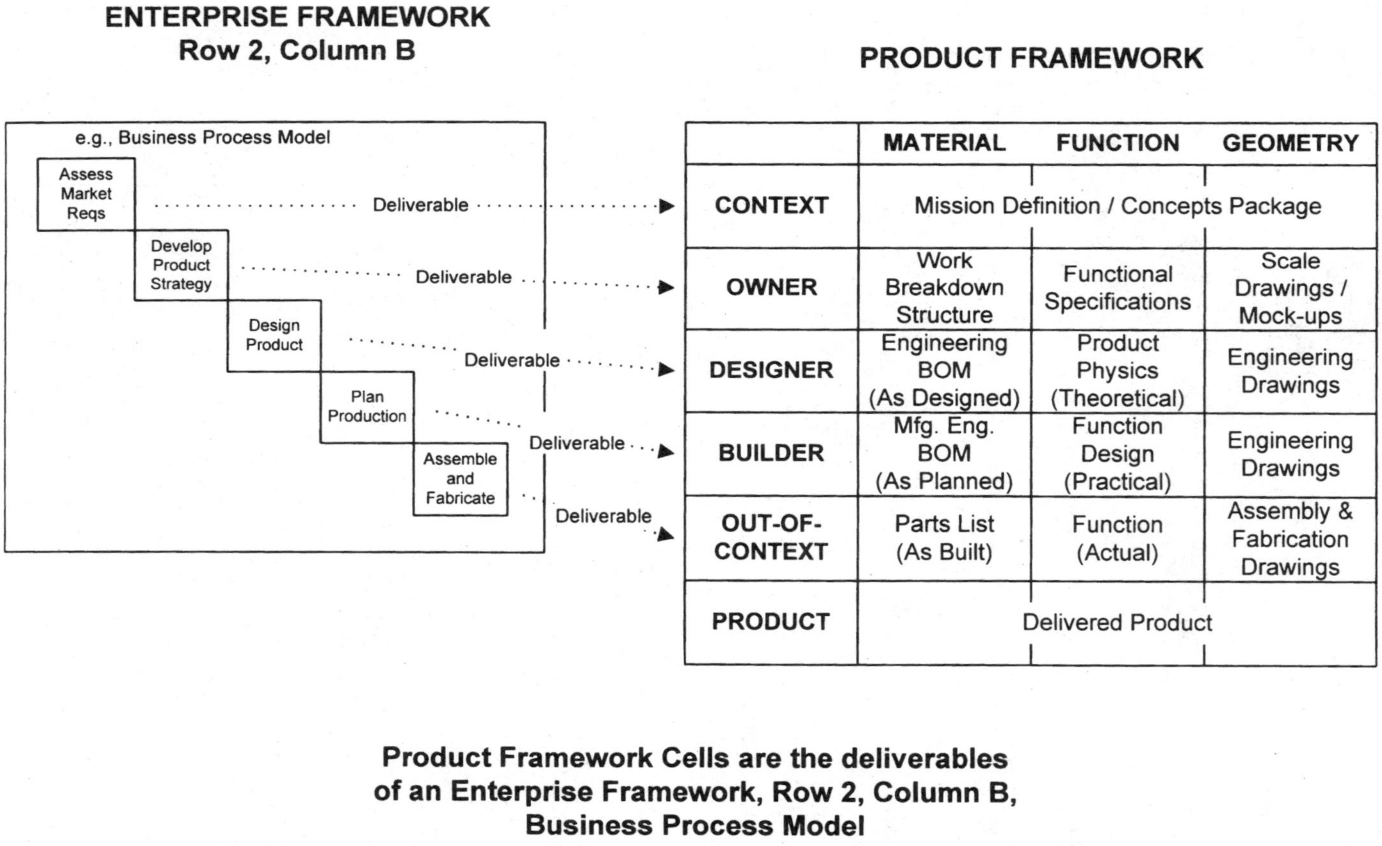

PRODUCT FRAMEWORK

	MATERIAL	FUNCTION	GEOMETRY
CONTEXT	Mission Definition / Concepts Package		
OWNER	Work Breakdown Structure	Functional Specifications	Scale Drawings / Mock-ups
DESIGNER	Engineering BOM (As Designed)	Product Physics (Theoretical)	Engineering Drawings
BUILDER	Mfg. Eng. BOM (As Planned)	Function Design (Practical)	Engineering Drawings
OUT-OF-CONTEXT	Parts List (As Built)	Function (Actual)	Assembly & Fabrication Drawings
PRODUCT		Delivered Product	

Product Framework Cells are the deliverables of an Enterprise Framework, Row 2, Column B, Business Process Model

**ENTERPRISE FRAMEWORK
Row 2, Column B**

Figure 4-6   Product Framework Relationship to Enterprise Framework Business Process Model.

process is to produce the enterprise's product, it necessarily requires producing the design artifacts for the product. The product design artifacts are the cells of the Product Framework as shown earlier in Fig. 4-3.

Figure 4-6 is a graphic representation of the relationship between the Enterprise Framework business process model and the design artifacts of the Product Framework. In a similar fashion, the Enterprise Framework column-A models, that is, the models of the material, things, or objects of the enterprise, would include models of the design artifacts of the product, the contents of the cells of the Product Framework, and very significant things produced and managed by the enterprise. Figure 4-7 is a very high level, generic, partial list of things from the Product Framework that would be part of the row-2, column-A semantic model of the enterprise.

Application

In addition to identification of all the relationships between the things, a robust semantic model of the enterprise would have considerably more detail than that of Fig. 4-7. This simplistic example is used merely to illustrate that the Enterprise Framework semantic model (row 2, column A) is comprised of, among other things, models of all the cells of the Product Framework. Of course, the complete, enterprisewide semantic model of the enterprise things would include not only product-related things as

Figure 4-7
Product Framework
Semantic Model
Components.

Work Breakdown Structure Components	Functional Specifications	Scale Drawings / Mock-ups
As Designed Parts	Theoretical Function	Engineering Drawings
As Planned Parts	Designed Function	Mfg. Eng. Drawings
As Built Parts	Built Function	Assembly & Fabrication Drawings

et cetera   et cetera

expressed in the Product Framework but also all the things that are *used* in the production of the product or are of significance to the operation of the enterprise as previously suggested, for example, in Fig. 4-4.

In a similar fashion, column C, the Geometry column of the Product Framework, which is represented by the row-2, column-C model of locations in the enterprise Framework would be a model of where the design artifacts, product models, and cells of the Product Framework are being produced. At an excruciating level of detail, this would likely be a model of the layout of the engineering and manufacturing facilities showing the placement of the machine tools and the routing of the parts as they are being fabricated and assembled into a product. The total enterprisewide location model would also include the locations of the non—product-related objects including customers, vendors, employees.

In summary, the row-2 models of the Enterprise Framework have a kind of metarelationship with the cells (models) of the Product Framework in that they are the models of what, how, and where the product models are produced over the process of producing the product itself.

Bear in mind that, as in the case of the Product Framework, the row-2 models of the Enterprise Framework would have to be transformed into row-3 as-designed (logical), row-4 as-planned (physical), and row-5 as-built (systems) models of the enterprise. In this fashion, the row-2 perceptions of the enterprise owners become the reality of the operating enterprise.

When the owners change their minds about how they want the enterprise to operate (e.g., row-2 models), the lower-row (rows 3 to 5) models must also be changed so that the desired changes can be manifest in the actual operation of the enterprise.

The absence of these ensuing transformations accounts for the frustration that management commonly has in actually instituting the changes it wants to effect.

Note that the end result of transforming the Enterprise Framework models from row to row and, ultimately, to row 6, is not only automated systems. If the technology constraints of row 4 are pencils, paper, and file cabinets, the resultant row-6 models would be manual systems. If the row-4 technology constraints are computer hardware and software, the resultant systems would be automated. The row-3, row-4, and row-5 models of the Enterprise Framework are the *implementation* of the enterprise, that is, the transformation of the owner's perception of the enterprise into the reality of the enterprise itself, automated or manual.

Figure 4-8
Enterprise Framework Meta-relationship with Product Framework.

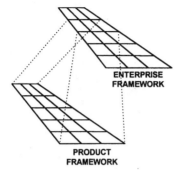

Ignoring the non—product-oriented objects like machine tools, customers, accounts, and vendors, Fig. 4-8 graphically represents the metarelationship between the Enterprise Framework and the Product Framework.

Engineering Administration

In a complex product manufacturing business, many organizations in the enterprise contribute to building the various product models, but *engineering administration* is charged with the responsibility of maintaining the models. All changes to the product are channeled through engineering administration, which retains previous versions of the models, enabling changes to be traced back through history. This serves as a comprehensive repository of knowledge about the product that enables numerous and rapid improvements to be made in the product. Consider airplanes for example. In the short period of 100 years, structures made of wood and cloth-covered components rapidly evolved into structures made of titanium and composites that can fly to the moon, enabled by the accumulated knowledge about the product as captured in the design artifacts.

Airplanes which were built decades ago are still flying, and business travelers rarely give a second thought to the age of the jet itself. The ability of these airplanes to remain functional is attributable to the rigor with which each of the models is maintained. Through this approach, incorporation of new requirements traverses through each of the five views and each of the six dimensions, so that the features are integrated into the overall design. The users of the planes take this for granted—the users of an enterprise (systems) should also be able to take this for granted. An organization for managing the enterprise models is needed. (See Fig. 4-9.)

Figure 4-9
Change Management.

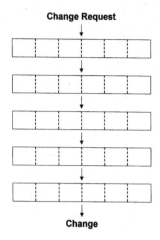

Data Administration

In most enterprises, there presently is no organization equivalent to engineering administration that is charged with managing the enterprise models. In some enterprises there is a data administration organization that attempts to manage the enterprise data as embodied in the column-A models of the Enterprise Framework, but the enterprise's perception of the role of data administration tends to be very limited. Data administration in many cases is constrained to be passive, overhead, and focused on input and transaction support. Its focus should be broadened to include all the column-A models, managing change, and supporting output, to facilitate analysis and exploitation of the company's investment in its data.

This limited perception of data administration is very reminiscent of the early appearance of material organizations in the manufacturing industry as it began to actualize the standard-production concepts. The enormous capital investment in material demanded attention and controls in order to protect profitability. Over time, the concept of material management broadened substantially to optimize the actual material inventory and manage the models from which to quickly adapt and rapidly assemble items to order.

Enterprises generally have not yet discovered or associated these aggressive, proactive material management concepts with data administration. They are just now becoming sensitive to the enormous capital investment in data (or information) whose value has been dissipated because of inattention and the erroneous assumptions that resulted from leaving the Enterprise Framework, column-A models implicit.

Data Warehouse and Operational Data Store

This is the pressing issue causing the avalanche of activity around the data warehouse and the operational data store. The data warehouse is a clever strategy that attempts to rectify the sins of the past and redeem some value out of the material (e.g., things, data) of the enterprise. With the introduction of tools which can directly access data in the legacy operational systems, there is a strong temptation to use these tools to extract information for queries reports and to call the result a data warehouse. Applying the tools is easy, but the result is not an architected data warehouse. It is just another quick fix for an immediate problem, and it compounds the overall complexity of the information-processing environment.

The operational data store is a further extension of the data warehouse concept to apply the strategy to support operational processes. As was noted in Chap. 2, this extension would often be unnecessary had the operational systems been built on explicitly stated models in the first place.

The fundamental and lasting Enterprise Framework solution to the data problem is explicitly to produce the column-A models and manage them over time. This would free the enterprise from all the data transformations, reconciliations, interfacing, maintenance, etc., associated with the legacy systems and redirect energy and resources on analysis, harvesting, mining, exploiting the data to its maximum advantage. (See Fig. 4-10.) Paradoxically, data administration tends to have the skills required for such an expanded role, but in many cases it lacks either the vision from within or the charge and direction from the enterprise to effect the fundamental solution to the data problem.

Referring to the Enterprise Framework in its entirety, the column-A data models are only a small subset of the descriptive representations that are relevant for designing and changing the enterprise. Therefore, the challenge of model management goes beyond the normal scope, and even the expanded scope, of data administration.

Figure 4-10   *Using Data to Its Maximum Advantage.*

The Challenge

One cannot help but observe that if an enterprise expended the equivalent amount of energy managing the Enterprise Framework models as an airplane manufacturer expends managing its Product Framework models, the enterprise could have a comprehensive knowledge base upon which to realize dramatic increases in the state of the art of enterprise design. Until the enterprise learns how to retain and manage its knowledge base of design artifacts, it is likely relegated to an enterprise design and performance equivalent to that of wood-structured, cloth-covered-component airplanes.

This raises the question,

> **Who in the enterprise is charged with producing and managing the design artifacts, that is, the Enterprise Framework models, which are the knowledge base of enterprise infrastructure?**

Before answering the rhetorical question, it may be useful to observe that using the Enterprise Framework to organize (classify) the descriptive representations of the enterprise quite independent of those of the product is helpful for two reasons:

- It makes it possible to apply many of the lessons learned over hundreds of years of complex product engineering and manufacturing to the rather new science of enterprise engineering.

■ It makes it possible to disassociate product engineering issues from enterprise engineering issues, reducing complexity and confusion between the two separate but similar processes.

Now returning to the question, Who is charged with managing the knowledge base of enterprise infrastructure, the Enterprise Framework models?

Information Systems Department Framework

There is a third framework that has major significance to the enterprise—it could be thought of as the Information Systems Department Framework. Information systems (as an organizational entity) has all the characteristics of a complex enterprise in its own right. It has an owner, designer, builder; data, process, and network. The Zachman Framework logic could be applied to information systems, just like any other complex object, including the product or the entire enterprise. Figure 4-11 is

Figure 4-11
Information Systems Department Business Process Model Sample.

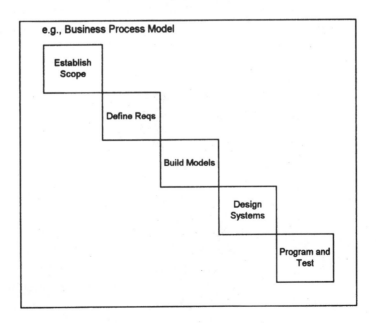

INFORMATION SYSTEMS DEPARTMENT FRAMEWORK
Row 2, Column B

e.g., Business Process Model

Establish Scope

Define Reqs

Build Models

Design Systems

Program and Test

an example of a row-2, column-B (business process) model of an Information Systems Department Framework.

The example in Fig. 4-11 is a very high level model of an information systems application development business process, without any of the inputs or outputs. Although the subprocesses in Fig. 4-11 are graphically arranged in a waterfall form, it is not meant to imply anything about the sequence, iterations, modularity, etc., of the process. This is the reason that no attempt was made to include inputs and outputs. That is, the example is not meant to be a commentary on which methodology—waterfall, spiral, or prototyping—is more or less preferable. The intent of the example is simply to illustrate the nature of the business processes relevant for an Information Systems Framework and to show that the logical deliverables of this particular information systems business process are actually the cells of the Enterprise Framework as depicted in Fig. 4-12. This is identical to the case made previously that the deliverables of the Enterprise Framework business processes are actually the cells of the Product Framework.

The Problem

It should be pointed out that there is a very big problem with the business process model example shown in Figs. 4-11 and 4-12. The problem is that the model is defined from an information systems perspective, and this could be expected because it was declared to be part of the Information Systems Department Framework. The first and second subprocesses read Establish Scope and Define Requirements, respectively. From the information systems perspective, that accurately represents the role of the row-1 and row-2 models of the Enterprise Framework. However, from the enterprise perspective, which is intended to be the perspective of the Enterprise Framework, the row-1 models are the specifications of the environmental conditions surrounding the enterprise which establish its priorities, parameters, strategy, and structure. The row-2 models are the design models of the enterprise itself, from the perspective of its owners.

Granted, the information systems interest in rows 1 and 2 of the Enterprise Framework is to extract scope decisions and requirements specifications for automated systems, but that is a very limited employment of the models. A more appropriate terminology for the process of defining the row-1 and row-2 models, which would reflect the enter-

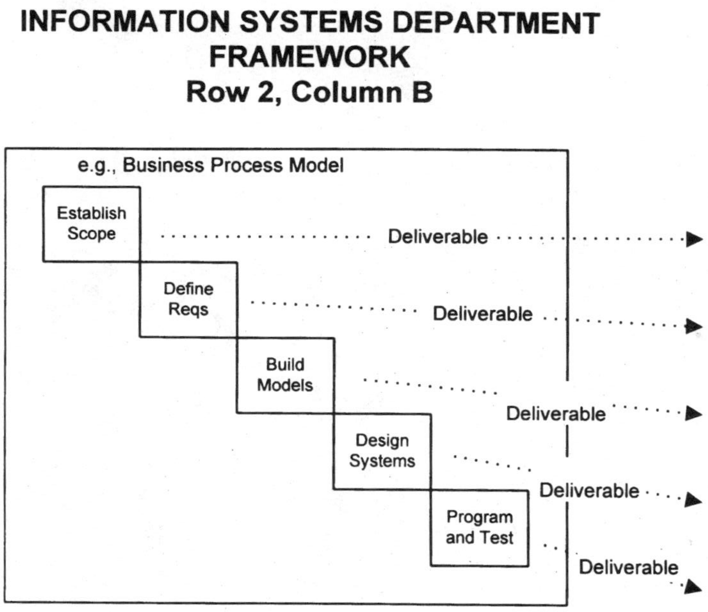

INFORMATION SYSTEMS DEPARTMENT FRAMEWORK
Row 2, Column B

ENTERPRISE FRAMEWORK

	MATERIAL	FUNCTION	GEOMETRY
CONTEXT	e.g., List of Things	e.g., List of Processes	e.g., List of Locations
OWNER	e.g., Semantic Model	e.g., Business Process Model	e.g., Business Logistics Model
DESIGNER	e.g., Logical Data Model	e.g., Application Architecture	e.g., Distributed Systems Architecture
BUILDER	e.g., Physical Data Model	e.g., Systems Design	e.g., Systems Architecture
OUT-OF-CONTEXT	e.g., Data Definition	e.g., Program	e.g., Network Architecture
PRODUCT	Running Systems		

e.g., Business Process Model

Establish Scope — Deliverable
Define Reqs — Deliverable
Build Models — Deliverable
Design Systems — Deliverable
Program and Test — Deliverable

Enterprise Framework Cells are the deliverables of an Information Systems Department Framework, Row 2, Column B, Business Process Model

Figure 4-12 Deliverables of Information Systems Department Framework.

109

prise owner's perspective, might be something like Position within Environment and Design Enterprise.

This brings out a very important problem with the name of this third framework, the Information Systems Department Framework. Actually this third framework is *not* the Information Systems Department Framework! In fact, it is a framework for building all the architectural models of the enterprise itself. Some of these may fall within the purview of the information systems department, and some may not. The information systems department just happens to be functioning as an architect (in the architecture and construction sense of the word) relative to the enterprise owners. It is *transcribing* the owner's perspective of the row-1 and row-2 models of the Enterprise Framework and then making the designer's, builder's, and subcontractor's (rows 3 through 5) transformations, which constitute the implementation of the enterprise design (row-2 models).

Actually, the information systems department normally focuses only on the automated implementations of the enterprise and ignores the manual systems. However, the implemented systems, manual plus automated, (row 6 of the Enterprise Framework) become the *physical manifestation of the enterprise.* This is one of the things that is causing much management frustration. The enterprise as it is actually implemented or operating (the manual and/or automated systems as they are implemented, that is, row 6) is inconsistent with what management perceives or wants the enterprise to be (row 2). (See Fig. 4-13.)

In many cases, the information systems department is *not* functioning effectively as an architect. It is not truly transcribing the owner's perspectives of the row-1 and row-2 models as it should. The row-1 and row-2 models are not being produced, and, in many cases, the information systems department is not even producing the designer's (row 3) or

Figure 4-13
The Great
Disconnect.

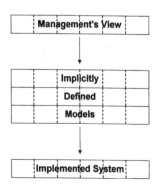

the builder's (row 4) models. The row-1, row-2, row-3, and row-4 models are being left *implicit,* which means that assumptions are being made, and those assumptions in some (possibly many) cases are not valid.

> **Without explicit models about the planner's view (scope), owner's view (business models), designer's view (system models), and builder's view (technical models), the likelihood of the implementation meeting the requirements is low to zero.**

In fact, in this scenario, it would be a miracle if management was not frustrated with the resultant systems implementations.

Typically, in present practice, no specific organizational responsibility is assigned to produce and manage the models of the Enterprise Framework. If there was such a formal endeavor, it could well be named the *enterprise Engineering enterprise,* that is, the human endeavors or enterprise focused on producing the architecture for the main enterprise. Therefore, in place of the Information Systems Department Framework, a more appropriate name for such a framework might be the Enterprise Engineering Framework. Figure 4-14 changes the original information systems department business process model to reflect the enterprise perspective and renames the framework the Enterprise Engineering Framework.

The business process model (row 2, column B) of the Enterprise Engineering Framework, if it were formally defined, would be the explicit specifications of the process (or methodology) that would be followed for defining the main enterprise and transforming it into a physical reality. This would be done by defining the Enterprise Framework row-1 and row-2 models and transforming them through rows 3, 4, and 5 into row 6, that is, into running systems (automated or manual) which are the main Enterprise.

Application

The semantic model (row 2, column A) of the Enterprise Engineering Framework would describe the contents of the Enterprise Framework cells (models) so they could be produced as desired, stored in a database, and maintained and/or changed over time. Figure 4-15 is an example of a high-level list of things in the Enterprise Framework that would have to be modeled in the Enterprise Engineering Framework semantic model.

Notice that the contents of Fig. 4-15 belong to a set that is related to the enterprise and its systems, whereas the contents of Fig. 4-8 belong to

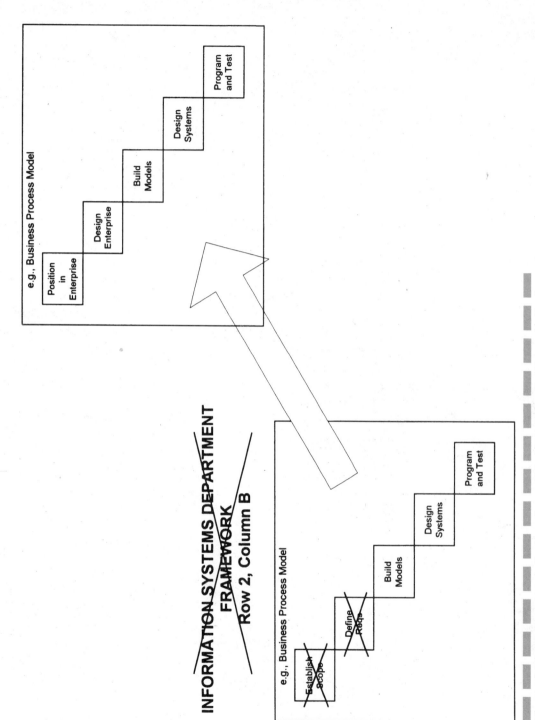

Row 2, Column B

e.g., Business Process Model

| Position in Enterprise |
| Design Enterprise |
| Build Models |
| Design Systems |
| Program and Test |

INFORMATION SYSTEMS DEPARTMENT FRAMEWORK Row 2, Column B

e.g., Business Process Model

| Establish Scope |
| Define Reqs |
| Build Models |
| Design Systems |
| Program and Test |

Figure 4-14 Adjustments to Business Process Model to Reflect the Enterprise Engineering Perspective.

Figure 4-15
Enterprise Engineer-
ing Framework
Semantic Model
Components.

Business Objects	Business Processes	Business Locations
Logical "Entities"	Applications	Distributed System Functions
Tables	Modules	Hardware and System Software
Data Elements	Programs	Nodes

a different set, related to the product that the enterprise is producing. It only makes sense to separate these two different sets of things to simplify the engineering thought process.

The same logic that was presented for the Enterprise Framework establishes that the semantic model (row 2, column A) of the Enterprise Engineering Framework is a model of the models of the Enterprise Framework. The actual model would be far more detailed and contain all the relationships among the model components. The logical data model (row 3, column A) derived from this semantic model is commonly referred to as a *repository information model* in the information systems community because it is the logical data model of all the enterprise models which is required for storing the models in a repository; that is, it is a database for storing models. In a similar fashion, the location model of the Enterprise Engineering Framework specifies where the Enterprise Framework models will be produced and maintained.

Figure 4-16 replaces Fig. 4-12 to show the Enterprise Framework models as deliverables of the business process model of the Enterprise Engineering Framework, plus it adds the designer's view (row 2, column B, Application Architecture) of the Enterprise Engineering Framework.

This addition of a row-3 designer's view is a very high level generic model of an application architecture for the Enterprise Engineering Framework, not intended to imply anything more than make the point that tools (automated or manual) are the applications of enterprise engineering.

In summary, the row-2 models of the Enterprise Engineering Framework have a meta-relationship with all the models of the Enterprise

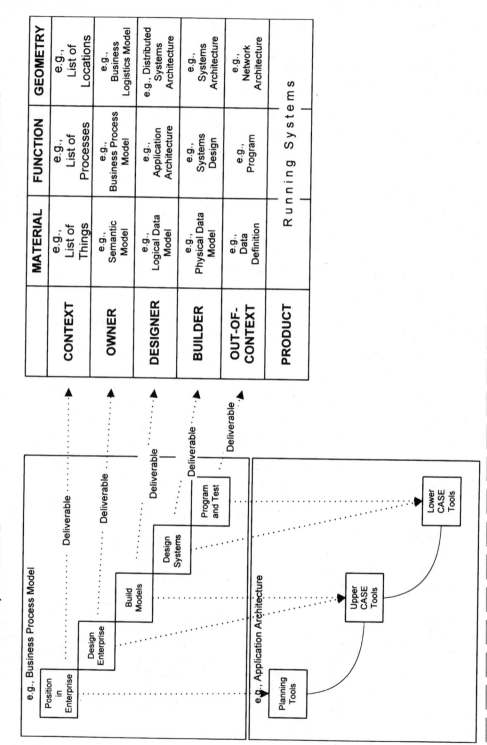

Figure 4-16 *Deliverables of Enterprise Engineering Framework.*

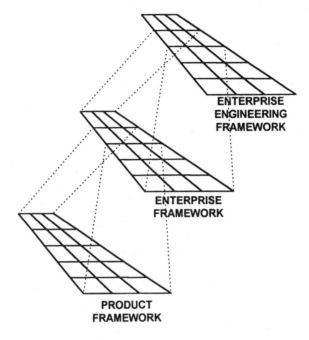

Figure 4-17
Meta-relationship among Product, Enterprise, and Enterprise Engineering Frameworks.

Framework. Figure 4-17 adds the Enterprise Engineering Framework to Fig. 4-8 and graphically depicts the relationship among the Product Framework, the Enterprise Framework, and the Enterprise Engineering Framework.

Summary

Once again, using a framework to factor out the idea of engineering the enterprise from the idea of the enterprise itself makes it possible to conceptualize the engineering of the enterprise as well as apply the lessons of the older disciplines to the process.

To summarize the employment of the Zachman Framework thus far:

■ The product is an object in its own right and has a framework of descriptive representations that are relevant to the product.

■ The enterprise is an object in its own right and has a framework of descriptive representations that are relevant to the enterprise. Further, the enterprise is producing the Product Framework representations as a function of its role in producing the product.

■ The enterprise engineering enterprise is an object in its own right and has a framework of descriptive representations that are relevant to engineering the main enterprise. Further, the enterprise engineering enterprise is producing the Enterprise Framework representations as a function of its role in producing the main enterprise.

Without using such a framework to separate out these complex objects to think about independently, it would be impossible to understand the issues and advance the state of the art of enterprise engineering. There is little wonder that the success rate for enterprise engineering is still minimal and the frustration of management regarding enterprise change remains high. The technical ability to build and store models coupled with the dire need to accommodate the increasing rate of change are the environmental factors that are making it possible and also mandatory to accommodate these enterprise complexities.

The Zachman Framework is not dissimilar to other organizational or taxonomic structures of the physical domain like the periodic table, the zoological taxonomies, or mathematical calculus that allow for dramatic theoretical advances in the face of otherwise unfathomable complexities.

The practical use of the Enterprise Engineering Framework is simply to think and communicate about the immediate issues of managing a changing enterprise, and in this vein, there is one more meta-framework that is significant to the enterprise, the Repository Framework.

The role of the Repository Framework is to employ the semantic model of the Enterprise Engineering Framework as the database design for the models of the Enterprise Framework and in so doing, become a repository for enterprise knowledge. Since its role is to address the knowledge of the enterprise, it is also referred to as the Knowledge Management Framework.

Repository Framework

The same logic that has been twice applied already in this chapter could be applied once again to define a final meta-framework. Figure 4-18 is a graphic representation of the set of four frameworks that exist in every enterprise and that are vitally interesting in the management of change.

Figure 4-18
Frameworks Vital for
Managing a Dynamic
Enterprise.

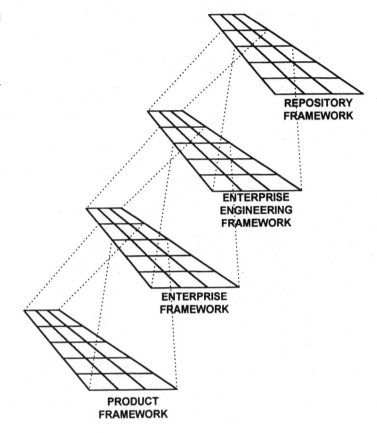

REPOSITORY
FRAMEWORK

ENTERPRISE
ENGINEERING
FRAMEWORK

ENTERPRISE
FRAMEWORK

PRODUCT
FRAMEWORK

Application

The business process model (row 2, column B) of the Repository Framework is a model of building the models of the Enterprise Engineering Framework. It would clearly bear a striking resemblance to the business process model of the Enterprise Engineering Framework itself. Both of these process models would be describing processes for building enterprises. The only difference would be that in one case the resultant enterprise would be the main enterprise being built, and, in the other case, it would be an engineering enterprise that is building the main enterprise. The process models would be different in instance but the same in nature. This is the reason that it would make no sense to identify any more metaprocess models. Everything that can be learned would have been learned.

By the same token, a location model (row 2, column C) in the Repository Framework would be different in instance but not in nature as compared to the locations model of the Enterprise Engineering Framework. Once again, it would make no sense to identify any additional metalocation models.

However, the material or thing model of the Repository Framework is materially different from the previous Framework material models. Only one thing is required to model all things of all the cells of the Enterprise Engineering Framework: "thing." (See Fig. 4-19.)

Adrienne Tannenbaum, the author of *Implementing a Corporate Repository: The Models Meet Reality,* calls this model the "Zen of Meta Modeling." It is the basic model at the heart of repository technology. It is the universal metamodel in that it is a model of any of the models of any of the frameworks. A database deriving from this model could store any or all models. However, this does not obviate any of the intermediate metamodels because it is at such a high level of generality it would not express sufficient definition required for change management.

Figure 4-20 is an illustration of the power of metaconcepts when it comes to change management. Every model in every framework is completely extensible. The figure illustrates that changing any model in any framework may be as easy as adding an instance to a database.

Furthermore, the metastructure lends itself to location independence. Location is simply tracked as an attribute of a thing which provides the ability to put any thing in any place at any metalevel and always be able to find it wherever it is located.

Although conceptually, this four-level repository metastructure is fairly straightforward, it is complicated to implement, and therefore it is not recommended as a do-it-yourself project for just any enterprise. Tools and services are available to help any enterprise that is serious about managing change.

It should be noted that this four-level structure bears a strong resemblance, if not an identity, with the four-level structures of various information resource directory system (IRDS) standards activities.

Figure 4-19
"The Zen of Meta-Modeling" (Adrienne Tannenbaum).

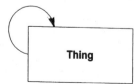

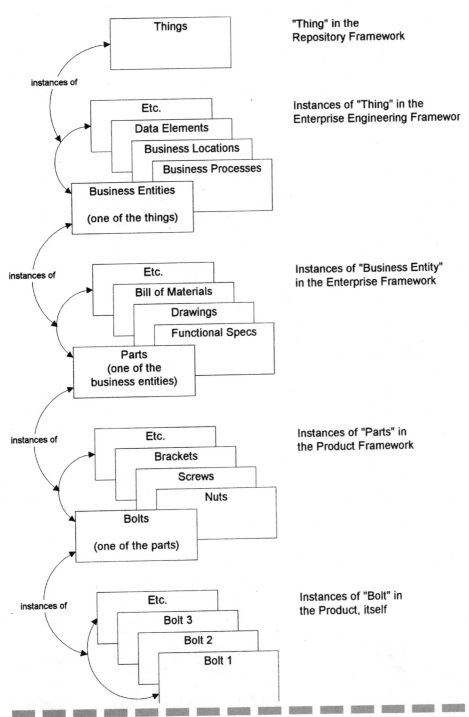

Figure 4-20 Power of Metaconcepts for Change Management. Changing any model in any Framework may be as easy as adding an instance in a database.

Domain of Information Resource Management. Many people think the domain of information resource management is simply one of managing the data of the enterprise. This would entail managing the column-A models of the Enterprise Framework with a somewhat enlarged vision of what is currently thought of as data administration. It would likely include not only the administrative aspects of defining and enforcing data standards but also

- Producing the total set of column-A models
- Keeping them synchronized
- Managing model change
- Migrating out of the legacy environment into an architected environment
- Establishing a capability for assembling to order input and/or output processing systems

Still, this is a rather limited perspective for information resource management.

Managing the Knowledge Base of the Enterprise. Specific responsibility must be assigned for managing the knowledge base of the enterprise, or else the enterprise will never have a knowledge base from which to realize value. Even in the very early stages of the knowledge age, it is becoming apparent that failure to manage knowledge will be at least as devastating as was the failure to manage capital in the industrial age, as knowledge is the capital of the knowledge age.

The domain of information resource management is the management of enterprise knowledge which includes:

- Knowledge about the product as embodied in the set of models describing the product, the Product Framework
- Knowledge about the enterprise as embodied in the set of models describing the enterprise, the Enterprise Framework
- Knowledge about the enterprise engineering enterprise and change management as embodied in the models of the Enterprise Engineering Framework
- Knowledge about managing knowledge as embodied in the models of the Repository Framework

This does not exclude knowledge about the external environment including knowledge about the marketplace, the regulatory environment, the economy, the industry, the technology and so on. However, for any of this external knowledge to be meaningful to the enterprise in any ongoing sense of the word, it must be integrated somewhere into the knowledge base internal to the enterprise as described in the preceding list.

The key to managing all the models of all the vital frameworks is the Repository Framework. The column-A models establish the storage structure for the models of the other frameworks. The column-B models establish the tools (or applications) for synchronizing and controlling the versions of all the other models. And, the column-C models establish the locations in which the models are produced and/or managed at any given point in time.

Analogy to Engineering Administration

As engineering administration is to the product, so should knowledge management be to the enterprise. (See Fig. 4-21.)

It could be argued that knowledge management should even manage the models of the framework first described, the Product Framework, as

Figure 4-21
Engineering Administration and Knowledge Management.

ENGINEERING ADMINISTRATION ROLE	KNOWLEDGE MANAGEMENT ROLE
▪ Doesn't necessarily build all or even any of the model but ensures the models are built and built to specification	▪ Doesn't necessarily build all the models of the enterprise but ensures the models are built and built to specification
▪ Stores the models and keeps them synchronized as change is introduced	▪ Stores the models and keeps them synchronized as change is introduced
▪ Serves as the control point for knowledge about the product that enables the product to be changed, improved, increased in sophistication, and adapted to the changing market requirements	▪ Serves as the control point for knowledge about the enterprise that enables the enterprise to be changed, improved, increased in sophistication, and adapted to the changing environmental conditions
▪ Integral with the change management process for the product	▪ Integral with the change management process of the enterprise
▪ Manages the knowledge base, the design artifacts, and the models of the Product Framework	▪ Manages the knowledge base, the design artifacts, and the models of the Enterprise Framework, enabled by advances in information technology

well, which have historically fallen within the purview of engineering administration. In this case, knowledge management would kind of subsume engineering administration. Because of the historical role of engineering administration and the fact that some of the product models (the drawings) are geometric rather than character-based, there is some rationale to ensure that the engineering administration specialization is protected however the change management process is engineered or however the organization is structured.

Figure 4-22 graphically depicts the comprehensive knowledge base of the enterprise, including

- The four frameworks of models
  - Product knowledge
  - Enterprise knowledge
  - Enterprise engineering knowledge
  - Repository, or knowledge management, knowledge
- The subjects (or objects) the enterprise is *using* as opposed to producing itself
- The common information systems department's names for the columns of models in each framework

Recognizing the fact that the role of knowledge management is the management of the comprehensive knowledge base of the enterprise, what is known as information resource management (IRM) today is likely to be known as knowledge management (KM) tomorrow, the cornerstone of which will be the set of frameworks vital to managing change.

Summary

Enterprises are complex, far too complex to consider in their entirety all at once for design, implementation, management, or adaptation to a changing environment. A framework is mandatory simply as a thinking tool to cut through the complexity without losing an integrated perspective.

Every enterprise has four such frameworks that are related in a very straightforward metafashion, even though it is sometimes difficult to conceptualize models of models (i.e., metamodels). However, it is fairly

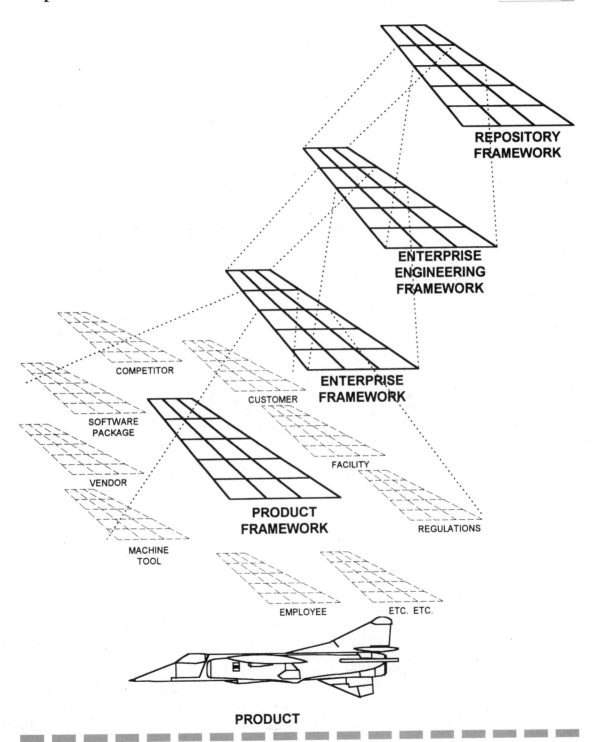

REPOSITORY FRAMEWORK

ENTERPRISE ENGINEERING FRAMEWORK

COMPETITOR

CUSTOMER

ENTERPRISE FRAMEWORK

SOFTWARE PACKAGE

FACILITY

VENDOR

PRODUCT FRAMEWORK

REGULATIONS

MACHINE TOOL

EMPLOYEE

ETC. ETC.

PRODUCT

Figure 4-22 Comprehensive Knowledge Base of the Enterprise

simple to think about any one framework at a time and then after the fact construct the metarelationship with another framework as was done for illustration purposes with the very high level model examples in this chapter.

If there is any one thing that makes the assimilation of high rates of change in an enterprise at all possible, it is the fact that the very same framework logic can be employed recursively, in different contexts, to form a basis for a repository implementation, storing all the models necessary for managing change. If there was no way to organize the models in a consistent, comprehensible, reliable manner, the resultant model would likely be so complicated that it would be very difficult to understand, let alone implement and maintain. With *no* models, accommodating high rates of change is simply impossible.

All the necessary logic for describing the four frameworks and their metarelationships can be developed using a three-column framework. Therefore all the discussion and illustration in this chapter have been limited to the three-column framework for convenience and simplicity. However, it must be remembered that the complete set of descriptive representations would be comprised of six columns of models.

It is beyond the scope of this book to address the process of building and managing all these models. However, it is appropriate to suggest that a deliberate strategy must be employed if the enterprise is ever to achieve an architected state for accommodating the changes that are already rampant in the early stages of the Information Age.

At some point in time, the enterprise is going to wish it had all the models, enterprisewide, horizontally and vertically integrated at an excruciating level of detail!

One thing is clear. It's not a prudent strategy to suspend satisfying short-term demands until all the models are built and stored in a repository. This is demonstrated in the forthcoming chapters with the evolutionary development of a data warehouse using the Zachman Framework, and its use as a foundation for building an architected environment. It is equally imprudent to ignore the issue of architecture altogether. It may take years or even decades to complete all the relevant architectural representations, that is, all the models of all the frameworks. Maybe the end-state vision will never completely be achieved. Maybe it is reasonable to leave some parts of some of the models implicit forever as the cost of producing them continues to be perceived to be greater than the risk of suboptimization or threat of change. However, in *every* case, a deliberate architecture strategy is mandatory and must provide for building the models incrementally and accumulating them over time. Hopefully, in all instances, a balance can be found between satisfying short-term demand and, at the same time, accumulating the architectural models and minimizing the effects of suboptimization of the enterprise in the process.

The knowledge age is here. A thoughtful and deliberate architecture strategy is the key. Knowledge management, in the most expansive sense of the word, is vital.

CHAPTER 5

Establishing the Data Warehouse Strategy

The Zachman Framework is more than a theoretical taxonomy. It is a practical tool which can help companies establish and manage an architected information management—or knowledge management—environment. The first step in establishing this environment is to define a strategy in the form of principles to guide behavior. These guiding principles, at least initially, may apply only to data warehouse activities. Over time, they should apply to the remainder of the knowledge management environment.

This chapter uses the Zachman Framework to identify areas in which principles should be established to define the governing philosophy for the data warehouse environment. Sample principles are presented, but it is not the intent of this book to establish the principles for a particular company. Instead, these samples are meant to help companies understand the topics so that each firm can determine if it needs to define a principle to address a particular area. Not all companies need explicitly stated principles in all the areas cited. If a statement of the guiding principle is needed, the company can use the sample provided as a starting point or create its own, based on its specific environment and needs. Once the guiding principles are established, they need to be communicated to ensure that people understand both the principles and the reasons they are being established.

What Is a Guiding Principle?

A guiding principle, as the name implies, is a statement of belief which is designed to steer or direct activities. A fully conceived guiding principle consists of a statement, the rationale for creating it, and the implications of following it.

The statement should be succinct. It should clearly state a direction so that someone working in the area understands the rules to be followed. Examples of succinct statements are

- All new data warehouse development activities will be funded jointly by information management and the benefiting business unit(s).
- Data warehouse designs will be based on a logical data model.
- The data warehouse will be updated only through controlled batch processes.

The guiding principle represents a direction that the company wants people to follow. Human nature is such that people will resist taking that direction unless they either are forced to do so or understand the reasons for doing so. Stating the rationale of the guiding principles is a way of helping people understand the importance of the direction being set so that they may commit to the principles as opposed to just complying with them. The rationale for the first guiding principle listed above could be stated as follows:

> A data warehouse is built to provide a business benefit. To ensure that business value is appropriately balanced with the cost, the business units which receive the benefits should provide a portion of the funding. A well-architected data warehouse is subject oriented, and, hence, its construction may require expenditures which build a foundation for the future but do not directly support the immediate business need. The information management department has funds for projects designed to benefit the company as a whole; those funds should be used to defray such costs.

The major implications of the guiding principles should also be stated. These statements help people better understand the direction and what it means to the way they, or others, perform their jobs. Some of the implications of the first guiding principle are

- Data warehouse projects will not be undertaken without a sponsoring business unit.
- The data warehouse project plan needs to accommodate activities which support the architecture but which may not directly contribute to the data warehouse being developed.
- The portion of the data warehouse development project to be funded by each of the business units and by information management should be negotiated during the project definition phase.

A complete statement of this guiding principle is shown in Fig. 5-1. The information provided helps people understand the direction being set, the reasons it is being set, and the manner in which it affects activities to be performed.

Once developed, the set of guiding principles should be compiled and communicated throughout the organization. The manner of presenting the principles should be adjusted to suit the audience. For example, since some of the guiding principles pertain to the development process, these could be deemphasized (or even omitted) in the set presented to upper management. A summary of the principles could be developed as a bulletin prominently placed throughout the company. This summary, along with the full set of principles could also be pro-

Figure 5-1
Sample Guiding Principle.

Guiding Principle:	All new data warehouse development activities will be funded jointly by information management and the benefiting business unit(s).
Rationale:	A data warehouse is built to provide a business benefit. To ensure that business value is appropriately balanced with the cost, the business units which receive the benefits sould provide a portion of the funding. A well-architected data warehouse is subject oriented, and, hence, its construction may require expenditures which build a foundation for the future but do not directly support the immediate business need. The information management department has funds for projects designed to benefit the company as a whole; those funds should be used to defray such costs. The portion of the project to be funded by each of the business units should be negotiated during the project definition phase.
Implications:	This guiding principle has the following implications:

- Data warehouse projects will not be undertaken without a sponsoring business unit.
- The data warehouse project plan needs to accommodate activities which support the architecture but which may not directly contribute to the data warehouse being developed.
- The portion of the data warehouse development project to be funded by each of the business units and by information management should be negotiated during the project definition phase.

vided electronically through bulletin boards, groupware, or the Internet or Intranet.

Motivations Dimension

The guiding principle presented in Fig. 5-1 addresses the Motivations dimension since it focuses on why a data warehouse may be built. Other areas in this dimension which could be addressed by guiding principles include funding of other aspects of the data warehouse and service levels to be provided.

Guiding principles addressing the Motivations dimension set expectations with respect to the funding and service.

Funding

Most of the costs associated with a data warehouse follow its implementation. Therefore, having a policy for the initial funding only does not ensure that the warehouse will remain a viable component of the information delivery architecture. Other related guiding principles are needed to address maintenance, enhancements, operation, and use.

Maintenance and Enhancements. For organizations that believe the data warehouse is built for the company as a whole, an appropriate guiding principle would be that "data warehouse maintenance needed to keep it operating within specifications is funded by the information technology department." This statement places the day-to-day maintenance responsibility within that department, while leaving open the question of funding for improvements.

Data warehouse enhancements should be implemented based on their business value. To ensure that requests adequately consider the costs, a guiding principle could be "funding for enhancements to a data warehouse to provide additional functionality or business value is to be secured by the requesting business unit."

Operation and Use. Just as the enhancement requests need to recognize the cost implications, so should the operation of the data warehouse itself, and a guiding principle can be developed to define the charge-back philosophy to specify the responsibilities for reimbursing the information technology department for related expenses. If a charge-back system is used for allocating costs, the cost structure should be such that it does not deter use. For example, a guiding principle which states that "funding for query and reporting tools is to be provided by the users of these tools" recognizes that the company is incurring a direct cost to provide the tools to the business community. In the case of this principle, the method by which charges are determined needs to be defined procedurally.

Service Levels

The designer's view of the Motivations dimension addresses the performance criteria. These can be stated in the form of service level objectives, and a guiding principle can simply state that "a service level agreement will be established as part of the development of a data ware-house."

The specific contents of the agreement (e.g., support responsiveness, response time, availability, recoverability) and the process for negotiating the agreement may be defined within the development procedures. The guiding principle simply states that the service level agreement should be created.

Times Dimension

The Times dimension addresses when events take place. Guiding princi-ples addressing this area pertain to the scheduling of the data ware-house—related activities and the retention of historical information.

> **Guiding principles addressing the Times dimension set expectations with respect to the currency and age of data in the warehouse.**

Historical View

Depending on the design, this data can be used to provide (1) a view of history using a perspective which existed at any point in time, (2) a view of history events using a current perspective, (3) a view of history as it existed at the time of an event, (4) a view of the current events using the current perspective. The first option can also be used to pro-vide a view of the current environment using an historical perspective (See Fig. 5-2.)

The third and fourth situations portray events as they occur. If a company is considering reorganizing its sales responsibilities, the second situation provides a view of historical activities in prospective sales terri-tory divisions to help determine the impact of the reorganization. If sales territories were changed midyear, the fourth situation helps to com-pare actual results to the projections which were made using the former territory boundaries.

From an implementation perspective, the first situation is most com-plex. It requires retention of historical perspective information, and the importance of retaining this information needs to be evaluated since it complicates the design and makes access more difficult. If a star schema is used, the second situation can be satisfied by simply storing perspec-

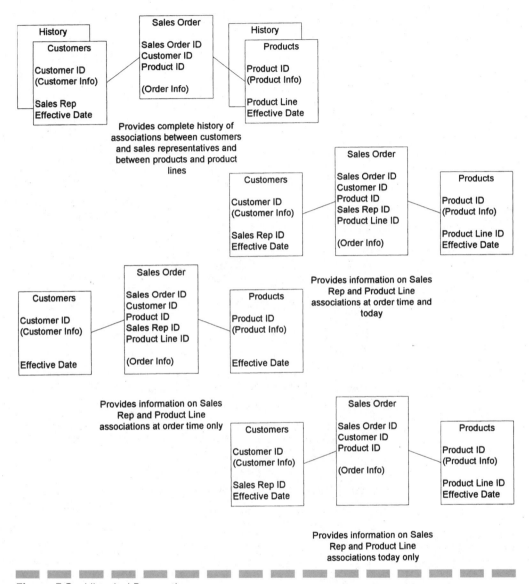

Figure 5-2 Historical Perspectives.

tive information in the fact table, and the fourth situation requires only current information in the dimension tables. With the first situation, the date becomes part of the key to the dimension table to attain record uniqueness (or a flag needs to be set to help find the current perspective).

The guiding principle for this area should provide guidance to reflect the philosophy toward the value of capturing and retaining historical reference information in the data warehouse. For example, the principle may state that "the data warehouse will retain a full history of the data elements it contains" or that "the data warehouse will provide a snapshot view of historical events, with additional views to be provided only when a business value can be demonstrated."

Historical Information

Capturing historical information in the data warehouse is critical. Managing this history is equally important. Guidelines concerning the amount of history to be retained at both a detail and summary level need to be established. These guidelines need to consider more than just the performance implications. Companies may have records retention policies which dictate that certain information should be purged periodically.

Historical information presents an additional problem. Since the operational systems and the data warehouse itself change over time, the information retained, its format, and its metadata may also change. An often-ignored issue with archived information is its retrieval. The retrieval mechanisms need to be maintained to access both current and archived information.

Operational systems can sometimes change data about an historical event. If these events are loaded into the warehouse using refresh logic (e.g., the historical events are reloaded each time), reporting repeatability from the warehouse is jeopardized. There may be circumstances in which attaining this ideal state is extremely complex. For example, if the source system provides no means of capturing changes, the logic required to use an append process may be prohibitively complex. To ensure the appropriate handling of historical information, guiding principles relating to retention, archive retrieval, metadata version maintenance, etc., need to be defined.

Data Currency

Another important issue within the Times dimension pertains to the timing of the data warehouse loading process. The timing of the data warehouse loads should be based on a number of factors, including the volatility of the source data, the use of the data in the warehouse, and referential integrity requirements. Each set of information should be analyzed to determine its timing requirements. Because the data warehouse is intended to support strategic decisions, loading frequencies of more than once a day should not be necessary. (If data is needed more frequently, consideration should be given to building an operational data store.)

An issue of data quality also impacts currency. Often, particularly with financial information, data is not certified until the end of a monthly cycle. Hence, any data extracted prior to that time is subject to change either due to corrections or due to an allocation process. If the data currency is more important than its correctness, extraction prior to month-end processing may be needed. The implications of this process need to be understood by the users of the data.

Data currency is one issue—load frequency and scheduling is another. For example, the data currency may dictate that data may be 3 days old, yet the load frequency may still be daily. This situation exists if the processing of information through the operational system has inherent delays.

Guiding principles addressing data currency may dictate, for example, that "updates to the data warehouse shall not be more often than daily" or that "when currency requirements dictate that preliminary data is needed in the warehouse, the metadata shall reflect the risks and a process for replacing it with final data shall be implemented."

Locations Dimension

The Locations dimension addresses the places of interest to the data warehouse and the flow of data among these places. Guiding principles addressing this area pertain to the servers, the communications facilities, and the access facilities.

Guiding principles addressing the Locations dimension define where the data resides and the facilities for retrieving it.

Servers

The data warehouse itself resides on a server, with different components potentially residing on different platforms. (See Fig. 5-3.) The atomic level

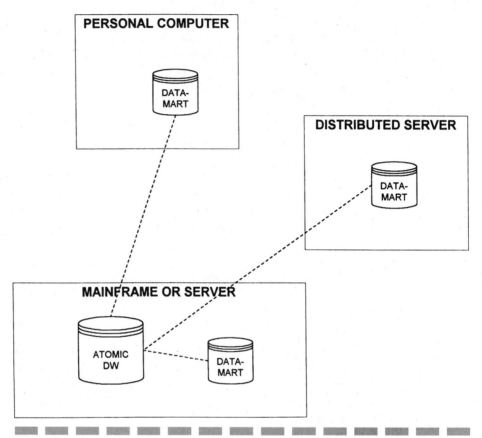

Figure 5-3 Data Warehouse Platforms.

of the warehouse, for example, could reside on a mainframe computer, and a datamart could reside on a personal computer.

Selecting the platform is not the only server issue. Each platform has an operating system and database management system, and it interacts with clients and other servers through middleware and communications facilities. The usage characteristics of a data warehouse differ from those of a transaction-processing system. To ensure appropriate performance for both environments, they should be separated at least at the database level and potentially at the server level.

Sample guiding principles addressing servers follow: "Data warehouse infrastructure components such as servers, communications protocols, operating systems, and database management systems shall conform to the corporate technical standards." "Operational data shall not be placed on the same database image as the data warehouse." "Unless the server is a mainframe, operational data shall not be placed on the same server as the data warehouse." "Access to the data warehouse will only be provided through the local area network and wide area network."

Indirect Data Access

Having data in the warehouse is useless unless people can get to it to support their decision analysis. In some cases, access is direct; in other cases, it is indirect. The direct access to the data warehouse is addressed in the People dimension. Since the indirect access is impacted by the placement of the components of the warehouse, it is addressed within the Locations dimension.

Indirect access to the data warehouse can be provided through extracts. These can be in the form of datamarts reflecting the needs of a group of people, personal data warehouses, extracts exported to spreadsheets, and feeds to operational systems. Valid reasons exist for each of these, and their implications need to be understood to ensure the integrity of the data.

Datamarts recognize that users of the data warehouse rarely need access to all the data. In a company which is divided by major product line, for example, the marketing group in each division may need only its own data. Rather than requiring that each division access the full data warehouse (and compete for resources with other users), a datamart containing detailed and/or summarized data of interest can be created. When created in this manner, the datamart becomes part of the overall data warehouse architecture. A guiding principle to communicate the belief in this approach may be "datamarts and personal data warehouses shall be created using controlled processes managed by the data warehouse group."

Personal data warehouses are an extension of the datamart concept. Within the marketing group, different people may be responsible for a subset of the customers or products. Exporting data to a personal data warehouse, potentially residing on a personal computer, provides them with additional flexibility and responsiveness. Taking the concept one step further, the people may need to perform what-if analysis, and, in this case, the data may be exported into a different environment, such as a spreadsheet. Once data is extracted from the warehouse, its integrity can no longer be guaranteed. Hence, a principle which states that "the integrity of data in data warehouse extracts is not assured unless the processes are managed by the data warehouse administration group" places users on notice that they have accepted the responsibility for the quality of the data.

Using the data warehouse to feed an operational system may also provide business value. The data warehouse integrates data from various sources. This integrated information may be useful in the operational environment for making decisions concerning treatment of customers. Through the integration process, for example, the total outstanding credit amount for a customer can be determined and a decision for further credit extension may be made based on this information. Similarly, the total monthly sales volume to a customer can be determined, and this may help recognize the importance of the customer to the company. Stating that "the data warehouse is a legitimate source of information for operational systems" clarifies the potential role of the data warehouse. (See Fig. 5-4.)

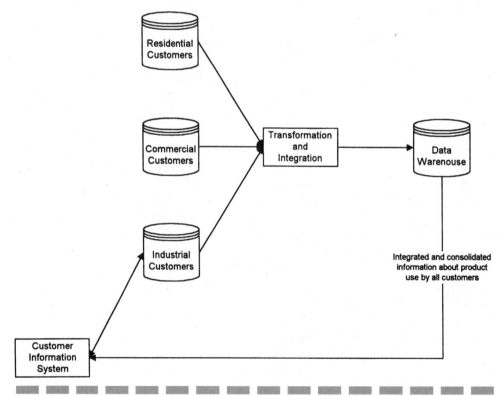

Figure 5-4 Data Warehouse Feed to an Operational System.

Activities Dimension

The Activities dimension addresses the way in which the data warehouse is built and operated. Guiding principles address the methodology of both the data warehouse and the operational systems.

> **Guiding principles addressing the Activities dimension define the process for building and supporting the data warehouse and anticipate the impact of this process on systems development and support activities.**

Data Warehouse Methodology

The data warehouse methodology itself is described in Chap. 6. The methodology consists of thirteen phases and is based on a set of guiding principles. The principles which relate to the "how" of building the data warehouse are

- The design of the data warehouse is based on a data model.
- Data warehouse development is an iterative process.
- Data warehouse support encompasses each step of the development process.
- Data warehouse development shall utilize reusable components whenever practical.

Data Model Foundation.   A data warehouse cannot be built without a data model. The data model provides the blueprint both for the initial data warehouse and for its expansion. With the model, the road map for the warehouse can be established, and progress along the road can be made one step at a time.

That same model also helps to coordinate efforts among data warehouse projects. By remaining cognizant of the portion of the model being addressed, each project can gain from the other's efforts, and the project scopes can be adjusted to minimize or eliminate any overlap.

Iterative Methodology.   The second principle recognizes a fundamental difference between the development of a data warehouse and the development of a traditional operational system. Within a traditional systems development life cycle, the implementation of the system is pre-

Figure 5-5
Data Warehouse
Development
Methodology.

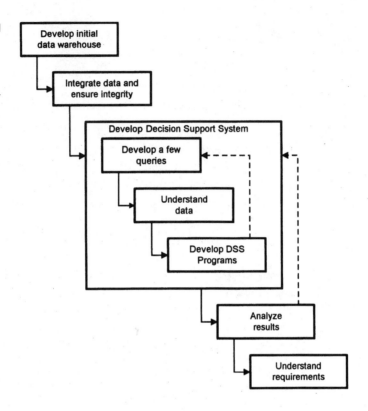

ceded by requirements definition, analysis, design, programming, testing, and integration.

With the data warehouse, the first effort focuses on implementation guided by a data model. Complexities introduced by integration can follow, with the integrity of the data verified as data is added. The decision support system which uses the data warehouse is also developed iteratively—a few queries are placed against the data, the data is then better understood, and a decision support system is developed. Results are analyzed, and only then are the true requirements understood. (See Fig. 5-5.)

Support Cycle. The support cycle of the data warehouse recognizes that each enhancement or iteration is, in fact, another data warehouse project. In some cases, the improvement scope is such that it takes months; in other cases, it may take hours. Even if the enhancement is small, each of the perspectives portrayed within the Zachman Framework need to be considered. (See Fig. 5-6.)

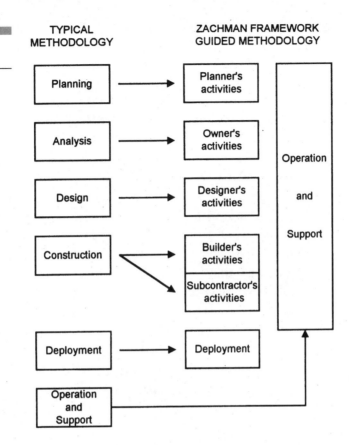

Figure 5-6
Support Cycle.

Reusable Components. Fundamental to the methodology is the concept of reusability. The fifth row of the Framework emphasizes this point by segregating the subcontracting work from the construction and assembly activities. Through the use of the model and metadata, reusability of components is enhanced.

Application Development Methodology

The application development methodology is also impacted by the data warehouse. The existence of the data warehouse influences the scope of systems being developed and requires that people working on systems development and support consider the impact on existing data warehouses.

The existence of data warehouses in general should be considered in defining the scope of new systems. For example, if the data warehouse can support some of the reporting requirements and if the data in the operational databases can be restricted to a very limited amount of history, then development of the operational system becomes simpler, its support less complex, and its performance better. With this in mind, the following guiding principles should be considered:

- New systems development projects will be divided into two projects whenever feasible—a transactional system and a data warehouse.

- The data warehouse is the preferred reporting source for strategic and historical information.

- History retained within operational systems shall be limited to 6 months unless more history is needed to directly support operational decisions.

- Systems development and support efforts shall address the impacts on existing data warehouses.

People Dimension

People interact with the data warehouse during its construction, implementation, and operation.

Guiding principles addressing the People dimension define the interaction between people and the data warehouse.

Direct Data Access

Having data in the warehouse is useless unless people can get to it to support their decision analysis. Direct access is provided through a set of available queries and reports and a set of query and reporting tools. The tool market is very volatile, and while establishing a firm standard may be advantageous in terms of support, training, and tool costs, it may also limit effective use of the warehouse. A principle such as "data warehouse users are encouraged to use the approved query and reporting tools, but specialized or other tools may be used at the user's risk as long as they conform to the infrastructure technical standards" recognizes the economies of scale available through tool standards as well as the potential for moving away from the standard for specific applications. To encourage the sharing of queries, a principle encouraging placement of reusable queries in a sharable library can also be delineated.

Interface

The look and feel of the data warehouse is presented through the interface. The interface design needs to recognize that the warehouse may be accessed by many people who use the warehouse to help them fulfill their responsibilities. Since the data warehouse is not their primary job responsibility, specialized training requirements should be limited, and a principle addressing this may be appropriate.

The data warehouse user will also need to access the metadata. If the metadata delivery mechanism is distinct from the data warehouse, coordinated use of the two will be more difficult. Hence, a principle dictating that the metadata will be delivered using data retrieval tools is appropriate.

Security

Inherent in the human interface is the potential need to block the interface, and security addresses this aspect of the data warehouse. Since the data warehouse contains both detailed and summary data, the security requirements for each may differ. If data from the warehouse is transmitted on public networks, security may also be needed for the transmission facilities. Guiding principles may be needed to protect this valuable asset of the company.

Entities Dimension

The Entities dimension addresses the physical content of the data warehouse.

> **Guiding principles addressing the Entities dimension define rules concerning the content of the data warehouse.**

The data model foundation has been addressed as part of the methodology. Other entity issues pertain to the quality of the data, the rules for combining disparate data, the data sources, the orientation, and the metadata.

Quality

Perhaps more important than the quality of the data in the warehouse is the predictability of its quality. The data in the warehouse is based on that which exists in the operational systems. While some of the data errors in those systems can be detected and addressed, others cannot without fundamental changes to those systems. Also, since data may be derived from multiple sources, the completeness of the data is difficult to attain. The cost of these improvements, therefore, needs to be balanced against the business value to be gained through better data.

Four basic situations can exist. In some cases, the data warehouse is being built as a prototype, and neither accuracy nor completeness are important. Another scenario is one in which the warehouse is used for trend analysis, and completeness is not critical, as long as a trend developed without it is viewed to be sufficiently accurate. Timeliness sometimes overrides quality. Financial data, for example, may be needed prior to its certification through a month-end process. As long as the business people recognize the risks, the complete data, though not fully accurate, is sufficient. The fourth option is to strive for complete and accurate data. This option is the most expensive and may not be attainable without major changes to the operational environment. (See Fig. 5-7.)

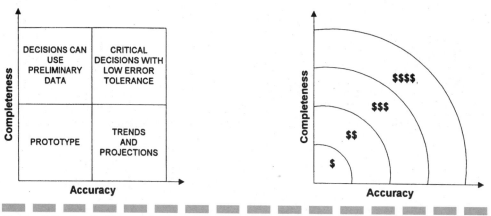

Figure 5-7   Quality Expectations and Cost.

A sample guiding principle concerning data quality may state that "the quality expectations for the data warehouse shall be set commensurate with the business needs and value." Since knowledge is reflective of the accuracy of information, the information about the data quality, combined with the data itself, helps companies transform their information into knowledge.

Data Sources

Setting the quality expectations for the data warehouse impacts the sources of data. Production-grade databases, whether provided by a centralized Information Systems Group, by a business unit's Information Systems Group, or by an outside source, all bring with them a degree of confidence in the data quality. Data from spreadsheets and ad hoc programs developed throughout the company, on the other hand, is not predictable in terms of quality. The relevant guiding principle, then, may be that "data for the data warehouse may be obtained from any production application or sanctioned external database."

Transformation and Integration

Once the sources of data are determined, the data from these sources must be combined through a transformation and integration process. Logically, these are two distinct processes. Transformation entails the molding of the incoming data into the desired form; integration involves the combining of the data from the various sources. The challenges in the transformation process are mostly technical, while the integration issues are mostly business related. (See Fig. 5-8.)

The physical separation of these processes and the creation of intermediary files with transformed but not integrated data is optional. If a company wants to enforce this method, then a guiding principle addressing it should be created.

Data Orientation

The data warehouse concept exists to support strategic decisions. Adding too much operational data into the warehouse encumbers its ability to meet its original objective. Another mechanism, the operational data

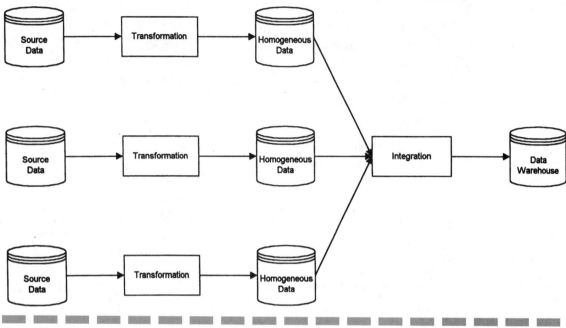

Figure 5-8 Transformation and Integration.

store, is better suited for that purpose. A guiding principle emphasizing the strategic orientation of the data warehouse can reinforce this concept.

Metadata

Metadata describes the contents of the data warehouse. Its access has been addressed in the People dimension. Its creation is part of the Entities dimension. The guiding principle for this characteristic should describe the types of metadata to be captured. Since metadata is such an important aspect of the data warehouse, a chapter is devoted to it later in the book.

Summary

The Zachman Framework defines an architecture for managing knowledge. The data warehouse is one of the instruments for obtaining that knowledge. Through a well-conceived and well-communicated set of guiding principles, the strategy for building, implementing, operating, and supporting the data warehouse is defined.

Several of the guiding principles address a broader horizon. Using the guiding principles developed for the data warehouse as a foundation and the Zachman Framework as a guide, principles can be developed for other aspects of the information technology environment.

Data quality is fundamental to transforming data into information and information into knowledge. Data becomes information when it becomes meaningful. It becomes knowledge only when it becomes reliable in terms of its accuracy.

6

Zachman Framework—Based Methodology

The Zachman Framework provides an architectural construct for the development of methodologies as well as an overall strategy. These methodologies could be used for development of a data warehouse, an operational data store, an operational system, or any other product. By mapping the methodology to the Framework, conscious decisions can be made concerning areas of emphasis and the sequence of activities. In this chapter, the methodology for building a data warehouse based on the Zachman Framework is developed. A similar approach can be used to relate other methodologies to the Framework.

The methodology provided identifies the major activities and how they fit within the Framework. Because of the nature of the data warehouse, the steps dealing with the data dimension are described in greater detail than the other activities. Standard project activities, such as project planning, leadership, and staffing, are not described, since these are not specific to the data warehouse methodology steps.

The data warehouse methodology is flexible, and with the aid of the Zachman Framework, the risk of postponing some activities is reduced.

This chapter describes the methodology. Its application is defined in subsequent chapters. Those chapters also describe reasonable compromises for attaining the desired results quickly without an undue risk.

Methodology Overview

The approach described in this chapter is consistent with the data warehouse development life cycle described in *Building the Data Warehouse.*[1] The concept emphasized in the development life cycle is that the development methodology needs to be data driven and that not all the requirements can be, or should be, identified in advance. The term *data driven* is not used in the traditional sense in which data issues are considered the most important aspect of the development cycle. Instead, the term is used to identify the primary target of a data warehousing effort—data for decision support.

The methodology consists of eleven major phases:

- *Commitment to proceed.* In this phase, the decision is made concerning the project to be undertaken. This activity includes a broad definition of the scope and confirmation of the availability of the needed support, funding, and resources.

- *Data model analysis.* In this phase, the existence of a solid data model upon which to build the data warehouse is confirmed. If one does not exist, a model is developed. This activity includes identification of the major subject areas, definition of the model boundaries, separation of primitive and derived data, and attribution of the relevant entities.

- *Breadbox analysis.* In this phase, the computer resources needed for the data warehouse are estimated at a high level to guide granularity level decisions.

- *Technical assessment.* In this phase, the ability of the technical environment to handle the projected data warehouse load with reasonable response times is reviewed. This process includes a review of both the loading implications and the ongoing interrogation of the warehouse.

---

[1]W. H. Inmon, *Building the Data Warehouse,* 2d ed. (New York: John Wiley & Sons, 1996.)

- *Technical environment preparation.* In this phase, actions are initiated to provide the needed hardware, software, and communications facilities. This phase could actually be addressed as a project in its own right, depending on the effort required.

- *Subject area analysis.* In this phase, the subject of the specific iteration to be addressed is confirmed. This process includes a review of the scope of the subject area and a determination of the potential need for dividing it into multiple efforts.

- *Source system analysis.* In this phase, the sources of the data are analyzed. This process includes a review of the key structure, transformation mapping, and handling of time variance.

- *Data warehouse design.* In this phase, the data warehouse itself is designed. This process includes the transformation of the base data model, which may be operationally oriented, into one which is suited for the data warehouse.

- *Specifications.* In this phase, the program specifications for migrating the data into the data warehouse are developed. Decisions concerning refresh and append strategies are made at this time.

- *Programming.* In this phase, the programming code for the transformation programs is developed. The process includes coding, compilation, walk-throughs, and testing.

- *Population.* In this phase, the data warehouse is populated with data, and decisions are made with respect to population frequency, archival and purging.

At first glance, the mapping to the Zachman Framework may seem limited, as shown in Fig. 6-1.

As described in Chap. 3, each methodology determines the emphasis or deemphasis of particular cells within the Framework based on the specific problem at hand, the operating environment which already exists, and the risks which a company is willing to take. The data warehouse methodology does actually address more cells in the Framework than is initially apparent. For example, the data model analysis phase considers the information needs (motivations) for the data warehouse, its users (people), etc., as well as the business cycles (times) if they are perceived to have an impact on the data warehouse. Similarly, the specifications phase addresses the response criteria (motivations) security and access requirements (people), and scheduling (times). A more accurate depiction of the coverage of the methodology is shown in Fig. 6-2 which recognizes that the depth of analysis for the Entities dimension is

	ENTITIES	ACTIVITIES	LOCATIONS	PEOPLE	TIMES	MOTIVATIONS
SCOPE DEFINITION	1			1		1
BUSINESS MODEL	2					
SYSTEM MODEL	2,3,4,6	3,4	3,4			
TECHNICAL MODEL	5,7,8,9	5,7,8,9	5,7,8,9			
OUT-OF-CONTEXT MODEL	5,10,11	5,10,11	5			

1. Commitment to Proceed
2. Data Model Analysis
3. Breadbox Analysis
4. Technical Assessment
5. Technical Environment Preparation
6. Subject Area Analysis
7. Source System Analysis
8. Data Warehouse Design
9. Specifications
10. Programming
11. Population

Figure 6-1 *Suspected Coverage of Methodology.*

greater than that of the other dimensions. As described in Chap. 7, this is particularly true for the first data warehouse project.

Planner's View

The planner's view is addressed by the first phase—commitment to proceed. Each of the dimensions is addressed, though the emphasis may vary depending on the company's particular situation.

Commitment to Proceed

At this point in the project, the basic concept of the data warehouse is formulated. The project sponsor plays a very key role in this phase, and,

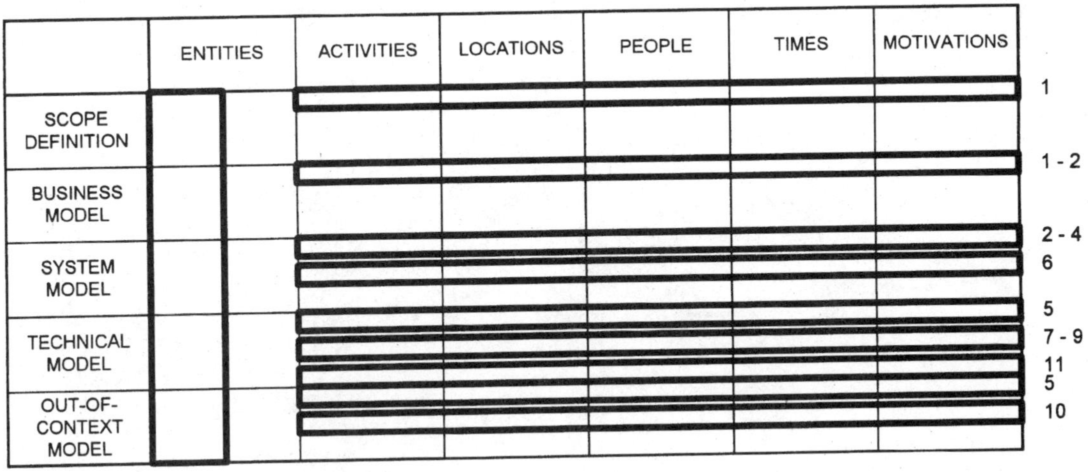

	ENTITIES	ACTIVITIES	LOCATIONS	PEOPLE	TIMES	MOTIVATIONS	
SCOPE DEFINITION							1
BUSINESS MODEL							1 - 2
SYSTEM MODEL							2 - 4 / 6
TECHNICAL MODEL							5 / 7 - 9 / 11 / 5
OUT-OF-CONTEXT MODEL							10

1. Commitment to Proceed
2. Data Model Analysis
3. Breadbox Analysis
4. Technical Assessment
5. Technical Environment Preparation
6. Subject Area Analysis
7. Source System Analysis
8. Data Warehouse Design
9. Specifications
10. Programming
11. Population

Figure 6-2 Actual Coverage of Methodology.

in fact, that person could be construed to be the primary planner, as described in Chap. 3. This person is thinking about things which could be built to improve the business, and through a partnership with the information technology department, is able to understand the role a data warehouse can plan in satisfying those needs. The major constraints facing this person are likely to be time and money.

The data warehouse, as a solution, addresses both of the major constraints. Philosophically, the data warehouse is approached as a series of short projects. Hence, the elapsed time between project conception and delivery of at least some business functionality is measured in months, not years. The cost of the initial data warehouse can also be limited, and value from that piece can be extracted prior to committing the funds needed to provide a more complete solution.

The sponsor may arrive at the need for a data warehouse through one of two mechanisms. Under one scenario, he or she may be faced with a business situation needing improvement and may solicit the help of

Figure 6-3 Partnership.

information technology. In the other scenario, a representative of the information technology department, who understands the leverage a data warehouse can provide, recognizes the potential business value of the warehouse for a particular business problem and approaches the sponsor with a proposal. Either way, the result is the same. (See Fig. 6-3.)

> **A business opportunity is identified, the data warehouse is deemed to be part of the solution, and a partnership between the business community and information technology is struck to provide that solution.**

The definition of the business opportunity directly addresses all the dimensions:

- Motivations are addressed through the identification of the business goals to be achieved, as well as the benefits to be attained.

- Times are addressed through the definition of those business goals, though a conscious effort may be needed to ensure that this is done.

- People are addressed by identifying the audience (business groups) of the data warehouse.

- Locations are addressed by being cognizant of the locations of the business groups.

- Activities are addressed by identifying the business processes being addressed and the related decision support activities which will employ the data warehouse.

- Entities are addressed by identifying the subject areas of interest.

As was noted earlier, the methodology does place an emphasis on the Entities dimension because of the nature of the data warehouse. For the planner's view to be considered complete, identification of the subjects of interest should be within the context of the total set of subject areas. If a subject area model for the company does not exist, the scope of the project should include its development. Development of a complete list of business functions is not needed. The data warehouse methodology focuses on only the business processes for which the decision support assistance is needed.

Developing a Subject Area Model. The need for a subject area model is apparent by examining the fundamental definition of a data warehouse—a subject-oriented, integrated, nonvolatile, time-variant collection of data.

> **The first important words of the definition are *subject oriented*. How can one proceed to build something which is subject oriented without knowing the subjects?**

Building a subject area model need not be a lengthy or costly task. A model, good enough to be used for guiding the data warehouse, can often be built in a day. Like other products of the development process, this model must be considered to be a living deliverable, and the potential exists for it to be revised as additional information is obtained.

To develop the subject area model, a group of people who understand the business and who are willing to invest a few hours because they understand the value of the model should be assembled for a facilitated session. At this session, the major items (subjects) are identified, and major relationships among them noted. The starting point for the list of subjects may be obtained from a number of sources. The company may have publications which identify its major subjects, or it may be in an industry which has commercial models available. If a starting point such as these is not available, another option is to start from a very generic list of subjects, such as the one which follows.

- *Competitors.* Companies which provide products and/or services which could be acquired by customers in lieu of the company's products.

- *Customers.* People and companies which did, do, or may acquire the company's products and/or services.
- *Facilities.* Physical places where activities by or on behalf of the company have been, are, or may be performed.
- *Financials.* Money which has, is, or may be received, retained, or expended by the company.
- *Human resources.* People who did, do, or may perform activities for the company.
- *Materials.* Goods and/or services which were, are, or may be consumed or used by the company in its operation.
- *Projects.* Organized sets of activities performed by or on behalf of the company.
- *Organizations.* Business groups which are responsible for or perform activities within the company.
- *Products.* Goods which the company did, does, or may provide to customers.
- *Services.* Intangible deliverables which the company did, does, or may provide to customers in conjunction with products.
- *Suppliers.* People and companies which did, do, or may provide materials to the company.

This list is not complete nor is it applicable to every company. The intention is to provide a starting point for discussion, which, with a skilled facilitator, could quickly lead to the list of subjects for the company.

Once the major subject areas are identified and defined, the major relationships among these are noted. A sample diagram of the relationships among the subject areas noted is shown in Fig. 6-4. The model should be such that if it were presented to a company executive, that person would agree that the major items of interest to the company and their relationships are captured. Within this model, for example, information pertaining to sales is embedded in the Customer subject area. If the visibility of Sales as a subject helps people better understand the model and relate to it, then Sales can be added. Similarly, if services are considered tangential to products, then the Products and Services subjects can be combined.

The subject area model should be maintained electronically, preferably in a tool which facilitates reuse of the information. Examples of such tools are CASE tools, repositories, in-house developed databases, and

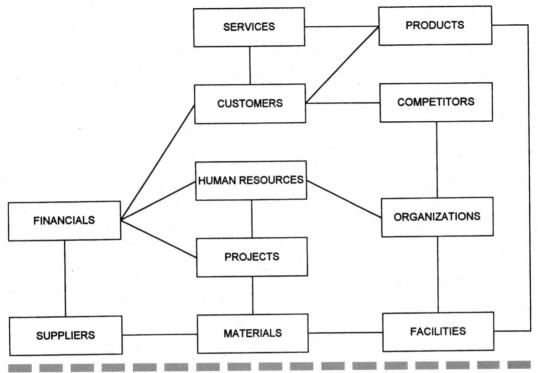

Figure 6-4 Sample Subject Area Diagram.

tools oriented to maintaining artifacts collected using the Zachman Framework.

Once developed, the subject area model is very useful for guiding data warehouse projects. The model serves as one of the foundations of the architected environment and greatly facilitates scope definition and the coordination of multiple efforts. In that context, it could be thought of as a jigsaw puzzle. (See Fig. 6-5.) All the pieces must fit together, and the relationships among the pieces are readily understood.

Owner's View

Some aspects of the commitment to proceed phase describe the owner's view, but the dominant phase addressing that perspective is the data model analysis phase. The steps within this phase portray a conscious decision to emphasize the data column. This decision is driven by a number of factors. First, the product of the data warehouse project is a

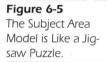

Figure 6-5
The Subject Area
Model is Like a Jig-
saw Puzzle.

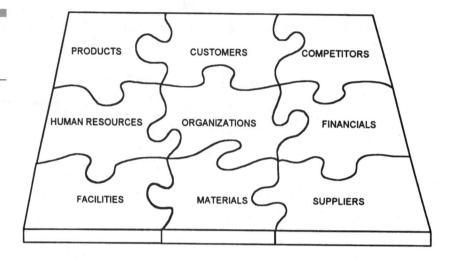

set of databases which conform to a set of characteristics suited for their purpose. Second, the nature of the data warehouse is iterative. The process and product both accommodate a fair degree of change if properly designed. This does not eliminate the need to address the other columns, but it does permit some of them to be addressed very quickly.

Data Model Analysis

If a solid data model exists, this step can proceed very quickly.

> **In the absence of a data model, time should be taken to create the data model, limiting its scope to the specific areas of interest.**

The data warehouse is being built to satisfy decision support needs. The existing decision support activities should be analyzed as part of the data model analysis. This exercise should provide information concerning the systems currently in place, the reports being generated, the perceived deficiencies, the users of the systems, etc. All six dimensions are addressed by answering questions such as

- What information is included in the queries and reports?
- Who is receiving the information?
- Where are those people located?
- When are the queries and reports executed?
- How much history is used in the analysis?

■ Why is the analysis performed? (What are the business decisions being addressed?)

Care should be taken in this analysis to ensure that the objectives of the data warehouse are not defined merely as "replace these reports." The focus needs to be on the information which the reports provide and the decisions that it supports. With that focus, the true information needs are more likely to be identified, and the mind-set is more likely to shift from one which is building a system which provides faster access to information in reports to a true data warehouse which provides information, as needed, to support business analysis.

Fundamental Entities.   The logical data model which describes the business items of interest within each of the subject areas and the business relationships among them is developed in the data model analysis phase. For each of the subject areas, 6 to 15 fundamental entities are likely to exist. Samples of the entities which could exist for selected subjects are delineated below.

■ *Customers.* Consumer, customer, customer account, customer contract, customer order, customer order item, distributor

■ *Facilities.* Factory, finished goods warehouse, office, raw materials warehouse, real estate, service center

■ *Human resources.* Agent, applicant, contractor, employee, former employee, skill, training course

■ *Materials.* Equipment, raw material, spare part, supply, waste, inventory

■ *Suppliers.* Manufacturer, purchase agreement, purchase order, purchase order item, material receipt, vendor

Within the business model, an identifier for each entity is typically defined. Care must be taken to ensure that this identifier provides for uniqueness under all circumstances. At this stage of development, the primary key attribute should typically be called "[entity name]_id." During the subsequent sourcing analysis, a determination can be made concerning the population of this attribute.

For any single data warehouse, data from more than one subject area is typically needed, and not all the data within a particular subject area is needed. For example, if the data warehouse is to address sales, some data from the Products, Services, and Organizations subject areas is probably needed, and data about prospects (within the Customers sub-

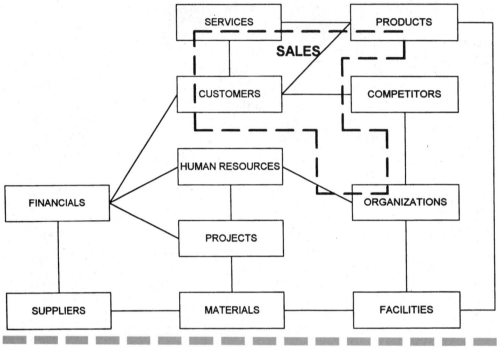

Figure 6-6 Subjects for Sales.

ject area) may not be needed. (See Fig. 6-6.) The model needs to be developed for each of the subject areas being addressed, but within those subject areas, the scope can be limited to those entities which are needed for the particular data warehouse segment. This step should not be considered complete until definitions for each of the entities of interest are developed.

Attributes.   Once the entities are identified and defined, the attributes, or business information, about each of the entities are addressed. As with the entities themselves, the focus should be on those attributes which are needed for the particular data warehouse segment. For example, in the sample attributes for the customer entity, only certain components of the address are shown.

- *Customer name.* The legal name of the customer
- *Customer number.* The customer's number in the company's records (This is also the number which is used within at least one of the supporting computer systems to uniquely identify each customer.)

- *Customer city.* The city in which the customer facility to which products are shipped is located

- *Customer state.* The state in which the customer facility to which products are shipped is located

- *Customer zip code.* The zip code, assigned by the United States Postal Service, of the customer facility to which products are shipped

- Customer TIN. The tax identification number of the customer, issued by the United States Internal Revenue Service

It is very likely that the operational systems contain other address information. For example, they may contain the street address and may also contain alternate addresses. If the objective of the data warehouse is to analyze sales, then the only required components of the address are likely to be those which facilitate locating the customer. With the information noted above, sales information could be provided by city, state, or zip code, or any higher-level grouping built on these classifications which may be supported by a reference table.

Business Rules. Once the business entities and attributes are identified, then the business rules governing them need to be defined. These rules can be presented in diagram form using an entity relationship diagram (see Fig. 6-7), or in textual form.

- A customer account includes one or more customers. All customers have a customer account.

Figure 6-7
Entity Relationship
Diagram.

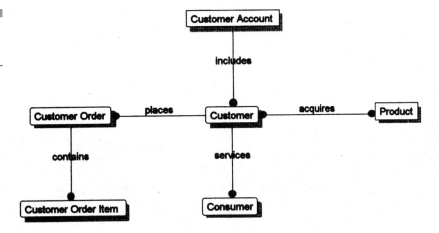

- A product is sold to one or more customers. A customer acquires one or more products.

- A consumer may be serviced by one and only one customer at any point in time. A consumer does not buy a product directly from the company.

Normalization.   The model discussed up to this point is limited to data needed for the data warehouse but describes the business in an operational sense. To transform this model for use in the data warehouse, a number of activities need to take place. Some normalization is needed so that the model can eventually reside in relational tables.

Normalization of the logical data model is recommended even if a star schema is used for presentation of data to the end user. The normalization process provides a better understanding of the data and builds a foundation for eventually using the data warehouse as a step in the journey to an architected environment.

Three entity types are introduced in the normalization process, and two of these, associative and attributive, have different roles in the operational and decision support environments. Subentities are similar in both environments. Subentities recognize that a particular entity may have different subtypes, all of which share some properties, and each of which has some unique properties. In a banking environment, for example, there are different types of customers. All customers share some information, such as account number, name, and address. There is some information, however, which is unique based on the type of customer. (See Fig. 6-8.)

The data warehouse contains historical information, and therefore all data in the warehouse must have an implicit or explicit time dimension.

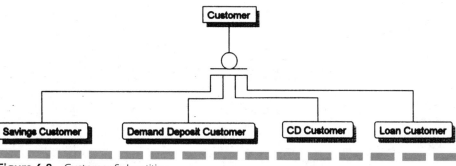

Figure 6-8 *Customer Subentities.*

The time dimension may take one of two forms. Some data, such as balance sheet information, represents a snapshot of a point in time. Other data, such as the profit statement information, is reflective of a period of time. The former requires one time identifier, while the latter requires two. The two identifiers for a period of time may be combined into a single attribute, such as day, week, or month, but that attribute actually represents a starting point and an ending point.

Associative entities are also created in the normalization process. These entities associate to other entities which have a many-to-many relationship. In the operational environment, the many-to-many relationship is created by the business rules. For example, a customer may buy many products and each product could be purchased by many customers. An associative entity which specifies a specific product acquired by a specific customer provides the needed uniqueness. As shown in Fig. 6-9, this entity could be identified using a product serial number. Data which would exist in this entity includes those items which are unique to this customer's acquisition of this product.

The data warehouse stores historical information. From an historical perspective, the previously identified entity is not unique if a product can be resold. Hence, for the data warehouse, a time dimension is added to the key to provide uniqueness. In the case of the product, the time dimension (purchase date) may already exist in the data. In some cases, a new field needs to be added altogether.

Attributive entities are also created in the normalization process to eliminate repeating groups of data. An attributive entity called *product component* may be created if a product has multiple components. This set of entities would have an instance for each component. In the data warehouse, with its historical perspective, the components may need to be tracked over time. The installation and (potentially implicit) removal date of each component become significant and need to be included as part of the entity identifier.

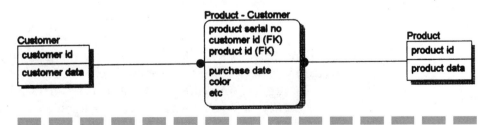

Figure 6-9 Associative Entity.

Data Model Analysis Summary. The method described for developing the data model is specifically geared for the data warehouse. Entities and business rules created to model the company over time should be designated as such to facilitate subsequent use of the applicable portions of the model for the operational environment. Similarly, if operational attributes are identified, they should be included in the model, but significant time should not be spent to refine their definitions until they are needed for operational systems. The version recursiveness rule of the Zachman Framework supports the dual representation.

Designer's View

The designer's view is addressed by several steps of the methodology. Completion of the data model analysis phase addresses the design implications of the model. These are explored in greater depth in subsequent chapters.

The breadbox analysis and technical assessment phases address the environmental items which must be designed for the data warehouse to perform as needed. The subject area analysis phase revisits the scope of the data warehouse iteration based on the information derived from the other phases.

Breadbox Analysis

The breadbox analysis provides a sanity check for the proposed approach.

A high-level estimate of the data warehouse size is made, and this information guides subsequent design decisions. If the data warehouse size appears to be too large, then the level of granularity is revisited. In building a data warehouse with point-of-sale data, choosing to capture sales volume data each minute requires more than 1000 times the records which daily statistics need. Moving to a monthly level reduces the number of records by 40,000. (See Fig. 6-10.)

Another option for reducing the size of the data warehouse at any one location is partitioning the data. For example, if regional information is being gathered, the lowest level of detail might be distributed to a regional server, with only summary information retained at a central

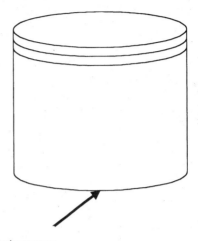

second-by second data = 31,500,000 records per year

minute-by-minute data = 525,000 records per year

hour-by-hour data = 8,500 records per year

day-by-day data = 365 records per year

week-by-week data = 52 records per year

month-by-month data = 12 records per year

year-by-year data = 1 record per year

Figure 6-10   Level of Granularity.

server. Thus, both the Entities and Locations dimensions are impacted by the breadbox analysis. (See Fig. 6-11.)

The breadbox analysis may also help to determine the contents of the various levels of the data warehouse architecture. The atomic level of the data warehouse contains the lowest level of granularity within the warehouse. Within the breadbox analysis, the contents of this level are determined, along with the amount of history which should be retained. The summarization levels contain less data, and some of the summarizations

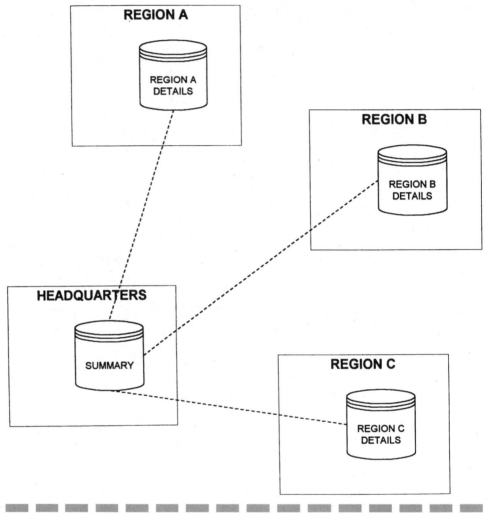

Figure 6-11 Physically Partitioned Data Warehouse.

could be considered as part of the breadbox analysis. (See Fig. 6-12.) (Other summarizations will evolve as the data warehouse is used.)

Technical Assessment

The technical assessment phase addresses many of the aspects of the data warehouse outside the Entities dimension. In so doing, the Loca-

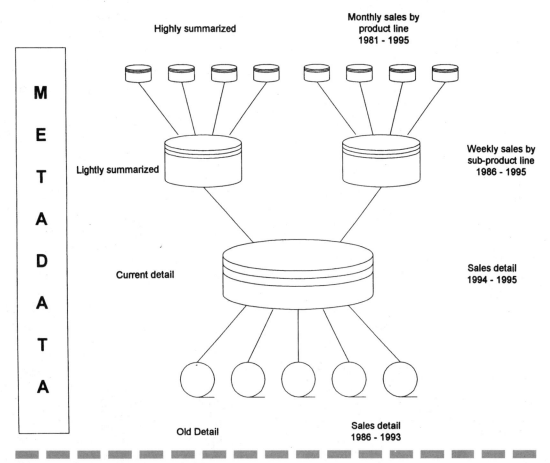

Figure 6-12   Data Warehouse Architecture.

tions, Times, and People dimensions are addressed. The performance requirements are established within the Motivations dimension.

The assessment needs to review both the loading of the data warehouse and its access within acceptable performance requirements.

Locations are addressed by identifying the places where data may reside and where its users reside. Once these are identified, the adequacy of the network for meeting the needs of the data warehouse must be determined. If deficiencies are identified, special projects to be worked as part of the technical environment preparation phase need to be defined.

From a technical perspective, the Times dimension addresses, among other items, the processing windows which are available for the data warehouse. Using estimates of the data volume, schedules of the source systems, and proposed operating schedules for the data warehouse, the analyst must determine if sufficient time is available to extract the data and to load it into the data warehouse. Based on the results of the analysis, additional equipment may be needed or modifications may be needed in the approach to the data warehouse.

The ability of the technical environment to provide the required security is one of the items examined in the technical assessment impacting the People dimension. If the data is extremely sensitive, encryption may be desired, and while the actual encryption process is relatively simple, administering the decryption facilities is not trivial.

Subject Area Analysis

The Subject Area Analysis phase revisits the scope of the data warehouse iteration based on the information derived from the other phases.

Based on the breadbox analysis and technical assessment phases, information for refining or developing models for each of the levels of the data warehouse architecture is obtained. The models for these levels can then be designed as part of the data warehouse design phase.

The subject area analysis phase is a quick reconfirmation of the scope based on the data to be included. The business issues and questions to be addressed by the data warehouse are defined or confirmed. The analysis should look at the business questions from multiple angles:

- Which business questions are being answered satisfactorily with the existing systems
- Which business questions are not being answered satisfactorily with the existing systems
- Which business questions need to be answered by the data warehouse
- Which business questions will not be answered by the data warehouse

The data model also should be reviewed to ensure that it contains enough data to provide a meaningful product and that it is still small enough to be implemented quickly. If the data addressed by the model is too limited, then a scope expansion may be in order. If the estimated delivery time is too long, then the project should be divided into segments if at all possible. Each segment should be designed for completion within 2 to 4 months so that business deliverables are continuously provided.

Builder's View

The builder's view is addressed by several steps of the methodology. The source system analysis and data warehouse design are performed, and the program specifications are developed. Corollary activities are also executed in the technical environment preparation phase.

Source System Analysis

All data in the warehouse is derived from some other source. That source may be an existing operational system, an operational data store, a new operational system being developed, or an external database.

> **The source system analysis is crucial for achieving the second and fourth attributes of the data warehouse definition (subject-oriented, integrated, nonvolatile, time-variant collection of data).**

In addition to the Entities dimension, the source system analysis has a significant impact on the Activities dimension (since the operational systems depict the business processes) and on the Times dimension (since the analysis must determine the sequence of processing).

Data Integration. One of the major benefits of the data warehouse is that it brings together data from multiple sources. This challenge has both a technical and a business aspect to it. From a technical perspective, the data sources may be on multiple platforms, they may contain data with the same name but different meanings, and they may contain data with different meanings but the same name. Additionally, the coding schemes, data types, and data lengths may vary. The data quality and completion may also vary based on the objectives of the source systems and the edit rules which permitted the data to be captured in the source systems to begin with. (See Fig. 6-13.)

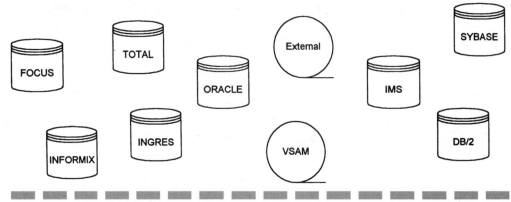

Figure 6-13   Source System Platforms.

The technical challenges of dealing with data sources on different platforms can be very significant. Since the source systems evolved over a long period of time, their platforms may include technologies of the sixties and seventies such as VSAM, information management system (IMS), and TOTAL, as well as technologies of the eighties and nineties, such as DB-2, Sybase, and Gemstone. From a database management system perspective, the sources may have sequential files, hierarchical databases, relational databases, and object databases. From a platform perspective, the sources may be on IBM-compatible mainframe computers, on other mainframe computers, on servers, or on personal computers. Similarly, the operating systems of the source systems may be MVS, VM, UNIX, or Windows-NT. Dealing with this potential variety in a single project can be quite a challenge.

Data names are another source of difficulty for integrating data. If sales data is to be collected from multiple sources, the analyst may jump for glee upon discovering that all the sources have a field called *net sales*. Further analysis, however, may reveal that net sales is a homonym and that the algorithm for deriving net sales differs from system to system. Similarly, synonyms may exist. The person responsible for the sale may be called *salesman* in one system, *sales representative* in another system, and *employee* in still another system. Only through a thorough analysis of the source data can the analyst ferret out the nuances of the element names and their meanings.

The identifiers used in the systems present another challenge. The first challenge is similar to the integration of elements having the same name. The term *customer* may have different connotations in each of the systems, so the first problem is to create a common set of definitions.

Even after the term customer is defined, the analyst needs to deal with issues of uniqueness and history. Uniqueness is often of interest only within the realm of the objective of the system. When data from multiple systems is joined, the uniqueness must take on a global perspective. Also, the history retention of each system is based on its requirements. Hence, for a system which retains only 2 years of history, the potential exists to reuse numbers. If the data warehouse contains more history, the source system identifier must be modified. If each of the source systems deal with only a specific type of customer, their identification scheme may be at the subtype level, while the warehouse needs an identification scheme at the supertype level.

Coding schemes also need to be integrated. This can be a straightforward task if the systems merely use different codes for the same item. If, however, the classification scheme itself differs, integrating the encoded data entails more than just developing a common set of codes.

Some of the other challenges of integration include data formats (dates, for example, may be represented in several ways in the source systems, particularly if international divisions are involved), incomplete information (some attributes may exist in only some of the systems), data format conversions (some data may be in EBCDIC and other data may be in ASCII).

From a business perspective, data owned by different business units is being brought together, possibly for the first time. Some resistance should be expected, and the process of determining the conditions under which data can be included and excluded is fraught with problems. Resolving the business integration issues can sometimes overshadow the technical integration issues. For example, if from a technical perspective overlapping coding schemes exist, the business people need to determine the business rules for the classifications. Once those are determined, the technical aspect of implementing them may be (but is not always) simple.

One approach for dealing with the integration and ownership issue is to provide a staging area which splits the integration into two steps. In the first step, data from different sources is maintained separately but is transformed into a common view. In the second step, the data from the different sources is actually integrated. This approach provides for the common enterprisewide view. Through the use of common formats, it can facilitate a transition period in which the query programs developed for the corporate view of the data can be used against individual source views of the data. Over time, people will hopefully recognize the value of the integrated information.

Time Variance. Data in the warehouse needs to reflect a historical perspective, but the source systems do not always provide the needed information. With the limitations of the source systems and some ingenuity, the time identifiers for the data warehouse need to be designed. When the time identifier is not contained in the databases of the source system, it can sometimes be deduced by controlling the time of the extracts. For example, if information on each day's activity is needed and the source system contains only the impact of the activity (e.g., year-to-date sales volume rather than each day's volume), then a daily extract is needed, and the data available from the source system is used to calculate the daily activity information. The periodicity of snapshot data may also impact the extract frequency, unless data is retained within the source system to re-create the needed data.

Other approaches for capturing the needed data include modifications to the source systems and extraction from log tapes. Modifications to the source system may be made to allow for the date to be added to selected records. Additionally, if the source system is using a database management system which utilizes log tapes, the log tapes could become the sources of data. Both these scenarios help not only to provide the time dimension, they also help to reduce the processing which must be done each time data is moved into the data warehouse.

Technical Environment Preparation

Preparation of the technical environment entails the set of activities which are needed to address the deficiencies identified in the technical assessment phase. This effort is a subproject in itself. The areas impacted are often not under the control of the data warehouse project manager, and the skills needed are also different. These activities address each of the six dimensions of the Zachman Framework.

> **The data warehouse project manager needs to have an oversight responsibility for the technical environment preparation efforts to ensure that facilities are available when they are needed, but these activities should be managed separately.**

The Motivations dimension provides information concerning the performance criteria to be satisfied. Aside from ensuring that the environment can meet these criteria, the technical environment preparation effort may also look into performance monitors to ensure that the objectives continue to be met.

The Times dimension impacts the execution of the individual scripts and jobs and necessitates an understanding of the processing windows available. Related to this activity is the need to have job schedulers which can sequentially execute jobs residing on different platforms. For example, the UNIX load job may need to detect completion of a mainframe extraction job prior to executing.

The People dimension identifies the audience. Knowing the audience, issues such as the client interface requirements and security facilities can be addressed. While the data warehouse project implements the client interface, the environment must support the types of interfaces which are needed. Similarly, while the data warehouse project implements the security facilities such as encryption, the environment must support the encryption and decryption of data if this technique is to be used.

The Locations dimension impacts the communications facilities. Factors to address include the communications lines and their ability to handle the bursts of data which the warehouse loading and use may create, as well as the client and server features needed to ensure compatibility.

The Activities dimension addresses the processing capabilities of the technical environment. The computer processing capacity needs to be sufficient to handle both the loading of the data and its access.

The Entities dimension addresses the databases themselves. If the data is to be distributed, for example, each of the servers on which the data is to reside must have the needed disk space, database management system, and operating system. In addition, to facilitate movement of data from one server to another, standards dealing with directory paths and database management system parameters should also be established.

Each of the technical environment items builds on the top views defined for the data warehouse and has a separate set of activities for the builder's and out-of-context views.

Data Warehouse Design

The database schema is developed in the builder's view. This schema is based on the data model previously developed, some results from the source system analysis phase which cause design changes due to the existing system constraints, and adjustments needed to ensure adequate performance and flexible access. The database schema may be founded on relational modeling concepts or on dimensional modeling concepts.

Relational Modeling Foundation.   The logical data model previous-ly developed undergoes additional transformations at this time.

1. *Create data artifacts.* The operational system handles current data. Over time, both the data relationships and the data contents may have changed. To the extent that these impact the retention of history within the data warehouse, the data warehouse design must accom-modate them. The addition of an attribute for the time dimension to the data warehouse information handles some of the needs.

If the relationships change, then multiple database structures may be needed at the atomic level. Users of the data warehouse are typical-ly interested in either the view of the data at the time it was created or the view of the data with current reference information. The changes over time are rarely needed. Therefore, while the atomic level of data may have the complex structures to support the rare times when the changes are needed, the tables provided to end users through summaries and aggregations can be tailored to the most fre-quently needed views.

Data artifacts also need to ensure that relationships are preserved even if the source system no longer retains the needed data. For example, if vendors are purged from the source system after 2 years of inactivity, and the data warehouse retains some purchase order infor-mation for 10 years, at least some information about the vendor must be retained in the data warehouse after it is purged from the source system to ensure that the vendor foreign key in the purchase order can be resolved.

2. *Add derived data.* Data views in the warehouse should support the typical users' needs. Hence data is often derived, summarized, and aggregated. Performing these functions in advance not only improves performance and simplifies access, it also improves consistency by ensuring that everyone is using the same algorithms. The nature of the data warehouse is such that not all the aggregations can be defined at the onset. The structure needs to be able to accommodate by adding to these as time progresses.

3. *Organize data for loading and retrieval efficiency.* The source system analysis phase identifies issues with the data sources. One conse-quence of this analysis is the extract frequency and sequence. Consid-eration of this information in the database schema can significantly simplify the extraction, transformation, and loading process.

Since the data warehouse is a retrieval system rather than a data entry and maintenance system, the data in the warehouse needs to be organized accordingly. This will usually mean that data from multiple tables in the source system are merged into a single table in the warehouse, and that data which may be in a single table in the source system may be parsed into multiple tables in the warehouse. The structure of the table itself may be different in that arrays are sometimes appropriate for the data warehouse.

4. *Partition data.* The access needs of the end users and the underlying technical infrastructure may provide options concerning the physical location of the data. If the volume of the warehouse warrants, consideration should be given to partitioning the data and distributing portions of it to remote sites. Even without data distribution, partitioning the data may be advisable, if most of the access is on a small (e.g., current quarter) subset of the data.

5. *Identify indexes.* A data warehouse is designed to get data out. Further, as a read-only database, it does not carry with it the overhead of transaction-based systems with respect to indexes. Based on anticipated use, indexes should be liberally defined. With usage, these can be modified to meet the needs. There are some database management systems which can accommodate indexing of virtually every field.

While the stepwise progression could lead to a database schema which resembles a star schema, a more streamlined approach can be used for the star schema if one is to be built.

Using the previously developed models as a base, to guard against stovepipe decision support systems, a star schema can be developed by defining the dimensions and facts needed to support the business process which the data warehouse addresses at the granularity level previously defined.

Dimensional Modeling Foundation. Dimensional modeling techniques are often appropriate for the summarization levels within the data warehouse. These techniques manifest themselves in a star schema which is described in Chap. 2. In a data warehouse environment, examples of fact tables include

- Order line items
- Sales line items
- Shipment line items
- Inventory activities
- Inventory levels

- Purchase order line items
- Insurance claims
- Insurance policies

Examples of dimension tables, which provide reference information for the fact tables, are

- Customers
- Products
- Employees
- Warehouses
- Stores
- Business units
- Time

These dimension tables often apply to multiple fact tables. Using the data model as the foundation of these tables supports their reuse across the multiple schemas. With this reuse, the process of building the dimension table is executed once, and that table can be replicated wherever it is needed.

Within the star schema, the time dimension offers an easy way for data warehouse users to obtain information within meaningful date ranges without complicated SQL. For example, a retail organization may be interested in tracking year-to-year sales results during the period between Thanksgiving and Christmas. Since the date for Thanksgiving is different each year, the request becomes complicated. If a flag to indicate this period is created in the time dimension table, the request is simplified since this flag is used to resolve the dates. (See Fig. 6-14.)

Programming Specifications

The specifications address moving the data from the operational systems to the data warehouse. For each element in the data warehouse, its source and derivation is documented. In its simplistic form, this documentation can take the form of a five-column table. (See Fig. 6-15.)

While many of the transformations will be simple, particularly if there is only one source, a number will be complicated, and surprises with the data should be anticipated. The greatest source of complication is in the integration of data from multiple sources and in the handling

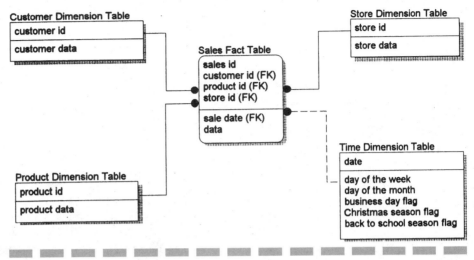

Figure 6-14 Times Dimension.

of source system data problems. If a staging area with a multistep process is developed, the transformation map in Fig. 6-15 is needed for each transformation.

The specifications address more than just the Entities dimension.

- Implicit in the target table (and hence database and server) designation is the location of the target environment. If special processes are needed to move the data to a particular server, the specifications need to address this.

SOURCE TABLE	SOURCE ELEMENT	TRANSFORMATION RULE	TARGET TABLE	TARGET ELEMENT
Customer	cust_no	Move as is	Customer	cust_id
	cust_name	Move as is	Customer	cust_co_nm
	cust_rep	Move as is	Customer	cust_rep_nm
(N/A)		Generate using system date	Customer	xfrm_dt
Product	prod_no	Move as is	Product	prod_id
	prod_name	Move as is	Product	prod_nm
	prod_type	Move as is	Product	prod_type_cd
Product Type	prod_desc	Generate using the product type code and description in the reference table	Product	prod_type_ds
(N/A)		Generate using system date	Product	xfrm_dt

Figure 6-15 Transformation Map.

- The specifications also need to address the operating schedules. They define the jobs which need to be executed, their interdependencies, and their dependencies on jobs within the operational environment.

- Performance considerations are also addressed. The load process typically must operate in a finite amount of time. The time available may dictate the need for parallel processing, the manner in which the indexes are loaded, etc.

- The data warehouse jobs need to be monitored by operations personnel, and the needs of these people must also be considered. For example, the specifications may address operational information to aid in recovery activities. Another people-related issue is security. Depending on the sensitivity of the data, security may need to be handled during the transformation process by encrypting some or all of the data.

With the advent of code generators for data warehouse transformation programs, these specifications could also take the form of parameters for those code generators.

Two sets of programming specifications may be needed— one for the initial load and one for the ongoing operation.

The ongoing operation addresses the day-to-day loading of the data warehouse. The initial load addresses the gathering of historical information which is needed at implementation time. Some historical information may be available in the systems to be used as the day-to-day sources. Other historical information may need to be retrieved from archives, and these archives may not conform to the format of the current sources. Hence, additional transformations and quality checks may be necessary.

Technical Environment Preparation

The effort required for preparing the technical environment can range from nothing to extensive. If all the required facilities exist, then no work is needed. More often, some work is needed to ensure that the environment is ready for the data warehouse. The work which is needed is based on the deficiencies identified during the technical environment assessment related activities previously noted.

Subcontractor's View

Within the subcontractor's view, the individual components of the data warehouse are developed.

Programming

The programming defined in the specifications is performed at this time. If a code generator is available, then the programs are developed using that generator. If not, then the programs are developed using the appropriate language(s). In addition to the programs, the databases and tables are defined at all appropriate locations.

The programming activities also include compilations, walk-throughs, and testing at various levels. Upon completion of the programming activities, some data should be available on the data warehouse tables.

Technical Environment Preparation

Components of the technical environment area are also developed in the Subcontractor's view based on the work identified at the higher-level views.

Builder's View Revisited

Once the individual components of the data warehouse are built, they can be assembled to provide the data warehouse system. Once this process is complete, data warehouse population can take place.

Population

Two basic structures may be needed to address the data warehouse population.

Initial Population.   The implementation project needs to provide the base data for the data warehouse. As previously noted, special programs may need to be developed to handle the initial load.

Even if all the data is available in the sources to be used on an ongoing basis, special processing may still be needed due to the amount of data which is initially being captured.

Ongoing Population.   The ongoing population of the data warehouse assumes that the tables exist and that information must either be brought into the data warehouse in a refresh or append mode. Examples of refresh activities are data which is used for reference and for which no history is needed. Examples of append activities are data concerning events of interest. Each load cycle should concentrate on bringing in the events since the previous load cycle.

Metadata

No discussion of a data warehouse methodology can be considered complete without mentioning metadata. Because of the importance of metadata, it is treated as a separate topic in Chap. 10.

Tool Support

Numerous tools are available to support data warehouse development and the capture of artifacts to populate the Zachman Framework cells. General-purpose, as well as data warehouse—specific, repositories can store the artifacts. Modern full-function repositories are extensible and as such can support a metamodel which is compatible with the Framework. Within such a repository, an entity or object can be created for each cell, and attributes of that entity can be created to capture the elements of interest for each cell. Some of the repositories also provide a means to electronically load metadata from other sources.

Another option is to use a tool such as Structure for Information Systems Architecture by Framework Software, Inc., of Redondo Beach, California. This PC-based tool facilitates capturing or referencing the artifact information for each cell of the Zachman Framework. Figure 6-16 shows some of the details about each artifact (in this case the goal of the customer service department) which can be captured. CASE tools address some of the cells, though they rarely encompass the entire Framework.

Figure 6-16
Scope—Motivations
Artifact. (Courtesy
Framework Software,
Inc. P.O. Box 3415;
Redondo Beach, CA
90277; (310) 374-
8076.)

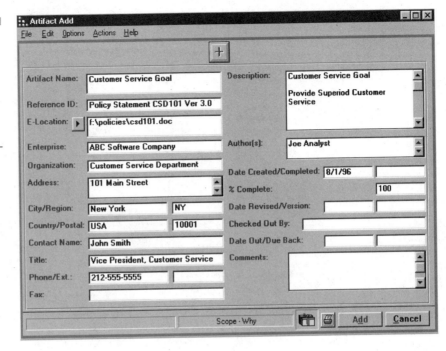

Performance monitors and schedulers facilitate handling the actual data migration flow and performance management, and metadata from these tools can also be used to populate appropriate Framework cells.

Summary

The Zachman Framework provides an architectural construct for the data warehouse methodology. The base methodology fits very well into the Framework. (See Fig. 6-17.)

The value of this exercise is not just in mapping the methodology into the appropriate steps but in using that process as the launching pad for applying the methodology. In Part 3 of the book the methodology is applied toward the building of the data warehouse. It is also adapted to support development of the data warehouse query system, a metadata system, the operational data store, building legacy system replacements, improving business processes, and supporting total quality management.

Planner's View	COMMITMENT
Owner's View	DATA MODEL ANALYSIS
Designer's View	BREADBOX ANALYSIS / SUBJECT AREA ANALYSIS / TECHNICAL ASSESSMENT
Builder's View	SOURCE SYSTEM ANALYSIS / DATA WAREHOUSE DESIGN / TECHNICAL ENVIRONMENT PREPARATION / SPECIFICATIONS
Subcontractor's View	PROGRAMMING
Builder's View Revisited	POPULATION

Figure 6-17   Methodology Method.

PART 3

Applications

CHAPTER 7

Building the First Data Warehouse

A data warehouse effort is typically initiated to satisfy a quest for information; an operational system development effort, on the other hand, is launched to improve the way computer technology is used in a set of business processes. The first data warehouse, either within the company as a whole or within an area of the company, often has an additional objective which is to demonstrate how an architected decision support database can be developed quickly and provide business value. This chapter describes construction of such a data warehouse and deviations from the standard methodology which are warranted for this effort.

The Development Life Cycle

The methodology described in Chap. 6 provides a top-down approach.

The methodology recognizes that with a data warehouse that is based on a solid data architecture the risks introduced by making assumptions concerning the other dimensions are minimized.

The need to make these assumptions is paramount in the first data warehouse. With the first project, the momentum for building data warehouses is generated, and it is essential to deliver results quickly. As Fig. 7-1 points out, the emphasis of the initial effort is on building the database. Artifacts for some of the other columns are actually gathered as the data warehouse is exercised.

Within a traditional systems development life cycle, the implementation of the system is preceded by requirements definition, analysis, design, programming, testing, and integration. With the data warehouse, the first effort focuses on implementation. Complexities introduced by

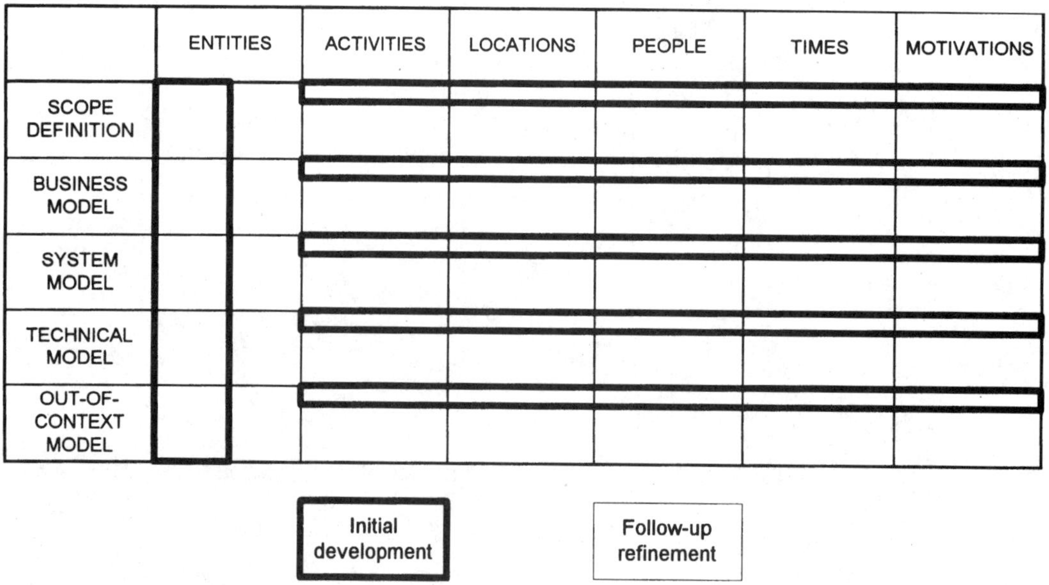

	ENTITIES	ACTIVITIES	LOCATIONS	PEOPLE	TIMES	MOTIVATIONS
SCOPE DEFINITION						
BUSINESS MODEL						
SYSTEM MODEL						
TECHNICAL MODEL						
OUT-OF-CONTEXT MODEL						

Initial development

Follow-up refinement

Figure 7-1   Iterative Methodology.

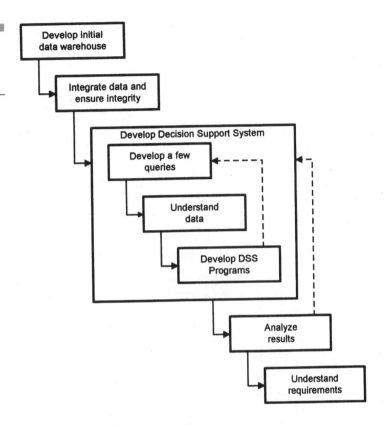

Figure 7-2
Data Warehouse
Development
Methodology.

integration can follow, with the integrity of the data verified as data is added. The decision support system which uses the data warehouse is also developed iteratively—a few queries are placed against the data, the data is then better understood, and a decision support system is developed. Results are analyzed, and only then are the true requirements understood. (See Fig. 7-2.)

Commitment to Proceed

The commitment to proceed defines the scope of the data warehouse and obtains the necessary funding and support. One of the best places to start is with the basic purpose of the effort—What is the business issue that is creating the need for the data warehouse?

Motivations

A person or organization which requests construction of a data warehouse has business reasons for the request. For example, the sales and marketing organization of a single product line may want a data warehouse to help achieve its goal of becoming the dominant vendor for its product line. In line with that goal, specific information, not easily retrievable from the operational system, may be requested. Answers to the following questions may be requested:

- Who are our largest customers?
- What are the buying trends of our products for our largest customers?
- Is there any correlation between the sales of product A and the sales of product B?
- What was the effect of the discount offered in August of last year?

Questions such as these could be answered by the data in the sales system, but the base system is not designed to handle them. These questions are very limited in scope. As can be seen in Fig. 7-3, the business goal is an artifact of the planner's view, while the information needs are artifacts of the designer's view.

Figure 7-3 also points out that some of the motivations are implicit. For example, the information needs assume that all the objectives of interest will relate to the goal of becoming the dominant vendor of its products. Other objectives, such as those which may deal with other product lines or information about other vendors will therefore not be addressed by the first data warehouse.

Before proceeding further, the developers and business representatives need to assess the risk of stating the information needs while assuming (or implicitly defining) the business objectives upon which they are based. Developing a thorough set of objectives may require access to people who do not understand the data warehouse and who may not be familiar with the effort. While this is desired if a traditional systems development life cycle is followed, the team may feel confident that the criteria are on target and that it will be in a better position to identify the objectives after it demonstrates some of the capabilities of the data warehouse. That approach is consistent with the data warehouse development life cycle, and it recognizes the risks of the implicit assumptions.

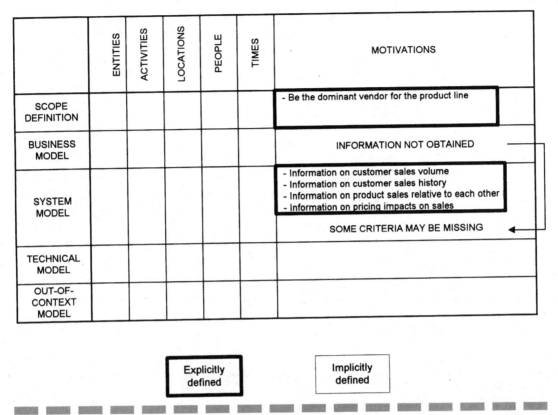

Figure 7-3 Motivations Dimension.

People and Locations

The initial set of business users of the data warehouse can frequently be identified quickly, and the complete set can rarely be identified in advance. The risks introduced by incomplete information about the users have two potential ramifications. The first impacts the design of the data warehouse and its interfaces, and the second impacts the supporting infrastructure.

The sales and marketing organization of the product line may be thinking only of its needs when requesting the data warehouse. Within that department, the needs of sales managers, marketing managers, and sales and marketing analysts could be met. By limiting the scope to that view, the needs of other departments, corresponding departments responsible for other product lines, or departments responsible for monitoring product shipments may be ignored. The data warehouse design, therefore, may meet only some of the business needs.

An incomplete set of users could also impact the technical infrastructure. The business users of the data warehouse dictate the functionality needed at each location. If all the users are at one location, a centralized approach may be appropriate. If, however, some of the users are located at remote locations, a distributed approach may be dictated. (See Fig. 7-4.)

Recognition of the absence of information concerning the user groups enables the development team to make conscious decisions concerning the initial scope. Introduction of all the user groups would provide a more complete data warehouse, but it also lengthens the development cycle. Confining the initial set of users will produce a practical (though possibly incomplete) data warehouse. Since it could be produced quickly, the data warehouse could be viewed as a working prototype.

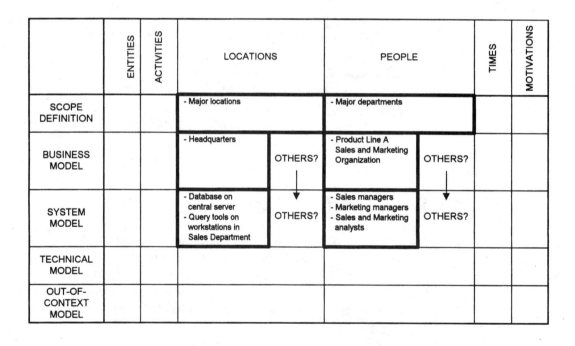

Figure 7-4 People and Locations Dimensions.

Another factor to consider is funding. If the data warehouse is requested by one division, that group may not be willing to fund expansions to address other areas, and the other divisions may not be sufficiently educated or motivated to fund efforts to address their own areas. The limited-scope data warehouse, in that case, both meets the needs of that group and provides a means to demonstrate the value to other departments.

Entities

The first phase of the data warehouse development should identify the subject areas to be addressed. As noted in Chap. 6, if the company does not have a subject area model, time should be taken to develop one. While the first data warehouse can be built without it, there is a risk that the warehouse will become a stovepipe decision support system rather than an integrated and subject-oriented source of information for decision makers.

> **If a company chooses to skip development of a subject area model, the data warehouse will be built based on the models implicit in the source system.**

As Fig. 7-5 shows, the absence of information adds to the risk of the project. The approach used in data model analysis provides a reasonable compromise for the first effort.

Activities and Times

The data warehouse does not directly address operational business activities. It does, however, address tactical and strategic business activities. Complete development of a data warehouse, therefore, requires the delineation of these activities and their timing from a business perspective. If the data warehouse is being built to address a specific set of criteria, the business activities may not be explicitly defined. Instead, the only known thing may be a set of reports which the users will be requesting. If the data is in the warehouse, then the major impact of needing to support additional activities will be the addition of new data aggregations or summaries. To attain performance expectation, database reorganization or tuning may also be needed, and depending on the volume of data involved, this is not a trivial item. Leaving these

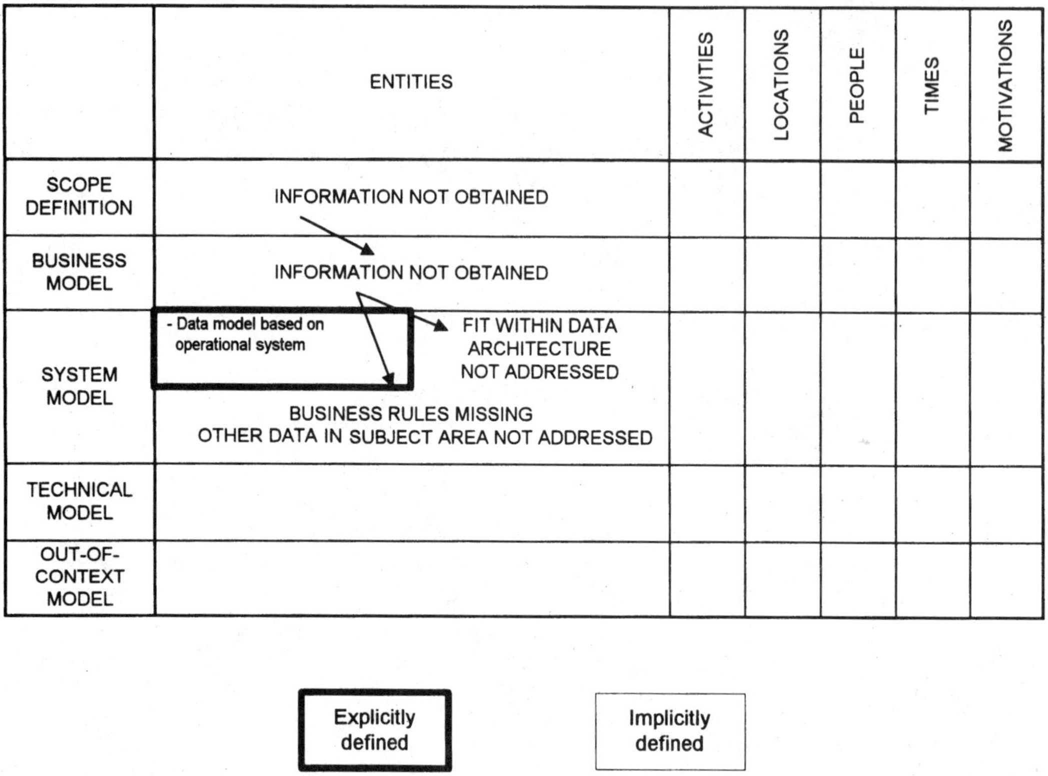

	ENTITIES	ACTIVITIES	LOCATIONS	PEOPLE	TIMES	MOTIVATIONS
SCOPE DEFINITION	INFORMATION NOT OBTAINED					
BUSINESS MODEL	INFORMATION NOT OBTAINED					
SYSTEM MODEL	- Data model based on operational system FIT WITHIN DATA ARCHITECTURE NOT ADDRESSED BUSINESS RULES MISSING OTHER DATA IN SUBJECT AREA NOT ADDRESSED					
TECHNICAL MODEL						
OUT-OF-CONTEXT MODEL						

Explicitly defined   Implicitly defined

Figure 7-5   Entities Dimension.

models implicit is consistent with the data warehouse development methodology. (See Fig. 7-6.)

Risk Assessment

As with any systems development project, skipping steps adds an element of risk to the project.

The Zachman Framework provides a context for evaluating the risks, comparing them to the benefits of the approach, and making the appropriate business decision. It is also very useful in communicating the expectations concerning the product of the effort.

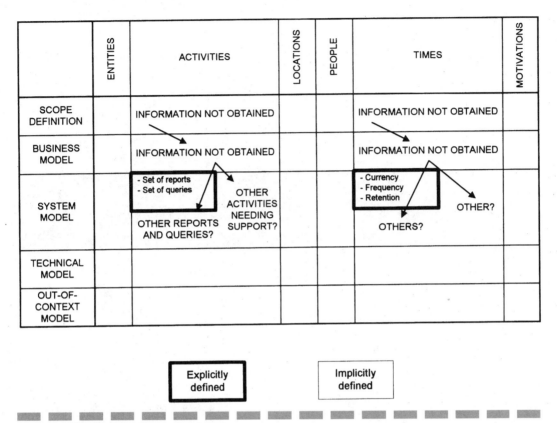

Figure 7-6 *Activities and Times Dimensions.*

It provides another very useful function. When the information is eventually obtained, it provides a place for evaluating the information in context with work already performed.

Figure 7-7 shows that the greatest areas of exposure are within Entities, Activities, and Times. Within the limited scope, information is available concerning the business users and their locations, and within a limited depth, information concerning the motivations is also known. The major driving factors for proceeding with the limited information are the low cost and short duration. Properly managed, the remaining deliverables for a limited-scope data warehouse can often be developed in 2 to 4 months, assuming the technical infrastructure to support the data warehouse exists.

Following the short-duration effort, demonstrations—both to the requesting business users and to others—can show the strengths of the

	ENTITIES	ACTIVITIES	LOCATIONS	PEOPLE	TIMES	MOTIVATIONS
SCOPE DEFINITION			major locations	major departments		goals
BUSINESS MODEL			network locations	dept		
SYSTEM MODEL	partial data model	operational system activities	node functions	sections	currency frequency retention	business rules
TECHNICAL MODEL						
OUT-OF-CONTEXT MODEL						

Explicitly defined   Implicitly defined   To be developed

Figure 7-7   Risk Assessment Information.

data warehouse in general and the limitations of the focused approach. If no expansion of the data warehouse is needed, then the development effort could proceed into production. A more likely scenario is that people will see the value of data access using data warehousing techniques. In this case, the missing information in the upper views needs to be gathered, and then an incremental approach for adding functionality to the data warehouse needs to be planned. (See Fig. 7-8.) Subsequent chapters address the expansion.

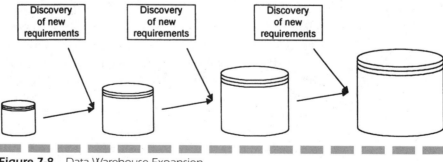

Discovery of new requirements   Discovery of new requirements   Discovery of new requirements

Figure 7-8   Data Warehouse Expansion.

Project Sponsor Implications

The project sponsor needs to recognize—and accept—the risks. He or she serves as the visionary.

The sponsor needs to understand the potential value of the data warehouse and needs to assess whether or not the approach being taken is likely to deliver that value—eventually.

The project sponsor must also clearly communicate the scope and objectives of the initial effort to ensure that expectations are appropriately set. Once people see the data warehouse, they are likely to point out deficiencies. If the expectations are properly set, then the impact of the deficiencies is minimized. Additionally, using the Zachman Framework to identify implicit information helps to communicate what was skipped and helps to plan for addressing these areas in subsequent iterations.

Project Manager Implications

The project manager for the initial data warehouse effort also needs to recognize the risks and must remain sensitive to the conscious acceptance of these risks to enable quick delivery of the results. Along with the project sponsor, the project manager must continuously promote the data warehouse.

The project manager must be prepared at all times to explain both the scope of the initial effort and the scope of a typical data warehouse effort.

This is critical in setting expectations so that people recognize that the missing steps do need to be completed to deliver on the promise of an architected data warehouse.

Source System Analysis

The traditional development of the data warehouse uses the data model as the foundation. For the first effort, if a single system is to be used as the source, the data model can be developed using the physical schema of that system's databases. The first step of this process, then, is to understand the data in the source system. Information about the system's operating environment and about its data needs to be gathered.

The operating information addresses the hardware and software platform on which the system is operating, its schedule, operating dependencies, etc. In addition, information about the suspected integrity of the data should be gathered. If the source system data is suspect, its quality must be clearly understood by the end users, or steps need to be taken to improve it.

If the source system uses a relational database management structure, information about the database names, database schema, database constraints, and database size needs to be gathered. The table sizes and contents then need to be examined, and finally, the attributes themselves need to be understood. A corresponding set of information is needed for other database structures.

The data warehouse will be built from the attributes of the source system. Therefore, it is extremely important to understand their definitions from the perspective of the system and to ensure that these definitions match the needs expressed for the decision support environment. For example, a system may create fictitious customers to handle interdepartmental transfers. If the decision support system is expecting customers to be external to the company, the data must be analyzed to transform it to the decision support definition.

Data Model Analysis

The logical data model is developed in this phase. The bottom-up construction of this model is based on the analysis of the source system. In that analysis, each of the attributes is identified and defined.

> **Rapid development of a data model demands constraining its scope to that needed for the decision support activities by removing purely operational data.**

Removing Operational Data

The operational data contains information which is needed for operational activities but which is of limited value for decision support. For example, in the case of the sales data, textual information about the cus-

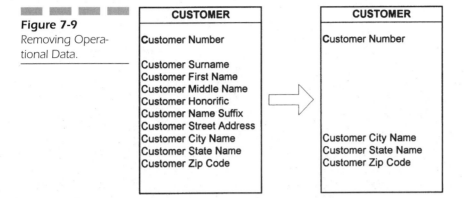

Figure 7-9
Removing Operational Data.

tomer interaction may be retained within the operational system but is typically not needed in the data warehouse. Only a small portion of the data elements of the source system are usually needed within the data warehouse. (See Fig. 7-9.)

While this activity may seem trivial, it is extremely important. The data warehouse will contain historical information. If all the data is captured, then the files will tend to grow very, very quickly. Careful thought needs to be given to each and every element brought into the data warehouse. Remember that data warehouse development is iterative. If the data is readily available, the predisposition should be to omit it if no clear need is expressed or suspected. This approach may result in needing to modify the data warehouse later to absorb it, but at that time, its use will be obvious. Including an element which *might* be needed may result in the element remaining in the data warehouse forever, unless a concerted effort is made to detect unused elements.

Identifying Business Entities and Attributes

The remaining elements are grouped into business entities and placed in the appropriate subject area. Each entity should relate to a business item of interest, such as a customer, consumer, or customer account, all of which fall into the customers subject area. Working together, the business analyst and data analyst should then develop an entity relationship diagram which depicts the portion of the data in the operational system of interest in the data warehouse. In the process, some changes may take place such that the attributes in the business model do not completely match those in the operational system. (For example, the definition of customer may shift to the external focus.)

Each of the entities and attributes should be defined, and these definitions should be compared with the definitions implicit in the operational system. To the extent that the definitions agree, the subsequent mapping is facilitated. Definition mismatches indicate a disparity between the business view of the data and the data as represented in its systems. The impact of any disparity needs to be assessed to determine actions necessary to either correct them, explain them, or obviate them.

Part of the creation of the business entities entails the designation of the unique identifier. The source system may have a customer number which uniquely identifies its customers. That number may be valid if its definition and the business rules for its creation, maintenance, and deletion are acceptable. If, however, the analyst is aware that other systems use different customer numbering schemes, or if the numbers are recycled, this may be a good time to create a universal identifier.

Adding a Time Dimension

The operational systems may not contain a time dimension. This dimension often needs to be deduced based on the content, structure, or timing of the operational system. For example, the time of the extract could be used to generate the time for the snapshot.

Risk Assessment

Figure 7-10 demonstrates the impact of combining a subject area model with the bottom-up development of the logical model. A comprehensive data model is a prerequisite for a full data warehouse. Without one, the warehouse cannot be truly subject oriented and integrated. Developing a limited-scope data warehouse from a single operational system does, however, have some advantages. The warehouse can be built quickly, and its use may help demonstrate the value of a full-fledged data warehouse development effort. The data model developed based on the operational system is a good starting point for an enterprise-level model. Even if each effort builds its models bottom-up, if time is taken to integrate the models as they are built, an enterprise model will eventually be created, and points of intersection can be readily identified. This will be demonstrated in the discussion of the data warehouse expansion in Chap. 8.

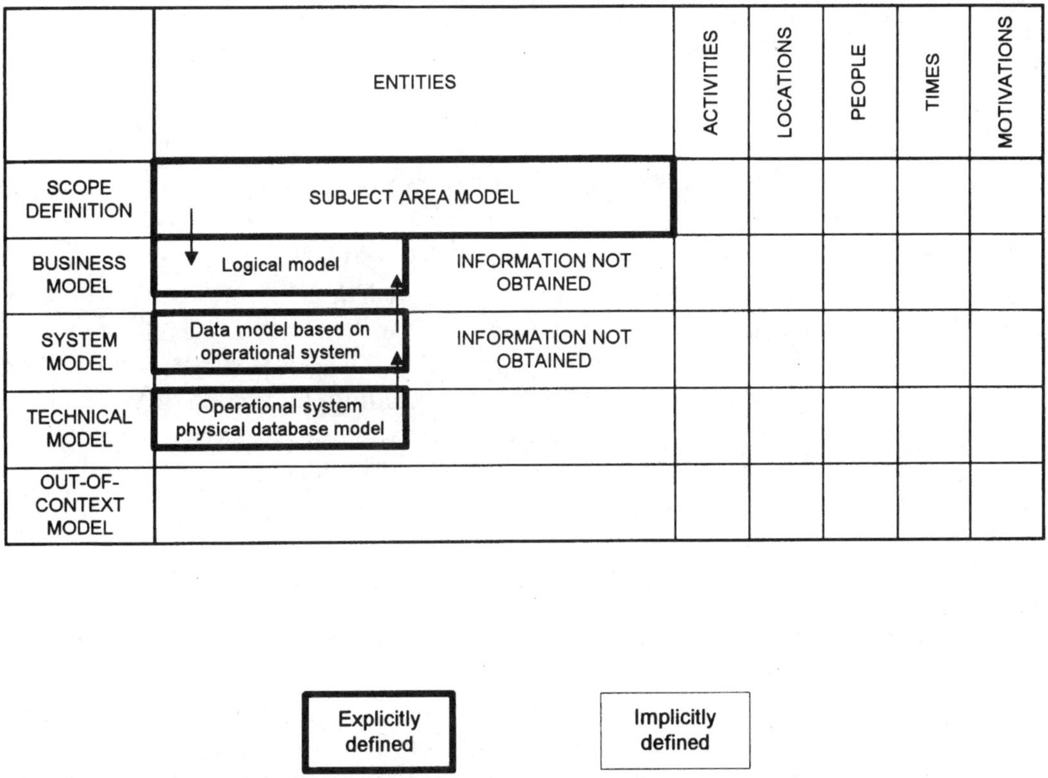

	ENTITIES		ACTIVITIES	LOCATIONS	PEOPLE	TIMES	MOTIVATIONS
SCOPE DEFINITION	SUBJECT AREA MODEL						
BUSINESS MODEL	Logical model	INFORMATION NOT OBTAINED					
SYSTEM MODEL	Data model based on operational system	INFORMATION NOT OBTAINED					
TECHNICAL MODEL	Operational system physical database model						
OUT-OF-CONTEXT MODEL							

Explicitly defined	Implicitly defined

Figure 7-10   Bottom-up Model Impact.

Technical Assessment and Technical Environment Preparation

During the commitment to proceed phase, certain assumptions were made concerning the users, locations, schedules, etc. These assumptions need to be reviewed to ensure that a warehouse with acceptable performance can be built within these constraints. If the environmental modifications are extensive, then serious consideration should be given to adjusting the scope. For example, if the objective is to provide access at many remote locations and some of these locations do not have the required connectivity, consideration should be given to either eliminating these locations during the initial rollout or providing them access using other facilities such as (relatively) low-speed telephone lines.

Breadbox Analysis

During the breadbox analysis phase, the size of the proposed data warehouse is reviewed to ensure that it is reasonable given the existing environment. If the analysis reveals that the warehouse is likely to stretch the limits of the infrastructure, then the level of granularity should be reconsidered. As noted in the methodology, changing the granularity from hourly to monthly reduces the number of records by over 700. If the level of data needed to support the strategic decisions is monthly, the level of granularity should reflect this need.

Subject Area Analysis

In the subject area analysis phase, the scope of the current iteration is confirmed. Information gathered from the previous modeling activities, the assessment of the infrastructure, and the breadbox analysis are used to confirm that the scope of the effort is appropriate. If not, then appropriate scope adjustments need to be made.

Source System Analysis

Sequentially, the source system analysis phase is generally conducted at this time. For the initial effort, the methodology was adapted to use the source system as input to the data model. If there are still open questions concerning the source systems, they need to be answered at this time.

Data Warehouse Design

Chapter 6 details the data warehouse design activities. For the initial data warehouse, some compromises are feasible. Using a logical data

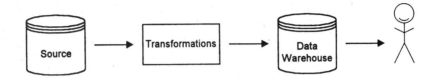

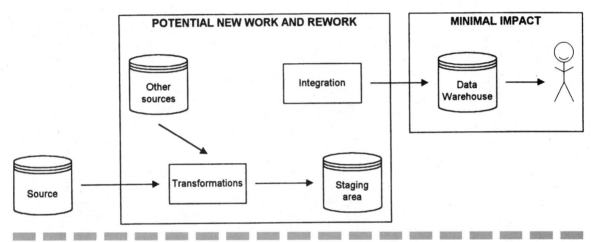

Figure 7-11 Staging Area Omission Impact.

model as a foundation, the physical model can be derived. Eventually, the data warehouse design will probably need to accommodate a staging area to facilitate integration. For the initial effort, a conscious decision can be made to skip this step. Skipping this step enables the analyst to postpone many of the integration issues. There may be some rework required later, but if the data warehouse model is developed well, the impact of this rework should have a minimal negative impact on the users. (See Fig. 7-11.)

If the objective of the first data warehouse effort is to provide a prototype, handling data artifacts can be postponed to a subsequent iteration. Data artifacts are often needed to ensure referential integrity when the history retained in the data warehouse is greater than that in the operational system. If, for example, the operational system deletes customers after 2 years of inactivity, the data warehouse, with 5 to 10 years of history, faces the prospect of having a reference which cannot be resolved. For the initial effort, the scope of the warehouse could be limited to 2 years of data, with a subsequent iteration handling the artifact resolution.

Specifications

After the data warehouse design and source system analysis are completed, the programming specifications can be defined. These specifications define the way in which the data will flow from the source systems to the data warehouse. The data warehouse design phase addresses the Entities (target database) dimension. The specifications also need to ensure that the warehouse, once completed, satisfactorily addresses all six dimensions.

Activities

The transformation rules are defined in the programming specifications. For the initial data warehouse, these should be fairly straightforward, since integration has been postponed to a subsequent iteration. Several complications may arise, and each needs to be handled expeditiously.

One likely complication is due to definition changes between the source system definition of an element and the element's definition in the data warehouse. If the difference is predictable and mathematical, an algorithm may be developed to handle the difference. An example of such an instance is that the operational system may exclude commissions in the revenue figures while the data warehouse includes them in the revenue figures and also maintains them as a separate attribute.

Other complications may arise due to changes during the life of the operational system. If freight cost, for example, was segregated as a separate item only during the past year and if history beyond that is needed in the initial data warehouse, the transformation program must deal with two separate rules—one for when the freight cost was a separate item and one for when it was not.

A common complication is the absence of information. If the sales representative is an optional field in the sales system, then rules to compensate for its occasional absence must be developed. Options include creating a sales representative named "unknown," derivation of the sales representative from other information such as the sales region, or omission of the field completely from the initial data warehouse.

The transformation rules, when completed, should be such that the developer could either use them to code the transformation programs or to determine parameters for a code generator.

Motivations

Within the technical model, the operating conditions and required performance characteristics are defined. These conditions impact the technological choices made in building the data warehouse and could be documented through service-level agreements which can be used to subsequently measure the actual performance relative to agreed-upon expectations. Common conditions which could apply to a data warehouse include response time, availability, and call-out requirements. Figure 7-12 provides a sample set of operating conditions for a data warehouse.

People

The direct individual users of the data warehouse are identified for the technical model. This information directly supports the database design as well as the look and feel of the data warehouse. The impact on the database design manifests itself in decisions concerning granularity, partitioning, and indexing. The impact on the look and feel shows up in the access tool and the front-end menu decisions. (See Fig. 7-13.)

Figure 7-12
Data Warehouse Operating Characteristics.

PERFORMANCE AREA	CONDITION
Availability	• Monday - Friday: 7 a.m. to 7 p.m.
	• During the week-end following month-end closing: Saturday, 7 a.m. to 7 p.m.
Performance - Standard Queries	• Type A queries: 15 seconds
	• Type B queries: 60 seconds
	• Type C queries: 15 minutes
	(assumes that a type is defined for each standard query)
Performance - Ad hoc Queries	• No performance guarantees provided
Problem resolution	• Problem resolution is provided during normal working hours, except that call-out support is provided during the month-end data extraction process

Figure 7-13 User Interfaces.

Locations

In the technical model, the locations need to be considered even if an existing mature infrastructure is being used. This consideration is necessitated by the need to physically place databases, query tools, and programs on the appropriate platforms; to ensure that the needed communications facilities are in place; and to ensure that the clients and servers have the needed resources to meet the performance expectations.

Times

The scheduling of the data warehouse programs is detailed in the technical model. This may entail defining the addition of extraction programs into the operational program job stream, or it may require the specification of new jobs related to the data warehouse. The prescribed process should also define a means for verifying the successful execution of the jobs.

Technical Model Culmination

Upon completion of the technical model, the operating architecture of the data warehouse is defined. The stage is now set for specifying and developing the individual components. (See Fig. 7-14.)

Programming

Programming addresses the fifth row of the Zachman Framework, which deals with the out-of-context model. The individual components are developed such that they fit within the framework defined by the

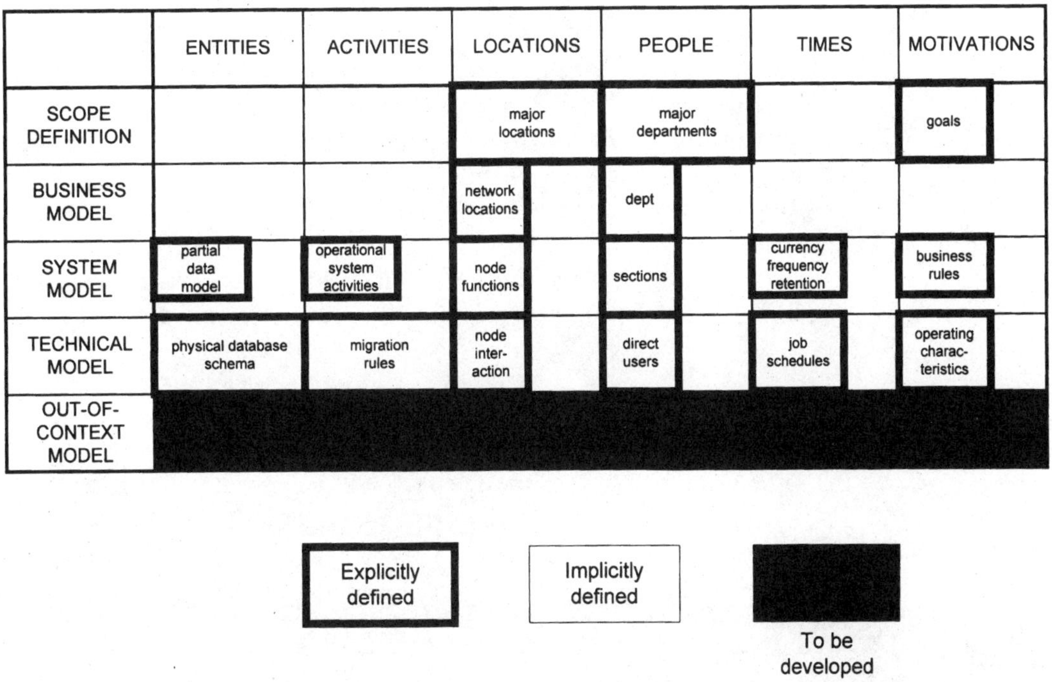

	ENTITIES	ACTIVITIES	LOCATIONS	PEOPLE	TIMES	MOTIVATIONS
SCOPE DEFINITION			major locations	major departments		goals
BUSINESS MODEL			network locations	dept		
SYSTEM MODEL	partial data model	operational system activities	node functions	sections	currency frequency retention	business rules
TECHNICAL MODEL	physical database schema	migration rules	node inter-action	direct users	job schedules	operating charac-teristics
OUT-OF-CONTEXT MODEL						

Explicitly defined	Implicitly defined	To be developed

Figure 7-14 Technical Model Culmination.

Figure 7-15
Out-of-Context Model
Artifacts.

DIMENSION	ARTIFACT
Entities	• Physical database definitions
Activities	• Program modules
Locations	• Operating network
People	• Access authorizations
Times	• Interrupts
Motivations	• Module-level performance conditions

technical model. The major governing factors at this stage are those which deal with integration and implementation. The artifacts associated with each of the six dimensions are delineated in Fig. 7-15. One of the salient aspects of considering the out-of-context model separately from the technical model is the increased potential for components to be reused. This approach should also reduce subsequent maintenance and rework when the data warehouse is enhanced and expanded.

As with the previous models, the Zachman Framework does not dictate a sequence for addressing the six dimensions. The sequence is typically dictated by the methodology, and the order in which the dimensions are delineated does not imply a particular sequence of execution.

Since the subcontractors are working on out-of-context tasks, the dimensions at this level interact with each other best through the technical model. For example, if the database being built does not conform to the physical schema, the best way to ensure that all the programs reflect the change is to change the physical schema first, then reflect the change through all appropriate dimensions of the builder's model, and then modify the appropriate out-of-context dimensions. (See Fig. 7-16.)

Entities

In the out-of-context model, each of the physical databases is defined within the appropriate database management system. Once the data

Figure 7-16
Impact of Out-of-Context Model Change.

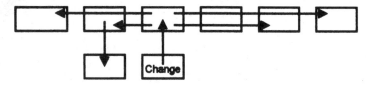

warehouse begins to operate, data will be physically loaded into the defined databases.

Activities

The programs for loading the data warehouse are developed at this point. The data migration programs are those which will read data from the operational system and create the data for the warehouse databases.

Locations

All the facilities needed for the operation of the data warehouse are interconnected during this stage of development. It is not uncommon for a data warehouse effort to be a company's first foray into the client/server arena. Depending on the maturity of the infrastructure and the access already available to the prospective users, much of this work may be done outside the specific data warehouse project.

People

The individual users and their required interactions with the data warehouse are identified in the technology model. In the out-of-context model, the users and their authorized activities are defined to the operating environment to ensure that appropriate security controls are in place.

The security controls to be implemented can have a profound effect on the data warehouse technical and out-of-context models. If the security is to be achieved through passwords, then the impact on the other models is probably minimal. If, however, the determination to achieve the desired security level through encryption is made at this point, several of the other models will need to change. The Zachman Framework facilitates identification of the impact of this decision.

Times

The scheduling details of the technical model are transformed into control language and scripts to trigger appropriate jobs at the appropriate

time and sequence. Since the jobs may be executed on different platforms (e.g., MVS and UNIX), the mechanisms to coordinate activities
among these platforms need to be developed.

Motivations

The performance characteristics for each of the modules developed by
the subcontractors are defined in the out-of-context model. Examples
include the data extraction program run times and the query performance characteristics. These may prove useful during integration activities to identify specific areas for improvement.

Out-of-Context Model Culmination

Upon completion of the out-of-context model, the components needed
to build the data warehouse are available. (See Fig. 7-17.)

	ENTITIES	ACTIVITIES	LOCATIONS	PEOPLE	TIMES	MOTIVATIONS
SCOPE DEFINITION			major locations	major departments		goals
BUSINESS MODEL			network locations	dept		
SYSTEM MODEL	partial data model	operational system activities	node functions	sections	currency frequency retention	business rules
TECHNICAL MODEL	physical database schema	migration rules	node inter-action	direct users	job schedules	operating charac-teristics
OUT-OF-CONTEXT MODEL	database definition	programs	operating network	access authorizations	interrupts	module operating characteristics

Explicitly defined   Implicitly defined

Figure 7-17 Out-of-Context Model Culmination.

Technical Model Revisited—Population

Once the data warehouse components are assembled into a system, the warehouse tables can be populated. Frequently, the process for the initial population of the data warehouse differs from that for the ongoing population. For simplification purposes, the transformation discussion assumed that the source system will be providing data both for the initial warehouse population and for its ongoing updates. Even though the programs may not change for the two objectives, some of the scripts are different, since *append* jobs become *create* jobs the first time the tables are loaded.

Summary

Building the data warehouse from a single source system is very different from building a fully integrated data warehouse.

The coverage of the methodology in this chapter differs slightly from the one presented in Chap. 6 in that some steps are taken out of sequence and a number of activities are abbreviated. The simple case does provide an immediate business benefit and can also enhance the visibility and value of the data warehouse. The area addressed by the data warehouse now needs to be assessed to identify potential improvement opportunities. (See Fig. 7-18.)

The expedient approach satisfies information retrieval requirements quickly, but the resultant environment may not be desirable for the long term.

- *The data warehouse may not be subject oriented.* It may contain data from several disparate subject areas.

- *The data in the warehouse is not integrated.* The data warehouse does not fully address any subject area; it only uses data which is processed by the sales system for the particular product line, even though there may be other databases with similar information.

- *The data is not gathered at the source.* The data warehouse only collects data after the data has been processed by the sales system for that product line.

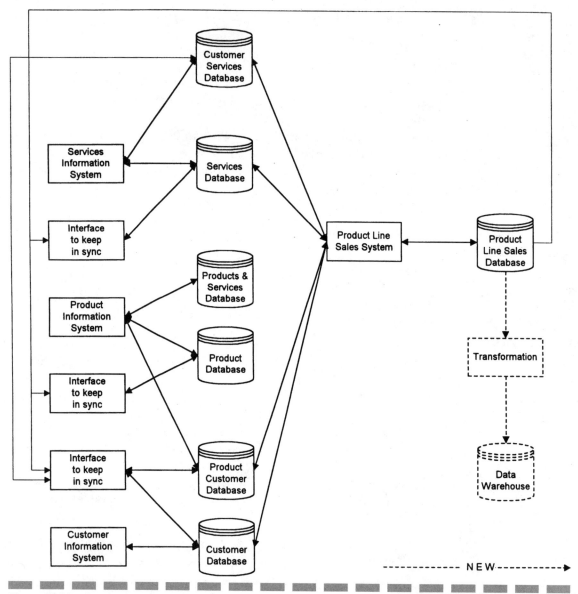

Figure 7-18   Resultant Environment.

- *The business goal may not be adequately addressed.* The business objectives have not been defined.

- *The business rules may not be properly represented.* Only a single group's interests are being represented.

- *The business tactical and strategic activities may not be adequately addressed.* The activities have not been defined.

- *The business cycle dependencies may not be adequately addressed.* The business events and cycles have not been defined.

Extension of the front-end activities to more fully address the top two rows of the Zachman Framework can be done as the next iteration, and this should lead to a much better result. Chapter 8 addresses the next iteration.

8

Extending the Data Warehouse

Chapter 7 described how the Zachman Framework can help in building the first data warehouse using a single source. It also pointed out the value of doing this and some of the pitfalls in terms of follow-up work. This chapter deals with the follow-up work needed to expand the data warehouse by including additional

- Objectives
- Data elements
- Sources
- Users
- Summaries

All five of these expansions can transpire as iterations for a warehouse which substantially is addressing a single subject. The value added by applying the Framework for this type of venture is that the organization is poised to expand the data warehouse, not just within the initial subject but also into additional subjects as well.

The first part of this chapter addresses expansion within a single subject and explores the implications on the following phases:

- Commitment to proceed
- Data model analysis
- Subject area analysis
- Source system analysis
- Data warehouse design
- Specifications

While work needs to be done in the other phases as well, the basic activities are the same as previously described, except that they build on the newly obtained information. The implications of expanding into additional subject areas are explored at the end of the chapter.

Commitment to Proceed

As with any project, the best place to start is in the scope definition which is addressed primarily by the commitment to proceed phase. This is the phase in which people come to agreement on the objectives of the data warehouse and, at a high level, on the business processes to be supported and on the data warehouse contents, user groups, and locations. When expansion is contemplated, the motivations should be considered first.

Motivations

In the first data warehouse effort, the motivations focused primarily on the criteria, or information needs. (See Fig. 8-1.) Motivations for subsequent iterations may be developed in either of two manners. One way resembles the traditional systems development life cycle using a top-down approach, while the other builds on the data warehouse life cycle. Using the traditional systems development life cycle approach, the company would take the time to identify the corporate and departmental objectives associated with the business goal of becoming the dominant vendor for the product line. This method is useful for determining the overall data warehouse scope, determining the data warehouse iterations and their priorities, and defining individual data warehouse projects to address them.

	ENTITIES	ACTIVITIES	LOCATIONS	PEOPLE	TIMES	MOTIVATIONS
SCOPE DEFINITION						- Be the dominant vendor for the product line
BUSINESS MODEL						INFORMATION NOT OBTAINED
SYSTEM MODEL						- Information on customer sales volume - Information on customer sales history - Information on product sales relative to each other - Information on pricing impacts on sales SOME CRITERIA MAY BE MISSING
TECHNICAL MODEL						
OUT-OF-CONTEXT MODEL						

```
Explicitly
defined
```

```
Implicitly
defined
```

Figure 8-1 Motivations for the First Data Warehouse.

Another approach is to build on the data warehouse momentum and let it evolve naturally. The natural evolution entails using the data warehouse and noting expansion opportunities as it is used. With this approach, subsequent iterations are determined through criteria, or information needs, which are not adequately addressed by the warehouse segment(s) in production. The original questions addressing the criteria were

■ Who are our largest customers?

■ What are the buying trends of our products for our largest customers?

■ Is there any correlation between the sales of product *A* and the sales of product *B*?

■ What was the effect of the discount offered in August of last year?

Exploration of information derived from answering these questions could lead to additional ones, such as

- Is there a difference between the order size for our largest customers and our next tier?
- Is there a correlation between the sales of our division's product line and the sales of division B's product line?
- What is the effect of each holiday season on sales of our product line? How has this changed over the last 3 years?

This approach still leaves some of the objectives unstated. Using the Zachman Framework as the architectural construct enables companies to continue this gradual expansion, adding criteria as they are uncovered, until circumstances dictate that significant benefits can be derived by identifying the remaining objectives. (See Fig. 8-2.)

The expanded questions such as these lead to iterations of the data warehouse to include additional data elements, new sources of information, new users, and additional summaries and aggregations.

The inclusion of additional data elements is addressed by the Entities dimension. Since no new subject areas are being addressed, this impact of the additional data and summaries can be initially addressed in the data model analysis phase. Similarly, the inclusion of new information sources can be handled in the source system analysis phase.

People

The inclusion of another division's product line does add to the system users, and support of that division for the expansion needs to be garnered within the commitment to proceed phase. The support is needed, even if the other division is merely a contributor of data. The division needs to understand that it has an added responsibility with respect to the integrity of the data which it is contributing to the data warehouse. It may also need to contribute resources to the effort. Involvement of the other division also provides another area of opportunity for the company—that division, through inclusion of its data, will be able to capitalize on the work already done to quickly gain information about its product line. Additional criteria may also be added based on the characteristics of that product line's sales.

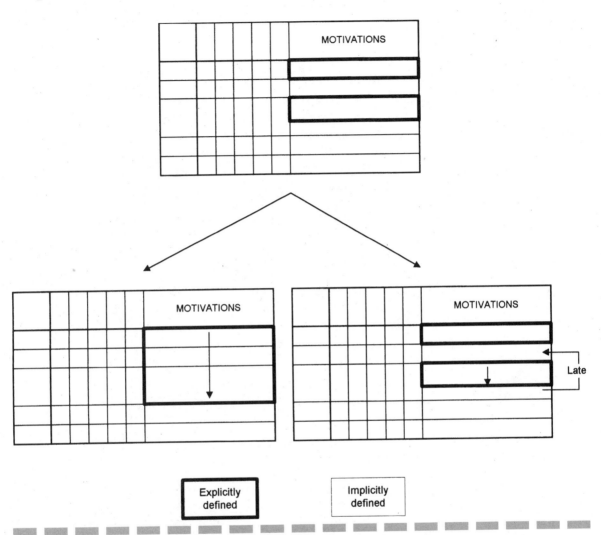

Figure 8-2 Motivations Expansion Options.

Data Model Analysis

Based on the work performed in the first data warehouse project, some information is available in the logical data model. The information in that model, however, was based on the data which existed in the source system. At this time, a top-down approach for reviewing and further populating the data model is appropriate to better represent the business entities and attributes of interest and their relationships.

Entities

The entity definitions previously formulated were based, to a large extent, on the meaning of the item within the source system. These definitions need to be carefully reviewed to ensure that no ambiguity exists. Eliminating the ambiguity helps developers in that they can better understand their task, and it helps end users, since they can better understand the information they are retrieving. Some of the potential areas of ambiguity with respect to the customer entity which should be addressed are

- Is there a distinction between the party which acquires the product and the one who uses it? (If so, one may be called *customer* and the other *consumer.*)

- Are the people using the product considered the customers (or consumers) or is the company for which they work considered the customer (or consumer)? (For example, if a company buys 100 copies of a software package for use by 100 of its employees, are there 100 consumers or just one?)

- If a customer has multiple subsidiaries, is each subsidiary considered a customer?

- If a customer has multiple locations, is each location considered a customer?

- If a product is acquired internally, is the company itself considered a customer?

If these ambiguities are not addressed, the information in the data warehouse becomes unpredictable. For example,

- If internal departments are considered customers and if revenue is exchanged for internal acquisitions, the revenue figures produced by the data warehouse will not match those in the company's profit statement.

- If staffing decisions are based on the number of customers, different conclusions could be reached depending on the definition.

- If statistics relating to claims and complaints are measured in terms of the number of customers, different conclusions could be reached depending on the definition.

Attributes

The existing attribute definitions are also based, to a large extent, on the meaning of the item within the source system. These definitions, too, need to be carefully reviewed to ensure that no ambiguity exists.

> **Eliminating the ambiguity of the attributes helps developers in that they can better understand their task, and it helps end users, since they can better understand the information they are retrieving.**

As with the business entities, the definitions of each element must be created and reviewed with great care. For example, a term such as *software product revenue* could have multiple meanings, particularly if contracts typically bundle services with the sale. Refinement of the definition helps the developers understand how to build the data warehouse and helps avoid confusion among data warehouse users. (See Fig. 8-3.)

Business Rules

The third component of the entity relationship diagram is the set of business rules. For the creation of the first data warehouse, only the business rules with a direct impact on the key structure were emphasized. For a software product, additional business rules, which may not

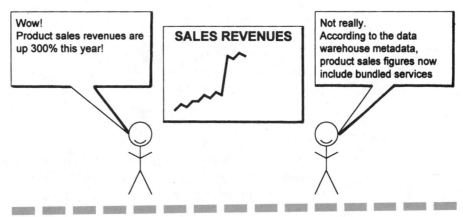

Figure 8-3 *Value of Data Definitions.*

have been discerned for the initial effort, are identified, and each of these has subtle implications. For example:

- *A customer licenses one or more software products.* This implies that the company does not provide services unless it also provides a software product. If the license on a product expires, the operational system may or may not consider the customer to still exist. Since the data warehouse has historical information, the customer exists in the data warehouse regardless.

- *A specific software product is licensed by one and only one customer.* This implies that if a product identified by a serial number is licensed, it can only be licensed to one customer. If the customer changes names or merges with another company, the operational system may merely use the new customer name. The data warehouse has to deal with two customers who, over time, licensed the product.

Data Steward

If possible, a data steward from an appropriate business organization should be appointed to be the final authority on the names, definitions, and business rules. A data steward is a person (or group of people) responsible for defining, setting policy, and enforcing policy for data. The scope of the data steward may include some or all of the items listed below, and some of the duties may be delegated.

The data steward is ultimately responsible for the identification of the business entities and their definitions. The entity relationship diagram identifies the relationships between pairs of entities. These relationships manifest themselves through the foreign keys of the physical database schema. It is the steward's responsibility to ensure that the relationships portrayed in the diagram accurately reflect the business rules. The definition of this relationship includes not just the connection which establishes the interaction. It includes the verb phrase which describes that interaction, the optionality which defines whether or not the relationship must always exist, and the cardinality which distinguishes between one-to-one and one-to-many relationships.

Once the business entities are sanctioned, the elements are grouped within these entities. This grouping helps to name them, to define them, and to ensure that they are perceived from a global perspective. The data steward is responsible for ensuring that the designation and definitions reflect the corporate perspective, even if the current effort is only concerned with a subset.

There is often a temptation to include extraneous data in the warehouse. Ultimately, the data steward may be called upon to balance the requests for information with the integrity of the warehouse and the cost of maintaining that information in the warehouse. For each element included in the data warehouse, its currency and history retention requirements must also be determined. The natural tendency in building a data warehouse is to request instant availability of data and availability of historical information from day one. The steward is responsible for ensuring that the currency and history retention requirements reflect an appropriate balance between the cost of providing the data and the business requirements of the data. Further, the steward needs to ensure that the data retained in the warehouse does not violate the company's historical retention policies.

Data for the warehouse may be available in multiple systems, and the owners of these systems feel that their data is the appropriate data to use. The data steward is responsible for designating the system of record for each element, as well as the rules for identifying and resolving differences when the same data exists in multiple systems. Since the data may be transformed on its way to the warehouse, the steward is also responsible for verifying the transformation rules being implemented to ensure that the integrity of the warehouse meets expectations.

Access to the data warehouse should be as open as possible to promote data sharing within the company, but there are legitimate needs for restricting access. These needs include legal issues such as privacy and warranty claims, as well as competitive issues such as pricing strategies. The data steward is ultimately responsible for determining who may access the warehouse and the level of protection needed for the data.

To be effective, the data steward must understand the business and technical issues, have the authority to take appropriate actions, and be respected in both the business and technical community.

The data steward's responsibility is awesome, and forming a data stewardship function is not easy. Like the data warehouse itself, data stewardship can evolve. For the first data warehouse, the project sponsor may serve as the steward. As the data warehouse expands, business units responsible for the data should be invited to provide people to participate as part of a data stewardship group. Initially, the group may function informally, but over time, procedures should be set, and the group should be formally recognized.

Subject Area Analysis

The subject area analysis phase ensures that the scope of the effort is appropriate. Through the commitment to proceed and the data model analysis phase, the scope of the project was defined. At this time, decisions need to be made concerning the way in which the project is to be worked. If the expansion is manageable, it could be handled in a single iteration. If not, then it may be appropriate to identify multiple iterations.

Source System Analysis

A common problem in many organizations is the existence of the same data (or data which appears to be the same but is not) within multiple databases. (See Fig. 8-4.) Figure 8.4 delineates the definition which "employee" may have within each of four systems, and refinements needed to facilitate integration and history retention within the data warehouse.

This phenomenon exists for various reasons, including technological restrictions which may have existed when a system was created, process-driven application development, security, and access restrictions. The

Figure 8-4
Potential Definitions of Employee.

SYSTEM	POSSIBLE DEFINITION	POTENTIAL REFINEMENT
Human Resource System	An employee is a person who currently performs work for the company and who is paid directly by the company for that work.	Adjust definition to include former employees, since the data warehouse contains history, and the people involved may no longer be employed by the company.
Applicant System	An employee is a person who is seeking employment with the company.	Either adjust the definition of employee to include people who might work for the company and be paid directly by it, or create another entity called "Employment Applicant".
Work Management System	An employee is a person who currently performs work for the company.	Create a superentity of "Person" which encompasses the definition in this system. Within "Person", create subentities of "Employee", "Contractor", etc.
Procurement System	An employee is a contact person at a supplier	Create a different entity called "Supplier Representative".

	ENTITIES	ACTIVITIES	LOCATIONS	PEOPLE	TIMES	MOTIVATIONS
SCOPE DEFINITION						
BUSINESS MODEL						
SYSTEM MODEL	Data model					
TECHNICAL MODEL	Physical database schema					
OUT-OF-CONTEXT MODEL						

Figure 8-5 Data Transformation.

data warehouse provides an opportunity to reunite the data, at least for information retrieval purposes. Within the Zachman Framework, the transformation which exists in the data column between the business and technical model addresses the sources of data. (See Fig. 8-5.)

To integrate all appropriate sources of data, the analyst must research the physical databases which contain the data of interest. For each data element or set of data elements, the best source(s) of information must be identified. The definitions of the data elements should also be reviewed to ensure that appropriate algorithms are built for moving data into the data warehouse. Figure 8-6 portrays three possible situations which may exist for the data.

- *A single system of record can be identified.* Even though multiple copies of the data exist, only one system is considered the official source. When this occurs, the source of the data is obvious, but there may be a need to explain why that source is selected. Also, if manipulations are done to the data in other operational systems, the disparities between results in those systems and results in the data warehouse must be explained.

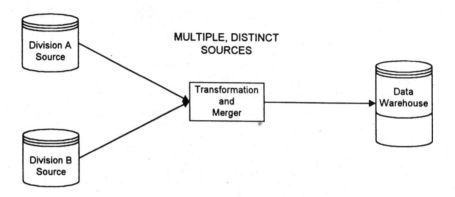

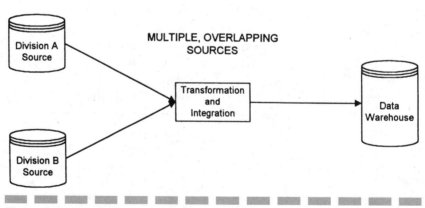

Figure 8-6 Data Sources.

■ *Multiple systems of record exist, each addressing a specific domain of the data.* Within the data warehouse, when the second division's products are included, all the product data is combined. In the operational environment, however, each of these divisions may be using a separate system. If the two sets of products are mutually exclusive, then information for the first division's product line is derived from that division's system, and information for the second division's product line is derived from that division's system.

Within a data warehouse, all customer data will also be combined. In the operational environment, however, there may be separate systems to deal with customers which buy a product from division *A* and those who buy a product from division *B*. If the two sets of customers are mutually exclusive, then data from the two systems could be merged, with each source system contributing data for its set of customers. A more likely scenario is that some customers buy products from both divisions at which case multiple, overlapping systems of record exist for this information.

■ *Multiple, overlapping systems of record exist.* Merging customers from multiple systems entails both business and technical considerations. From a business perspective, the information to be captured must be determined along with the rules for resolving conflicting information. From a technical perspective, the business rules need to be implemented, and technical issues need to be addressed. Some of the technical issues to be addressed, as noted in the methodology in Chap. 6, include handling missing data, decoding, and encoding.

The Zachman Framework provides a schema for capturing the information from this analysis. Tools such as repositories provide assistance in the mechanical and procedural data capturing activities. Once the system of record is identified, integration of the multiple sources becomes more feasible.

If the associated analysis has pointed out significant business benefits (e.g., motivations) which could be attained by adding more sources of data to the data warehouse, an effort to incrementally enhance the data warehouse could be initiated. If such an effort is not initiated, then the value to be gained without enhancing the data warehouse must be greater than the risks which remain due to the still incomplete level of information.

Data Warehouse Design

As with the initial data warehouse, the physical structure of the data warehouse needs to be designed. A data warehouse, when initially implemented, typically contains granular-level data and a very limited set of summaries. The summaries delivered with the warehouse are those which facilitate retrieval of data to produce reports people have thought about based on existing system capabilities or deficiencies.

Development of additional summaries could proceed in an evolutionary manner, or a concerted effort could be undertaken to identify other likely summary record requirements. (Even if a concerted effort is undertaken, additional summary requirements will unfold as the data warehouse is used.) With either approach, artifacts for the higher cells of the Motivations dimension can be collected and stored. The information collected will be extremely useful for subsequently developing an operational data store.

The data warehouse design should be conducted in multiple stages. The atomic level needs to address the granular-level data requirements. At this level, the tables need to contain all the information which is needed in the data warehouse or is needed to create the summaries within the data warehouse.

Staging Area

If the integration process is complex, a staging area may be appropriate. The staging area provides a separate set of tables to facilitate the integration process. (See Fig. 8-7.) Within the staging area, a number of functions can take place. Reference tables to facilitate the integration of the coding schemes can be maintained, so that when the data comes into the data warehouse, it employs a common scheme. Tables to ensure that data values fit within valid domains can also be maintained to help with the data integrity issues. If data from contributing systems is deleted on the way to the data warehouse, views of that data could be maintained in the staging area, too. If a staging area is used as part of the migration process, all activities performed in moving data into and out of the staging area need to be included in the metadata.

Star Schema

If a star schema is used to present the data to the user, a number of options exist. If the volume of the data is small and the facts are similar, a single fact table could be used to satisfy the needs of the two divisions. In this fact table, all sales involving either of the divisions' products

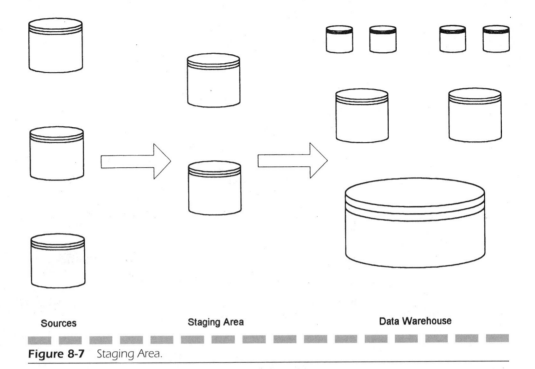

Sources   Staging Area   Data Warehouse

Figure 8-7   Staging Area.

would be included. Foreign keys would point to the dimension tables.

For a single fact table to be used, a single set of dimension tables should also be used. The customer dimension table, for example, should contain the superset of the reference information needed about customers. The product table, too, needs to contain the superset of data. If the attributes of the products are somewhat different, this may result in some null fields. Remember, relative to the size of the data warehouse, the dimension tables are small. Wasting a little disk space is usually better than creating multiple dimension tables to deal with the differences in attributes.

Even if a single fact table is not used, a single set of dimension tables should be considered. Keeping a single dimension table of product and customer information has several advantages. First and foremost, it promotes consistency and reuse. Everyone using the data warehouse will have a common product catalog. Queries against this information could be used by anyone with the access to the queries and these tables.

Use of the common tables simplifies maintenance and sets the stage for subsequent integration of other areas. The transformation and integration process for the dimension tables becomes valid across many applications. The table may be replicated, but since the table is included in the data warehouse architecture, its replication can also be included so that all steps in the process are appropriately managed. The model-driven design of this table also becomes the basis for the operational data store and the eventual migration from legacy systems which use this data.

Additional Subject Areas

The data warehouse developed to date focused on a vertical slice of corporate information.

A subject area model provides the foundation for taking a horizontal view.

The subject area model can be thought of as a jigsaw puzzle. (See Fig. 8-8.) The pieces (subjects) interact with each other in a predictable manner. This knowledge is particularly important if multiple, simultaneous efforts are launched. Once the data warehouse is shown to be a valuable tool, it is entirely possible for the demand to be so great that data warehouse projects are initiated in human resources, product management, and procurement management. Without the subject area model as a guide, each of these may be developed as a stovepipe decision support system. With the model as a guide, the people working on the procurement data warehouse become aware of an effort in the human resources

Figure 8-8
Using the Subject
Area Model.

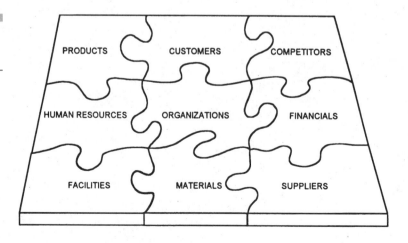

area. When the procurement project needs to deal with buyers and purchasing agents (who are employees), it should coordinate with the human resources project to ensure that either a common architecture is used or that it is deliberately not used, should the value of producing quick results outweigh the cost of rework. (The artifacts in the framework should record this conscious decision so that the integration can take place at a later time.) Ideally, the human resources project would develop the dimension table for employees, and that table would be used in a star schema for the procurement project. In this manner, employee information is consistently derived from a recognized set of sources, and its use throughout the data warehouse is managed by a set of controlled processes.

Summary

A data warehouse is never complete. It evolves over time, driven to a large degree by needs identified through its use. These needs may dictate the addition of data elements, the integration of additional sources of information, or the inclusion of additional users. (See Fig. 8-9.)

The data warehouse methodology and Zachman Framework combine to provide an orderly progression path along with a mechanism for capturing artifacts as they are available for use at the appropriate time.

The missing information does not pertain to the data warehouses being built. In the case of the Entities column, for example, it contains operational data. There is still some risk entailed by not addressing everything, but that risk is outweighed by the complexity, cost, and development time. The environment which results from integrating data from multiple sources is more complex than the previous one, but with an architected approach and effective use of the data steward, the complexity becomes manageable. (See Fig. 8-10.)

The data warehouse now addresses those aspects for which that concept applies best. With the data warehouse as a base and with the gathered artifacts captured in a structured manner, the company is poised to simplify the environment and to gain even greater leverage from its electronically stored information, as shown in the discussion of the operational data store in Chap. 9 and in the migration of legacy systems which is explored in Chap. 11.

	ENTITIES	ACTIVITIES	LOCATIONS	PEOPLE	TIMES	MOTIVATIONS
SCOPE DEFINITION	some subject areas	major functions	major locations	major departments	major events	goals
BUSINESS MODEL	partial entity relationship model	business processes	network locations	departments	business events	objectives
SYSTEM MODEL	partial data model	application function	node functions	sections	system events	business rules
TECHNICAL MODEL	physical database schema	migration rules	node interaction	direct users	job schedules	operating characteristics
OUT-OF-CONTEXT MODEL	database definition	programs	operating network	access authorizations	interrupts	module operating characteristics

Explicitly defined   Implicitly defined

Figure 8-9 Artifacts in Zachman Framework Cells.

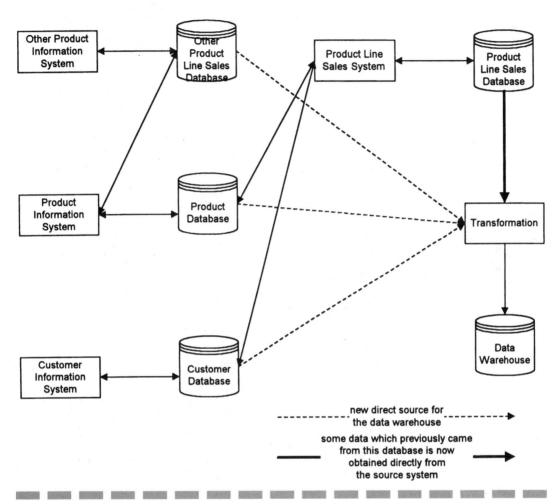

Figure 8-10 Resultant Environment

CHAPTER 9

Building the Operational Data Store

In addition to its use as an integrated and reliable source for decision support information, the data warehouse is an enabler for several other important activities:

■ Building an operational data store (ODS)

■ Migrating legacy systems to a new environment and improving data quality

■ Helping redesign major business functions and processes

■ Supporting total quality management

This chapter explores the ODS and how the information captured as artifacts in the Zachman Framework can help build an ODS. Other applications are explored in Chap. 11.

Contrasts and Similarities

There are both similarities and differences between the ODS and the traditional data warehouse. The data warehouse

- Stores historical and limited current integrated, subject-oriented information
- Is primarily oriented toward summaries
- Provides read-only access
- Is loaded no more frequently than daily from recognized production sources
- Is supported by metadata

The ODS

- Stores current and near-current integrated, subject-oriented information
- Is primarily oriented toward details
- Provides limited read-write access
- Is loaded very frequently—possibly in real time or near real time
- Is supported by metadata
- Provides a migration path to the data warehouse

Figure 9-1 provides additional information for distinguishing the data warehouse and the ODS from each other and from transactional databases.

Each of the cells of the Zachman Framework was populated with artifacts during the development of the data warehouse. Much of the information needed for developing an ODS is very similar. The differences can be discerned using information in Fig. 9-1, and the implications are identified in Fig. 9-2. In the latter figure, only the highest row of the primary dimension(s) impacted is noted. Within the philosophy of the Zachman Framework, all dependent rows may also be impacted, and there may be some residual impacts on other cells. The version recursiveness rule of the Framework permits the storing of artifacts relating to the ODS along with those relating to the data warehouse. Each of the impacted dimensions is explored individually. There may be some cross-column implications, and these need to be uncovered during the analysis.

CHARACTERISTIC	TRANSACTION SYSTEMS: OPERATIONAL DATABASES	OPERATIONAL DSS: OPERATIONAL DATA STORE	MANAGEMENT DSS: DATA WAREHOUSE
Audience	Operating personnel	Analysts	Managers and analysts
Data access	Individual records, transaction driven	Individual records, transaction or analysis driven	Sets of records, analysis driven
Data content	Current, real-time	Current and near-current	Historical
Data granularity	Detailed	Detailed and lightly summarized	Summarized and derived
Data organization	Functional	Subject-oriented	Subject oriented
Data quantity	All application-specific detailed data needed to support a business activity	All integrated data needed to support a business activity	Data relevant to management information needs
Data redundancy	Non-redundant within system; Unmanaged redundancy among systems	Somewhat redundant with operational databases	Managed redundancy
Data stability	Dynamic	Somewhat dynamic	Static
Data update	Field by field	Field by field	Controlled batch
Data usage	Highly structured, repetitive	Somewhat structured, some analytical	Highly unstructured, heuristic or analytical
Database size	Moderate	Moderate	Large to very large
Database structure stability	Stable	Somewhat stable	Dynamic
Development methodology	Requirements driven, structured	Data driven, somewhat evolutionary	Data driven, evolutionary
Operational priorities	Performance and availability	Availability	Access flexibility and end-user autonomy
Philosophy	Support day-to-day operation	Support day-to-day decisions and operational activities	Support managing the enterprise
Predictability	Stable	Mostly stable, some unpredictability	Unpredictable
Response time	Sub-second	Seconds to minutes	Seconds to minutes
Return set	Small amount of data	Small to medium amount of data	Small to large amount of data

Figure 9-1 Data Warehouse versus Operational Data Store. (Some information extracted from a presentation by Susan Osterfelt at 1995 Barnett Data Warehousing Conference.)

Activities

The most significant methodology implication of building an ODS is the expansion of information about functions and processes.

The data warehouse development objective is to provide data for strategic decisions. To support this objective, the emphasis of the Activities column is the migration of information from the operational environment to the decision support environment. The ODS, on the other hand, provides data for tactical and operational decisions and also supports

CHARACTERISTIC	MANAGEMENT DSS: DATA WAREHOUSE	OPERATIONAL DSS: OPERATIONAL DATA STORE	PRIMARY FRAMEWORK ARTIFACT IMPLICATIONS
Audience	Managers and analysts	Analysts	People - business model
Data access	Sets of records, analysis driven	Individual records, transaction or analysis driven	Entities - technical model
Data content	Historical	Current and near-current	Entities - system model
Data granularity	Summarized and derived	Detailed and lightly summarized	Entities - business model
Data organization	Subject oriented	Subject-oriented	(none)
Data quantity	Data relevant to management information needs	All integrated data needed to support a business activity	Entities - technical model
Data redundancy	Managed redundancy	Somewhat redundant with operational databases	Entities - technical model
Data stability	Static	Somewhat dynamic	Times - system model
Data update	Controlled batch	Field by field	Activities, Entities - technical model
Data usage	Highly unstructured, heuristic or analytical	Somewhat structured, some analytical	People - system model
Database size	Large to very large	Moderate	Entities - technical model
Database structure stability	Dynamic	Somewhat stable	Activities, Entities - technical model
Development methodology	Data driven, evolutionary	Data driven, somewhat evolutionary	(impacts sequence of development activities but not artifacts)
Operational priorities	Access flexibility and end-user autonomy	Availability	Entities, Activities, Locations, Motivations - technical model
Philosophy	Support managing the enterprise	Support day-to-day decisions and operational activities	Motivations - business model
Predictability	Unpredictable	Mostly stable, some unpredictability	(none)
Response time	Seconds to minutes	Seconds to minutes	Motivations - technical model
Return set	Small to large amount of data	Small to medium amount of data	Entities - technical model

Figure 9-2 Operational Data Store Design Artifact Implications.

some day-to-day activities. To support the day-to-day activities, information about these activities is needed. The information gathered for each of the five levels of the Zachman Framework is different, with each succeeding layer building on its predecessor. (See Fig. 9-3.)

Planner's Perspective

When the Entities were developed for the data warehouse, the starting point was the subject area model. For the Activities, the equivalent starting point is the identification of the major functions of the corpora-

	ENTITIES	ACTIVITIES		LOCATIONS	PEOPLE	TIMES	MOTIVATIONS
		DATA WAREHOUSE	OPERATIONAL DATA STORE				
SCOPE DEFINITION		LIMITED VALUE	MAJOR FUNCTIONS				
BUSINESS MODEL		LIMITED VALUE	BUSINESS PROCESSES OF INTEREST				
SYSTEM MODEL		TRANSFORMATION RULES	TRANSFORMATION RULES AND DATA FLOW FOR PROCESSES				
TECHNICAL MODEL		PROGRAM SPECIFICATIONS FOR TRANSFORMATIONS	PROGRAM SPECIFICATIONS FOR PROCESSES				
OUT-OF-CONTEXT MODEL		TRANSFORMATION PROGRAMS	PROCESS AND TRANSFORMATION PROGRAMS				

Figure 9-3   Activities Dimension Differences.

tion. As with the subject area model, corporations generally have a relatively small set of major functions. Some of the typical functions which exist are production, distribution, sales, marketing, human resource management, financial management, materials management, planning, information management, and facilities management. The set of business functions for a particular company can be developed relatively quickly. An examination of a company's organization chart provides valuable information for identifying the major functions. Care should be taken, however, to ensure that the decomposition diagram uses the organization chart merely as an input and that it consolidates the functional view regardless of the number of business units which may be performing a particular function. In some industries, an industry-specific model may be available. (See Fig. 9-4.)

The set of these functions populate the Activities dimension of the planner's perspective. As with the data warehouse, it is very useful to develop the list of the major functions and to define them. This set of functions provides a foundation for the operational systems which are developed, to help identify points of interaction. (See Fig. 9-5.) While identification and definition of all the functions is not essential specifically for the ODS, it could be useful, and its value increases as the corporation tries to use the ODS as part of its migration to the architected environment.

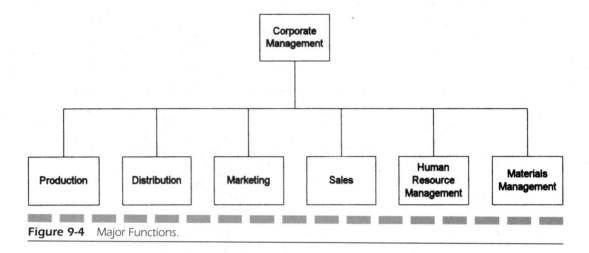

Figure 9-4 Major Functions.

Owner's Perspective

In the owner's perspective, the processes within each of the functions of interest are identified, along with their interactions, from a business perspective. The processes to be addressed should be limited to those of interest to the ODS as a whole or to the specific iteration being pursued. If an ODS to support training is being developed, a set of activities similar to those in Fig. 9-6 could be developed.

The details are developed successively through a decomposition process of the functions and processes. As each successive layer of func-

Figure 9-5
Function Interaction.

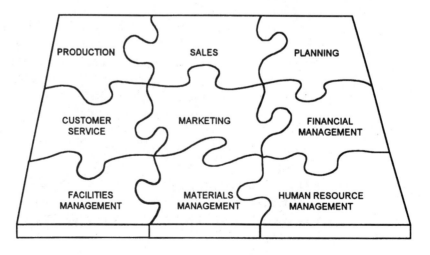

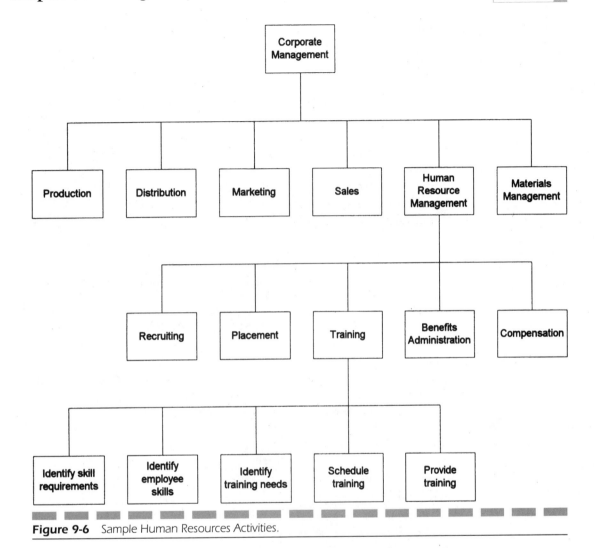

Figure 9-6 *Sample Human Resources Activities.*

tions and processes is identified, details are added only to those needed for the opportunity at hand. At the lowest level of decomposition, a process flow is developed for subsequent use in designing the system flow.

Designer's Perspective

In the designer's perspective, the business view of the activities is transformed into a systems view of the activities. This transformation entails assigning computer modules with the responsibility of handling each of the business processes. The modules are identified, along with the interaction between them. The interaction between them is generally through a flow of information between successive processes, and the data stores which are shown in the data flow diagram are actually reflective of databases which are developed in the Entities dimension.

The technical model also needs to address the transformation of data into the ODS. The development of the transformation rules is conceptually similar to that needed for the data warehouse, in that it involves an understanding of the data based on the Entities dimension information. The transformation for the ODS, however, is more complex for several reasons.

The inclusion of additional elements to support operational activities increases the transformation complexity.

The ODS contains more data elements. The data warehouse content should be limited to those elements needed to support strategic decisions. All the integration issues which exist for the data warehouse still exist for the operational data store, and they are compounded by their application to more data elements. The level of granularity also impacts the complexity. In the ODS, data may exist at the same level of granularity as the operational system; in the data warehouse, it often exists at a higher level of granularity. (The database implications are explored in the Entities dimension discussion.)

Data is loaded into the ODS more often. Decision support requirements can often be satisfied by monthly or weekly loads of information, and, at most, daily loads may be needed. Operational activities require more current data. (The reasons for these requirements are explored in the Motivations dimension discussion.) There are three classes of ODS, as illustrated in Fig. 9-7 and described in the sections which follow. The currency requirements of the ODS dictate the class of ODS to be developed.

Class-III ODS. The class-III ODS resembles the data warehouse in its transformation process. This class of ODS normally entails daily loading of information, and the load process involves transformation and integration which is similar to that needed for the atomic level of the data warehouse. Following the integration process, the data is loaded into the ODS in a batch mode. This process applies for applications whose primary purpose is to integrate data from multiple sources to provide a con-

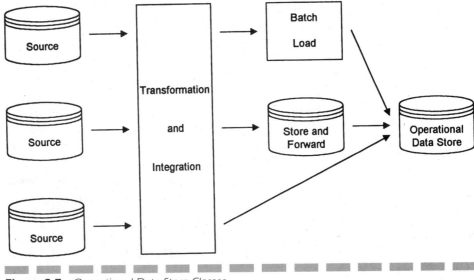

Figure 9-7 Operational Data Store Classes.

solidated view. The ODS table merges data from the disparate operational systems while retaining a cross-reference back to these systems. These typically apply to the type of information which would reside in a reference table. Information of this type needs to be relatively current but does not need to be up to the minute.

Class-II ODS. The class-II ODS employs a store-and-forward mechanism to load data into the ODS. The load frequency is often hourly, or possibly more often. Since a storing mechanism exists, integration still plays a major role in the transformation process. A class-II ODS is useful for providing current information to help develop a profile of customers. The operational systems, for example, may contain information on each sales transaction. In the ODS, tallies are updated hourly to identify total sales to a customer, the size of the largest sale, smallest sale, etc. This type of information may be very useful to customer service representatives to help them recognize the buying patterns of customers with whom they are dealing and to marketing and sales representatives to help them identify opportunities.

Class-I ODS. The class-I ODS loads information into the ODS synchronously. Data from multiple sources may be integrated, but transformation is very limited. These typically apply to factual information which needs to come from multiple sources, such as the credit extended to a particular customer whose purchases may be handled by multiple systems. Because of the synchronous nature of the updates, the integration process is different than that of the other classes of ODS and data warehouse. In the other cases, data from the source systems is gathered and processed together. In the class-I ODS, data is processed as it is received, and hence the integration process becomes a process of merging data from different sources into a common record. As with the class-II ODS, the data consists largely of tallies and aggregations, but for business reasons, very current information is needed. In the sales scenario, the ODS may contain information on the total debt of a customer so that a quick decision concerning credit terms can be made at the time a sale is contemplated.

Each of the classes of ODS is suited for a particular set of needs. The cost and complexity implications are significant. From a development perspective, the class-III ODS is similar to a data warehouse—the most significant issues will be in the integration of data from disparate sources and in the resolution of data definitions. Class-II ODS development shares these issues and adds some complexity. The integration process needs to address continuous feeds from the source systems rather than feeds at the end of a processing cycle. Further, cumulative tallies are created based on whatever information is available—there may not be a predictable pattern which enables detection of missing data. Backup and recovery become important factors in that the practicality of rebuilding lost data from load files decreases as the frequency of update increases. The class-I ODS is the most difficult to develop. In a sense, it becomes an operational system with its transactions emanating from another system rather than directly from a user's input. To ensure data integrity and adequate performance requires careful planning.

The operating characteristics of the three classes of ODS are also different. The class-III ODS consists of a batch process, and its scheduling can sometimes be controlled to take advantage of available processing windows. As the frequency of update increases, so do the operating costs. In the synchronous mode of the class-I ODS, the update transactions of the source systems begin to resemble transactions requiring a two-phase commit. Unless a fallback into a class-II ODS is designed into the process, any downtime in the ODS impacts all the source systems. A solid business case should exist for a company to contemplate development of a class-I ODS.

Builder's Perspective

The programming specifications for each module are defined in the builder's perspective.

By taking the modular approach and by recognizing that a modular approach is being taken, the potential for reuse is increased dramatically. The Framework emphasizes this approach through the use of the subcontractor's view.

Subcontractor's Perspective

The subcontractor's perspective entails development of the program modules out-of-context. This approach requires that each module or set of modules be specified such that it can be developed independently and still fit within an overall architecture. This approach, in addition to promoting reuse within the specific application, also sets the groundwork for the eventual migration to the architected environment. The assembly of the modules built by the subcontractors takes place in the builder's perspective, resulting in the operating ODS.

Summary of Activities

The preceding discussion takes a narrow path down the Activities dimension. The other dimensions were not discussed, but this does not mean that they do not exist nor that they do not impact the Activities dimension. For example, the content of the data to be moved into the ODS is determined in the Entities dimension, and the selection of the ODS class is driven by the Motivations dimension. Each of the remaining dimensions is now explored. (See Fig. 9-8.)

Motivations

Changes in the Motivations dimension are needed due to the philosophy of the ODS, its operational priorities, and its response time requirements, with the first impact of the first characteristic first manifesting itself in the business model.

Figure 9-8
Impact of Other
Dimensions.

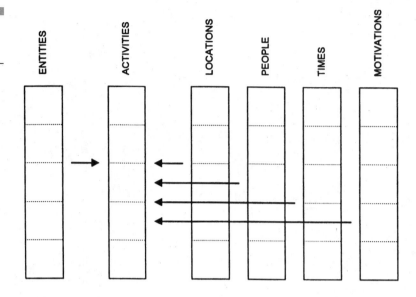

The philosophy differences are depicted through the business objectives. As a vehicle for supporting day-to-day decisions, the ODS objectives are different than those for a data warehouse. In the sales example, the data warehouse was being built to provide information for making strategic decisions. For the data warehouse, because of its iterative nature, it was not mandatory to identify the business objectives being pursued to support the business goals. Instead these could be left implicit, with the major focus being the information requirements.

An ODS supports activities, and the correlation between these activities and the objectives they aim to satisfy is important. For example, business objectives which support a goal of being a dominant vendor for a particular product include increasing market penetration and improving customer retention. Within these objectives, the application of the ODS and data warehouse differ, and hence their criteria, developed in the system model, also differ. (See Fig. 9-9.)

The criteria for the ODS have direct implications on other dimensions. For example, the need for information on a specific promotional campaign implies a level of timeliness and a level of detail. Using the ODS to actually produce promotional information requires elements (such as the address) which are not needed in the data warehouse.

The technical and out-of-context models also deal directly with the operating conditions and performance characteristics at the system and module levels, respectively. With the ODS, availability is often more criti-

DATA WAREHOUSE	OPERATIONAL DATA STORE
• Provide information to determine the most effective promotion media for a particular product group	• Provide information to determine the effectiveness of a particular promotion which was targeted at a specific demographic group
• Provide information to Identify the traits of customers who are likely to stop using the company's services	• Support actions to improve customer retention. For example, the operational data store could be used to generate specific promotions to a target audience.
• Provide information to detect sales trends for a product line and customer class	• Provide information to help a marketing representative prepare for a session with a major customer

Figure 9-9   Contrasting Criteria.

cal than with the data warehouse. Strategic decision analysis is generally a business day activity, though the business day may be a long one; operational activities, on the other hand, frequently require support 24 hours a day, 7 days a week. Also, while a decision support analyst may be satisfied with a 15-min response time for a query that previously took days to solve, the ODS user expects response times closer to those of on-line transaction-processing systems.

People

The data warehouse is designed to meet strategic information needs for making long-term decisions which are often based on trend analysis of historical information. The ODS, on the other hand, is used for operational decision support. As a result, the primary audience for the data warehouse consists of executives, managers, and knowledge workers, while the intended audience for the ODS consists of knowledge workers, lower-level supervisors, and even clerks.

The usage differences impact the human interface. The design of the screens needed to satisfy executive needs is different from the design of the screens needed to satisfy the needs of clerical personnel. The tools required to support these needs are also different, and that is addressed beginning in the system model of the People dimension.

Security is another issue which impacts the People dimension. The data warehouse is a read-only database, while the ODS supports updates.

Because of the types of users, the ODS often has more people accessing it. The security implications of these differences need to be addressed to maintain the needed data integrity level.

Entities

As might be expected, there is a major impact on the Entities dimension. The data content and granularity level differences manifest themselves in the business model.

Business Model

The ODS contains more detailed data than the data warehouse. (See Fig. 9.10.) If the scope of the entity relationship diagram for the data warehouse was limited to data elements pertaining to the data warehouse, it needs to be expanded to include elements in the ODS which are not in the data warehouse. It is imperative that the semantic intent of the Entities dimension of the business model stay intact. Attributes, entities, and business rules can be added to reflect the relationships at a point in time and over a period of time, but the basic structure remains. Otherwise, the semantic discontinuities that cause the legacy systems to be useless for management purposes are introduced.

As described in Chap. 6, the business rules included in the entity relationship diagram for the data warehouse reflect changes which may

Figure 9-10
Function Interaction.

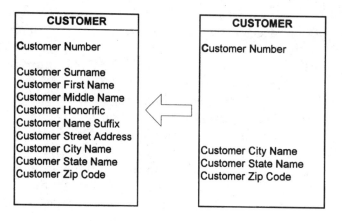

occur over time. The ODS is oriented toward current data, and hence the point-in-time business rules are more appropriate. The net result is that a set of models exist—one portraying a point in time and one portraying the historical perspective. The best approach is to start with the enterprise model and add what is necessary to support the operational requirements without changing the semantic intent. This is the key to the data warehouse—ODS architecture.

System Model

The major impacts on the system model are caused by changes in the business model. Since the system model consists of a transformed business model, the changes caused by the data content and granularity also impact the system model, and once again the key is to maintain semantic continuity.

Technical Model

The physical structure of the ODS does differ from that of the data warehouse. There is no problem with having more than one physical implementation of the same logical model. The major implication is that someone must assume the responsibility for keeping the two implementations synchronized semantically. The ODS schema is differentiated from the data warehouse schema by a number of factors:

- The data warehouse schema is designed for retrieval of many records with each transaction, while the ODS transactions tend to retrieve individual records.

- In the data warehouse, indexes are used generously to facilitate retrieval. The operational storehouse supports updates, and the performance implications of the indexes need to be considered. The update capability also impacts the requirements with respect to backup and retrieval. This is particularly true for class-I and class-II ODS.

- The data warehouse contains a significant amount of history and summarized information, while the ODS contains a limited amount of history and few, if any, summarizations.

- The performance requirements of the ODS are more stringent than those of the data warehouse.

These differences require another approach to the physical design of the ODS. A star schema is rarely applicable in a class-I or class-II ODS. Construction of a star schema requires a predictable and consistent supply of data. If, for example, sales transaction data is updated through a class-I approach, the customer dimension table must also be updated with that frequency to avoid receiving sales information before the customer information is available. The star schema in a mature environment also consists of shared and integrated dimension tables. The integrating and sharing process, by its nature, does not accommodate synchronous updates very well.

Out-of-Context Model

The out-of-context model is driven by the technical model which reflects the resolution of the aforementioned issues.

Summary of Entities

As with the Activities dimension, two sets of artifacts are collected within the Entities dimension, starting at the business model. At that level, the model encompasses the entities, attributes, and rules needed to address both the current view and the historical view. Model coordination is accomplished through the retention of the superset of entities, with the attribution and relationships being the key differentiating factors.

The model distinctions begin at the system model level and become even more pronounced at the technical model level. The common foundation for this model is of paramount importance for retaining coordination and continuity. (See Fig. 9-11.)

Times

The Times dimension addresses the scheduling of the updates to the ODS. The ODS is typically loaded more frequently than the data ware-

	ENTITIES		ACTIVITIES	LOCATIONS	PEOPLE	TIMES	MOTIVATIONS
	DATA WAREHOUSE	OPERATIONAL DATA STORE					
SCOPE DEFINITION	SUBJECT AREA MODEL						
BUSINESS MODEL	ENTITIES						
	OVER-TIME RELATIONSHIPS	POINT-IN-TIME RELATIONSHIPS					
SYSTEM MODEL	DATA WAREHOUSE SYSTEM MODEL	OPERATIONAL DATA STORE SYSTEM MODEL					
TECHNICAL MODEL	DATA WAREHOUSE TECHNICAL MODEL	OPERATIONAL DATA STORE TECHNICAL MODEL					
OUT-OF-CONTEXT MODEL	DATA WAREHOUSE OUT-OF-CONTEXT MODEL	OPERATIONAL DATA STORE OUT-OF-CONTEXT MODEL					

Figure 9-11 Entities Dimension Differences.

house, and as described in the Activities dimension, the scheduling is based on the ODS class.

Locations

The impact on the Locations dimension is derived from the audience change in that the locations of the ODS users may differ from that of the data warehouse users. In addition, the Locations dimension is impacted by the performance requirements and the database schema. To satisfy the needs of the ODS, the locations at which the databases are stored may be impacted.

The network load is another consideration. The data warehouse load pattern is based on occasional bursts of information, with the performance requirement being relatively lax. The ODS is similar to the operational system in its load pattern. The additional network traffic needs to be considered to ensure that the stringent performance requirements can be met for both the retrieval and the update.

Operating Environment

The ODS integrates data from multiple sources, just as the data warehouse does. Initially, the resultant environment could be very complex, as shown in Fig. 9-12.

To avoid a duplication of the integration process, the ODS can be inserted between the operational systems and the data warehouse.

In this mode, the integration of the data is handled in the migration to the ODS, with the transformations needed for the data warehouse addressing the reformatting of the information to support strategic decisions. (See Fig. 9-13.) This approach is practical with a class-II or class-III ODS, but not with a class-I ODS, since the data transformation in moving to that type of ODS is limited.

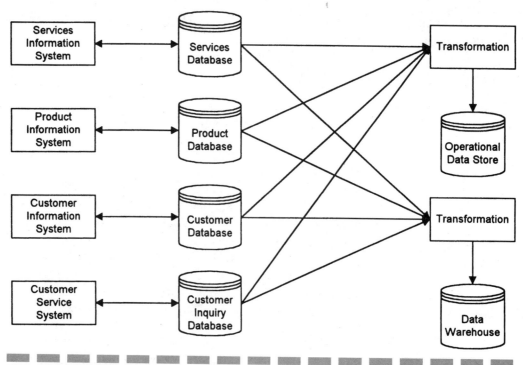

Figure 9-12 Transitional Environment.

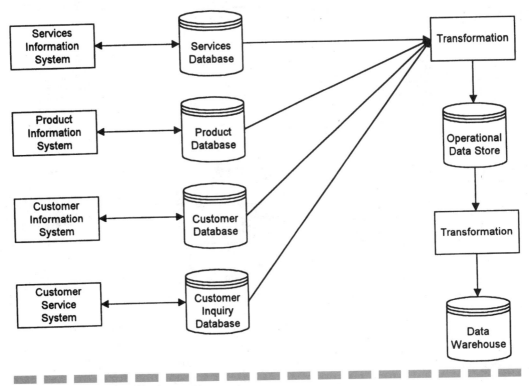

Figure 9-13 Resultant Environment.

Summary

The ODS expands on the concepts which initially led to the data warehouse. With the Zachman Framework as an architectural guide, it can build upon the design artifacts which were used to develop the data warehouse. Figure 9-14 shows the cells of the Framework which are impacted by each of the characteristics identified in Fig. 9-2. In each case, the top cell impacted is noted, recognizing that residual impacts exist in all lower cells and potentially in other cells at the same level. The absence of an impact in the top row should come as no surprise. The ODS is another mechanism for supporting business practices. The practices, from an enterprise perspective, are defined in the top row. While changes may take place occasionally in this row,

SCOPE DEFINITION						
BUSINESS MODEL	• Granularity	• Philosophy		• Audience		• Philosophy
SYSTEM MODEL	• Content • Update	• Update			• Stability	

**TECHNICAL
MODEL**
	• Access
	• Quantity
	• Redundancy
	• Usage
	• Size
	• Operational
	  priorities
	• Return set
		• Operational
		  priorities
			• Operational
			  priorities
						• Operational
						  priorities
						• Response
						  time

OUT-OF- CONTEXT MODEL						

Figure 9-14   Impact of the ODS Artifacts.

these changes are driven by business issues and not by the existence of an ODS.

Once built, the ODS provides an opportunity to simplify the environment, by serving as the focal point for the data integration needed by the data warehouse. It also sets the stage for the gradual removal of unarchitected legacy systems, as described in Chap. 11.

CHAPTER 10

Metadata

Metadata is the lifeblood of the data warehouse. Because of the use of the Zachman Framework for capturing artifacts, the discussion for developing the data warehouse did not elaborate on the metadata. Much of the metadata was implicitly mentioned by virtue of using the Framework as a mechanism for capturing it.

This chapter looks at the metadata for supporting the data warehouse. It identifies major types of metadata and proposes a metamodel for capturing and maintaining it. As with the guiding principles in Chap. 5, the information provided in this chapter should be used as a launching point—each company needs to assess its own requirements and priorities in building its metadata. The metamodel is developed by addressing each of the dimensions of the Framework with a focus on the data warehouse—related items. It should be expected that the resulting metamodel identifies relationships among the cells of the Framework. While relationships exist among all cells in any row, and between a cell and its vertical neighbors, only the relationships of interest are noted in the material which follows.

Importance of Metadata

Metadata has existed ever since the first computer program was written. In the early days, metadata took the form of written documentation and comment lines within programs. The primary objective of the metadata in the early systems was to provide information to explain program functionality to help maintenance programmers do their job. With modern tools, metadata can be generated and stored electronically to facilitate its creation, maintenance, and delivery. The delivery tools help achieve an objective of metadata for the data warehouse, which is to help the business analysts do their job as they use the warehouse. (See Fig. 10-1.)

> **While end-user access to metadata may be optional in a traditional system environment, it is crucial in a data warehouse environment.**

There are several reasons for the increase in importance. The first major distinction is that without metadata, the business user may not even know where to start. In the operational environment, the worker knows which system to use and has instructions for its use. In the decision support environment, metadata helps the analysts determine how the data warehouse can help them and where to find information in the data warehouse.

Figure 10-1
Modern Metadata
Tool.

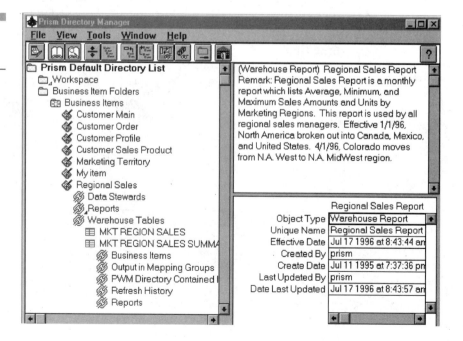

In traditional operational systems, end-user activities are guided through menus and transaction flows. Within the data warehouse, there may be some menus for standard reports, but sophisticated users create their own roads through the data as part of their discovery process. In traditional systems the definitions of the data elements are implicit through their use in the transactions or appearance on reports. Within the data warehouse, end users access some of the elements by name and need to be aware of their meaning.

The derivation is another area of difference. The user of the operational system is typically not concerned with the derivation. The operational system was built to meld into the workflow, and the definitions of the terms are implicitly the same as the ones used within that workflow. The data in the warehouse is the result of transformation, integration, and other manipulations. For the user to be able to understand the data, information about the derivation needs to be available.

The data warehouse contains extensive historical information. One of the roles of the metadata is to help the user understand differences in the data over time which may be the result of definition changes. For example, the metadata can help a financial analyst who notices that revenues tripled over a period of 3 years understand that part of the reason is that the enterprise acquired another company. The analyst would then be able to adjust the analysis to reflect an apples-to-apples comparison for trend analysis.

Metadata about the Data Warehouse

Data warehouses are built in pieces. Each segment of the data warehouse often has its own identity. For example, there may be a financial data warehouse, a sales data warehouse, and a human resources data warehouse. Information about the data warehouse itself is important in helping the analyst know where to start. The information can be divided into static information and dynamic information.

Some static information is included in the Data Warehouse Segment entity. This information includes the name of the data warehouse segment, a description about it, an overall statement about the quality of the data it contains, with other information to help its users understand areas of applicability. The Data Warehouse Role entity is derived through the People dimension and is explained in detail in that section. In essence, it provides contact information about each of the major par-

Figure 10-2
Data Warehouse
Alert.

ALERT!

Data from the Northern Region
was not obtained last night and
won't be available in the data
warehouse until tomorrow
morning.

ties involved in ensuring that the warehouse operate as expected. The
Business Entity entity contains information from the Entities dimension pertaining to the business information included in the data warehouse. The Server entity describes the physical server(s) being used to
support the data warehouse segment.

Dynamic information includes data on the operation of the data
warehouse. The Data Warehouse Operation entity is derived through
the Times dimension and is explained in detail in that section. It provides information concerning the completeness of the data warehouse at
any point in time based on conformance to the operating schedules. Static information may be accessible on demand; dynamic information
could be sent through e-mail, posted on an electronic bulletin board, or
sent to users when they log into the warehouse to alert them to the condition which may impact the use of the data. (See Fig. 10-2.)

The information about the data warehouse actually comes from several of the Framework dimensions. The metamodel in Fig. 10-3 recog-

Figure 10-3
Metadata about the
Data Warehouse.

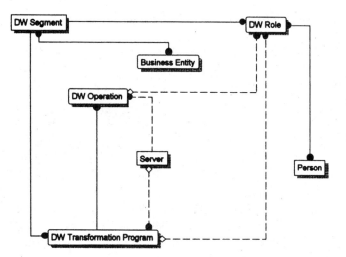

nizes this and separates the information into appropriate entities, some of which will be developed further as the metadata for each of the dimensions is developed. For simplicity, the models presented in Fig. 10-3 and throughout this chapter are at the entity level, and have been normalized only to the extent needed for illustration purposes.

Metadata about People

People comprise a very important part of the data warehouse metadata. The metadata about people identifies the participants in various aspects of the data warehouse. These include data stewards, database administrators, users, supporters, and sponsors. To minimize the repetition of information and to recognize that the same people may be in different roles, a single entity of Person is used along with a designation of the role. The organization hierarchy could be maintained within the metadata, but since this is typically the job of another business unit, the preference is to provide a link, such as employee number, into the system which maintains that hierarchy. Phone numbers are shown within the metamodel, but unless an electronic interface between the company's phone directory and metadata database can be created to populate these fields, the standard mechanisms for maintaining this information should be used.

A second important metadata component of people deals with security. People using the data warehouse need to be assigned into security groups, and these groups are granted privileges in terms of query use and database access. The metamodel in Fig. 10-4 presumes that views are

Figure 10-4
Metadata about
People.

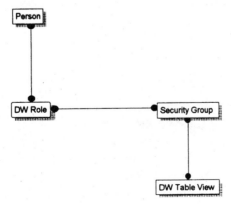

used for security control. If other controls are used, then the model can be adjusted accordingly.

Metadata about Entities

Entities represent the content of the data warehouse. In developing the warehouse, the entities were first described in the subject area model. In developing the subject area model, each subject was named and defined, and the relationships between pairs of subjects were identified. From a metadata perspective, then, an entity of Subject Area is appropriate. Information which would be contained in this entity includes the subject area name and abbreviation and its description. A relationship with itself portrays the subject area—to—subject area relationship. Through relationships, key personnel are associated with the subject area. While each area could be associated with the data warehouse, it is more meaningful to create the association at the business entity.

The owner's view is represented by the logical data model which addresses the business items (entities and attributes) of interest and the business rules governing their relationships. The designer's view entails the electronic view of the business items. From a data warehouse metadata perspective, these are typically more interesting than the business items themselves. For example, the data warehouse user is more interested in the information about customers than in the customers themselves. For each entity, information to be considered includes the entity name and abbreviation, its definition, and its type. From a metadata perspective, the entity types help to initiate the differentiation between the logical data model needed to represent the operational environment and that needed for the decision support environment. The entity types of interest are described in Chap. 6.

The attributes, or data elements, also need to be described within the metamodel. Attribute information of interest includes the business name and business definition. An interesting aspect about an attribute is its designation as decision support or operational. Through this designation, the same entity can be related to both types of attributes, and the metamodel of the data model is simplified.

Business relationships, which are included in the business model, are portrayed through their name (verb phrase), abbreviation, optionality, and cardinality. The relationship type (point in time versus over time) helps to distinguish between those relationships needed for the data warehouse and those needed for the operational environment.

The builder's view is represented by the physical database structure which is subsequently implemented in the subcontractor's view. From a metadata perspective, these can be combined into the representation of the physical databases—both of the source and of the target. In each case, information is needed for the database name, abbreviation, and description and the table name, abbreviation, and description. At the column or element level, in addition to the name, abbreviation, and description, information is needed concerning the data type, length, nullability, value domains, etc.

The metamodel in Fig. 10-5 depicts the Entities dimension information. To help complete the view, some information from the other dimensions is also included. Roles (People dimension) identify the peo-

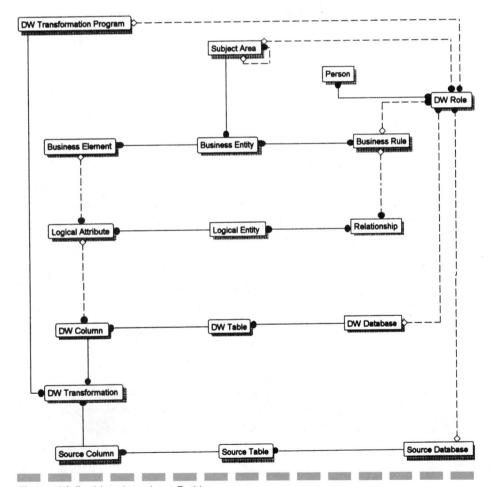

Figure 10-5 Metadata about Entities.

ple involved in various aspects of the warehouse, and transformation rules (Activities dimension) describe the movement of data from the operational environment into the data warehouse. For simplicity, this model also presents the sources as relational databases. The same concept could be applied to other database structures by adding the appropriate entities. The interaction of the metadata across dimensions is readily apparent. This becomes even more pronounced when metadata about activities is added.

Metadata about Activities

For an operational system, the metadata about the activities describes the business functions and processes. The metamodel in Fig. 10-5 includes some of this information because of its value beyond the data warehouse, but the focus for the data warehouse is the set of transformation rules governing the migration of the data from the source systems to the data warehouse. The primary information to be captured, then, is metadata about the source system and metadata about the transformation rules.

Source system metadata is captured during the source system analysis. Some of it pertains to the databases maintained by the source systems, and that was included within the Entities dimension. Other metadata pertains to the system itself and addresses information such as the program name, language, and author.

Transformation rule information is of great interest to the analyst using the data warehouse. This information traces the migration of the data from the source to the warehouse. The metamodel describes the simplistic form which delineates each step of the migration process. The user is typically concerned with the entire process and not each step. For example, temporary files which are of interest to the support personnel are meaningless to the business analyst. While this does not alter the metamodel, it does have implications for the way that data is presented to the business users.

The Activities dimension also addresses the decision support activities. As such, this column also needs to retain information about the standard queries and reports available to users of the data warehouse. Figure 10-6 provides an entity-level metamodel for the Activities dimension, with some of the related information from other columns included.

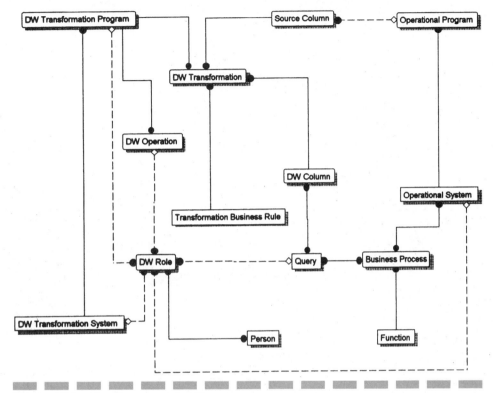

Figure 10-6 Metadata about Activities.

Metadata about Locations

The locations of the components of the data warehouse are also very important. Metadata about the locations includes the locations themselves as well as the data warehouse components, such as servers, processors, and clients at those locations, and the network connecting them. Some of this information is gathered during the technical environment assessment. It may be readily available if a company maintains an inventory of its computer equipment, and if so, the information should be maintained within that facility. It should be brought into the metadata maintenance facilities only if an electronic feed is available. Figure 10-7 portrays the entity-level metamodel for this information. As with the other metamodels, information from other dimensions is included for clarification.

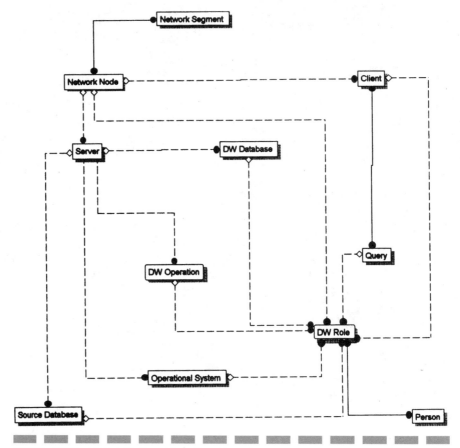

Figure 10-7 Metadata about Locations.

Metadata about Motivations

Motivations define the business goals and objectives which lead into the information needs. Initially, only the latter may be known. Eventually, the goals and objectives can also be documented. From a metamodel perspective, each of the levels of the Framework provides an entity, with appropriate attributes describing that entity.

The performance criteria for the data warehouse should be encompassed in a formal or informal set of service-level objectives. These represent the motivations of the technical model. By relating these to the actual operation information, appropriate actions can be initiated to ensure that the expectations are met.

Figure 10-8 Meta-
data about Motiva-
tions.

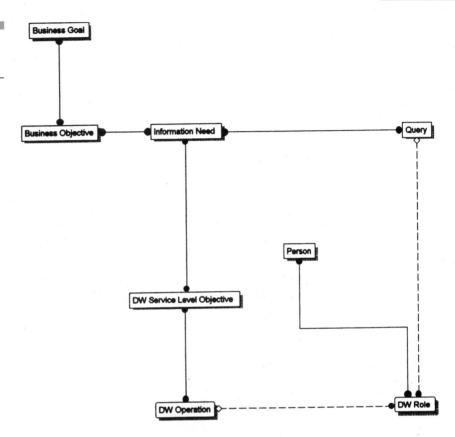

The operations entity contains the information about the actual performance. Actually, this is a very simplistic view since there are many
aspects to performance information. The operations and service-level
entities contain some attributes from the Times dimension too. Tools for
managing the data warehouse environment are evolving, and these can
be used to populate performance information of interest. Figure 10-8 provides the entity-level metamodel for motivations information, with some
relationships into pertinent information from the other dimensions.

Metadata about Times

The Times dimension defines the operating schedules for various jobs
associated with the data warehouse. For the most part, information

Figure 10-9
Metadata about
Times.

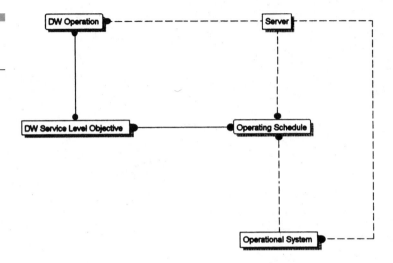

about this dimension is captured either as attributes within other entities or through relationships between pairs of entities. An entity with operating schedule information has been added. This entity could be populated with actual schedule dates and times, but the use of relative schedule dates and times is more practical. For example, if one job precedes another, an attribute within the job entity could identify the precedent job. (See Fig. 10-9.)

Combined View

The artifacts of the Framework come together to build a metamodel for metadata.

This metamodel is, in fact, the business entity model (column 1, row 2) of the Enterprise Engineering Framework described in Chap. 4. It is a model of the set of models about the enterprise which can in turn be used for managing the enterprise. This model and its implementation are managed through the Repository Framework. No single tool effectively manages all the components of the Repository Framework. Until such tools become available, preserving a metamodel which helps understand the relationships can help companies cope with the physical management of the metadata.

The metamodel developed in this chapter focused on the data warehouse needs, with minimal extension into other system requirements.

The method used to develop it could readily be extended into the larger view which would address the entire architecture. As was stated in the introduction, this model can provide a foundation, but each company should acquire or develop its own model based on its needs and its ability to capture and maintain the metadata.

Metadata Capture and Maintenance

Few deny the importance of metadata. The capture and maintenance of metadata, however, is not a trivial task. To understand the difficulty of this task, one should consider the success information technology has had in maintaining documentation (a form of metadata) about its legacy systems. The lack of metadata was not because of a lack of standards—there were volumes of standards. It was not even because of a lack of tools—primitive as they were, there were tools to capture at least some metadata. It was not because programmers did not like to document, though few would argue with that statement.

Historically, metadata was not created because it was not considered sufficiently important to explicitly define the models which were being used to build the information systems.

In some respects, today's environment is no different. Volumes of standards still exist, and programmers still do not like to document their work. It is management's job to decide that the effort required to create and maintain the metadata provides enough value to the organization. Management needs to realize that it is no longer optional!

The difficulty and discipline needed to keep metadata current must be considered in determining the amount of metadata to be maintained. If an item of metadata is not going to be maintained, it should not be included in the physical metamodel.

Every entity within the metadata metamodel should also contain information about the date the entry is made. The entry can be made manually or in an automated fashion, but the date is very significant. It is through this date that versions of the metadata can be maintained. In designing the physical metamodel, consideration should be given to maintaining versions of the information. In some cases, this is unnecessary; in other cases, it is absolutely essential.

Metadata for the Initial Data Warehouse

The components of the metadata described in this chapter are extensive, and the value of maintaining all this metadata needs to be balanced against the creation and maintenance cost. Metadata creation and maintenance tools are available, but their effective application requires significant expenditures and time commitments. A company undertaking its first data warehouse effort needs to carefully consider where its limited resources are spent. If the first data warehouse is limited in scope to a few (under 100) elements all coming from a single system, with minimal transformation complexities, the value of automated transformation tools which also generate the metadata is limited. In this environment,

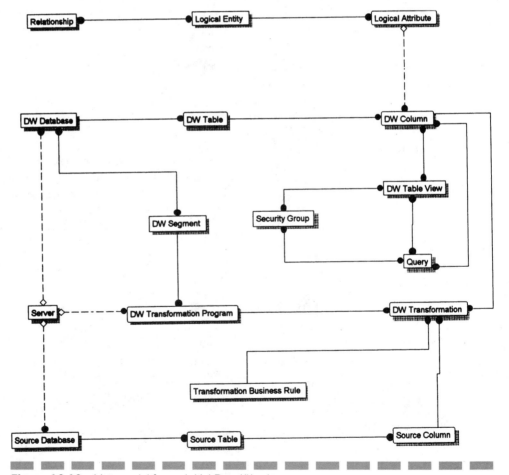

Figure 10-10   Metamodel for an Initial Data Warehouse.

the company should focus its efforts on providing a base level of metadata. This base level should be such that it is visible to the end user so that its value becomes apparent. It should also be easy to create and maintain, consisting primarily of by-products of the analysis, design, and construction activities. Figure 10-10 provides an example of such a metamodel.

The metamodel in Fig. 10-10 presumes that a CASE tool is used for the modeling effort. Sophisticated CASE tools have the ability to maintain information about both the logical view and the physical view. In the logical view, business definitions of the elements are maintained; in the physical view, the way the elements are represented in the data warehouse is handled. Assuming a CASE tool is used for the modeling activity, facilities of that CASE tool can be used to capture and maintain the metadata. To the extent that the CASE tool can accommodate the data model from the subject area level to the physical schema, maintenance of the information is facilitated.

The transformation rules describe the activities performed in the transformation programs. If a transformation matrix such as the one shown in Chap. 6 is used for defining the business rules, it provides a source of metadata as a by-product. Care should be taken to ensure that the programming activities actually reflect the specifications defined in the matrix.

The metamodel also includes information concerning access security. This information could be maintained within the security facilities which a company already has. The model also includes information about the data warehouse itself, and if need be, this information could be maintained manually, using electronic posting or broadcast facilities to make it available to the end users.

The metamodel is relational. Hence, one means of delivering the metadata to the end users is to place the metadata physical tables which contain information not otherwise maintained on the same server as the data warehouse and to provide a simple access to the database. Other options include loading information from the model into help facilities or printing a manual with the appropriate information.

Metadata for Multiple Data Warehouses

Once a company is committed to building several data warehouses, it should seriously consider acquiring tools to help in the transformation process and in the capture and maintenance of metadata. Several tools are available to perform these functions, though their breadth of coverage varies. CASE tools provide facilities for capturing information about the logical model components. Repositories provide facilities for capturing information from CASE tools and also information about the physical environment. Data warehouse code generation tools provide facilities to automate parts of the transformation process and to capture the associated metadata. Data warehouse management tools are evolving, and these provide vehicles for capturing operating information about the warehouse and for delivering the metadata.

In general, CASE tools provide fixed metamodels which may not adequately address the gamut of data warehousing needs. Repository metamodels, on the other hand, are often extensible and can be tailored to address the data warehouse metadata needs. The data warehouse code generators also have metamodels, some of which are extensible.

As with any packaged solution to a problem, a company should determine its metadata needs, compare them with the facilities being provided by the package, and make the appropriate decision.

Summary

The artifacts which populate each of the cells of the Framework are, in fact, a form of metadata. Because of the variety of artifacts, no single mechanism exists which is appropriate for storing and managing all the artifacts. Some, such as those needed in the planning view, are most appropriate in a report format (which may be either on paper or electronically in a word processor or spreadsheet). Others, such as those needed in the Owner, Designer, and Builder views are most appropriately stored in repositories and CASE tools. Still others, such as those needed in the Subcontractor view, are most appropriately stored in system libraries.

Each company building a data warehouse needs to address its metadata needs. In addressing these needs the company should consider its ability to capture and maintain the metadata and the value of this information to its intended audience. Based on that information, the company should determine its approach for managing this important aspect of the data warehouse environment.

11

The Data Warehouse as a Means to an End

In addition to its use as an integrated and reliable source for decision support information, the data warehouse is an enabler for several other important activities:

- Migrating legacy systems to a new environment and improving data quality

- Helping companies deal with a dynamic business environment

- Supporting total quality management

This chapter explores each of these areas, identifies major benefits which can be attained, and describes how the information captured as artifacts in the Zachman Framework can help companies generate knowledge.

Migrating Legacy Systems

Within the information systems arena, the legacy systems environment brings with it many problems. These systems are integral to the operation of the company, but the baggage they bring is becoming too great for companies to bear. And the prospect of replacing these systems en masse is far too expensive.

> **The data warehouse and operational data store provide a natural starting point for replacing legacy systems in an evolutionary manner.**

The Problem

In many companies, systems were developed over time to meet specific needs, based on technology and techniques which were available at that time. This approach led to the development of independent stovepipe systems, complex interfaces, and a lack of flexibility for meeting the requirements of fast-moving competitive corporations.

Another problem which plagues companies is that the documentation for these systems is often out of date or nonexistent. In other words, the artifacts for each of the cells of the Framework have been left implicit rather than being stated explicitly.

The Opportunity

The 1990s bring with them concepts, techniques, and technologies which can enable companies to move to a better-architected environment in an evolutionary manner. The first step in this evolution is the data warehouse, the next step is the operational data store, and the third step is the replacement of legacy systems. Tools such as repositories and architectures such as the Zachman Framework provide for a practical implementation of the vision that many had in the 1970s.

- The *data warehouse* provides an integrated, subject-oriented set of databases for tactical and strategic information retrieval.

- The *operational data store* provides an integrated, subject-oriented set of databases for operational information retrieval and a limited amount of operational interaction.

- The *legacy system replacements* can build on the integrated, subject-oriented approach of the data warehouse and operational data store and the client/server technology to support an increased amount of operational interaction.

- *Client/server technology* is an enabler for improving the delivery of information and knowledge to the business users.

The transformations needed to move to the new environment are identified in Fig. 11-1. The visible transformations are mostly in the data column. There is another very important difference between the legacy environment and the systems in an architected environment.

In the legacy environment, many of the models which occupy the cells of the Framework are left implicit. In the fully architected environment, explicit information is accumulated.

During the development of the data warehouse and operational data store, appropriate cells of the Zachman Framework were populated with artifacts, and much of the information needed for building the new operational system environment is similar. The major impacts on the artifacts of the Zachman Framework follow.

Scope Definition

The planner's view of the system has not changed. In the legacy environment, however, this view may have been implicitly defined, at least within the information systems community. From a corporate perspective, it is likely that the information for the planner's perspective is known. The company goals may not have been documented as part of the systems development process, but that does not mean that they do not exist. Often, these are documented in strategic plans, company communications, and annual reports. Before embarking on replacement of the legacy systems, the goals should be reviewed.

Even if it was explicitly stated, with the prospect of rebuilding the legacy systems, it is advisable to confirm the artifacts within this row of the Framework to ensure that it is reflective of the company's current—and future—needs and direction. The information in the planner's perspective can be used to establish priorities for addressing the needed systems improvements. For example, matrices can be used to assess the

CHARACTERISTIC	LEGACY SYSTEMS	REPLACEMENT SYSTEMS
Audience	Operating personnel	(same)
Data access	Individual records, transaction driven	(same)
Data content	Current, real-time	(same)
Data granularity	Detailed	(same)
Data organization	Functional	Subject oriented
Data quantity	All application-specific detailed data needed to support a business activity	(same)
Data redundancy	Non-redundant within system; Unmanaged redundancy among systems	(same)
Data stability	Dynamic	(same)
Data update	Field by field	(same)
Data usage	Highly structured, repetitive	Somewhat structured, mostly repetitive
Database size	Moderate	(same)
Database structure stability	Stable	somewhat stable
Development methodology	Requirements driven, structured	Evolutionary
Operational priorities	Performance and availability	(same)
Philosophy	Support day-to-day operation	(same)
Predictability	Stable	Mostly stable, with some unpredictability
Response time	Sub-second	Sub-second and seconds
Return set	Small amount of data	(same)

degree to which information systems are satisfying the corporate needs. These matrices need to be completed by the business community.

In Fig. 11-2, each of the major functions identified in the Activities dimension is first assessed based on its impact on meeting the corporate goals. This assessment is judgmental, and a series of assessments may be appropriate. For example, one assessment could identify the impact of the functions on meeting operational needs, while another could

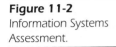

Figure 11-2
Information Systems
Assessment.

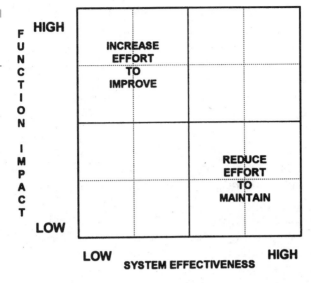

address the functions' impact on meeting strategic needs. The functions are placed on the vertical axis positionally, based on their impact.

On the horizontal access, the effectiveness of the systems in meeting the needs of that function are rated. The effectiveness should be measured relative to perceptions of the support systems. This rating is not for individual systems—it is for the collection of systems which support the function. For example, if a function is supported by two excellent systems but the interface between these systems is cumbersome, then the rating may be good or fair. If, on the other hand, three reasonably good systems support a function and their value is improved through their synergistic interaction, the assessment may be excellent.

The position of the rating provides valuable information for setting priorities for system improvements. Ideally, the ratings should be primarily in the bottom-left and top-right quadrant. These ratings indicate that the high-priority functions are being supported well, while the low-priority functions are not. Ratings in the bottom-right quadrant indicate that the support level of the systems is excellent but that this support is being provided for functions which have minimal impact on the operational or strategic needs of the company. In looking for resources, consideration should be given to diverting resources which are supporting these systems. Ratings in the top-left quadrant indicate that important functions are not adequately supported by information systems. Serious consideration should be given to expending resources on the systems for these functions.

In some respects, this analysis is similar to that performed in the tra-ditional information strategy planning approach. The major difference is that instead of spending months gathering the artifacts to perform this assessment, the artifacts have been collected as a by-product of building the data warehouse and operational data store.

Basing the assessments on the overall system support is extremely important since that support is being provided through a combination of the legacy systems and an operational data store and data warehouse, if these were developed to support this function. The overall system support considers the integration of all the systems needed to support the function and hence provides a better picture than an assessment of a single system.

Once an improvement project is identified, the typical project start-up and planning activities need to be pursued. These activities include identification of the key players, including the project sponsor, estima-tion of the needed resources, and development of a project plan. As part of this effort, the artifacts of the top row of the Framework, at least with respect to the function being addressed, are completed.

Business Model

As with the scope definition, the business model for the legacy system may not have been explicitly defined. Even if it was, it is very likely that one of the drivers for replacing the legacy system reflects a change in the business model. Some of the business model changes which could have an impact are business information changes (Entities dimension), changes in business objectives (Motivations dimension), changes in the business processes (Activities dimension), entry into national or interna-tional markets (Locations dimension), new organizational structures (People dimension), and changes in the business cycle (Times dimension).

To properly develop the replacement system(s), each of the dimension artifacts needs to be appropriately modified. Within the entities model, the data model is reviewed. This data model reflects those aspects of the function which needed to be defined to develop the operational data store and data warehouse. Since the current effort entails replacing the operational system, the model needs to consider any additional items of interest to the company relative to that function, along with the associat-ed business rules. Once the operational model is developed, its data warehouse equivalent should also be described. If the changes have a downstream effect on the data warehouse, changes in it may be needed even if the new system is not developed.

Within the activities model, the functional decomposition diagram is completed. As with the entities, the existing artifacts were limited to those needed for the funded projects. In the same manner, these artifacts need to be expanded to address the scope of the existing project which encompasses a greater portion of the enterprise.

A similar process is pursued with each of the remaining four dimensions. In the Motivations dimension, the objectives are explicitly stated; in the Times dimension, the business cycles are reviewed and appropriately adjusted; in the People dimension, organizational responsibilities are reflected; and in the Locations dimension, the locations which perform the function are identified.

Technical Model

The technical model both drives changes and is driven by changes.

The technical model drives changes because one of the fundamental catalysts for the migration of the legacy systems is technology. The technological innovations serve to change the technical constraints upon which the model was initially built. It is also driven by the system model because another catalyst is the company's need for more flexible systems, but for that driver to be properly reflected, the system model must first be modified to reflect both the business drivers and the technology drivers.

System Model

The system model is the focal point of the change. (See Fig. 11-3.) Some of these changes are driven by the business model changes, while others are driven by proposed technical model changes. These changes will, in turn, drive additional changes in the technical model. To the extent that the Zachman Framework artifacts for the systems being migrated either do not exist or need to change, they need to be incorporated at this time.

Motivations The operating criteria for the new system need to be examined. The subsecond response time which was economically avail-

Figure 11-3
System Model
Impacts.

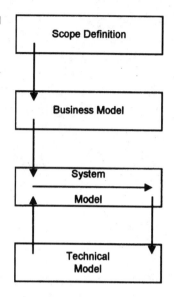

able in the mainframe world may be too costly to provide across the board in the client/server world. Additionally, a subject-oriented design may not operate as efficiently as a transaction-oriented design. These factors all need to be considered to determine the operating criteria for the new system. Often, compromises will need to be subsequently made in the technical model to meet otherwise conflicting criteria. If subsecond response time is still a requirement, then the design—and budget—need to reflect this requirement.

Locations With a distributed, client/server environment, different operations may take place at different locations. The functions to be performed at each node are defined in the system model. Depending on the interaction of the data from one location with the data from another location, options may be available to partition the data and improve the response time. That and other data design considerations are addressed in the Entities dimension.

Entities Two data models impact the system model—the point-in-time model for operational requirements and the over-time model for data warehouse or reporting requirements. Within the Framework, the two models are supported through the (version) recursiveness rule. Consideration of these models separately could provide additional ways of improving performance without significant additional costs. The business model, which encompasses all the views, is the glue that binds the multiple system models.

Operational systems typically contain the history needed to support the day-to-day activities. In some instances this entails only a few months' data. Sometimes, sales or customer service representatives need a few years' data to adequately support their customers. Prior to the introduction of the operational data store and data warehouse, this information was preserved within the operational system. Retaining that information in the operational system brought with it increases in maintenance costs since the databases are bigger and more complex. The size also impacts the operating costs which include the processing and storage requirements, as well as the costs associated with backup, recovery, reorganization, etc. Flexibility is decreased because of the database size and the need to consider the impacts of any change on the historical information. Inclusion of the history within the operational system is no longer mandatory.

In the architected environment, the historical information could be migrated to the data warehouse. Doing this reduces the volume of data of the operational system and eliminates several of the previously mentioned problems. Additionally, the data is placed into the environment which lets the appropriate model be applied for its organization. The point-in-time model governs the current information, and the over-time model governs the historical information. (See Fig. 11-4.)

Activities   The business model contains information on the business activities. In developing the new system, these activities should be analyzed from three perspectives. (See Fig. 11-5.) In the basic perspective, only those activities needed to support the day-to-day operation should be included. These are the activities which require interaction with the data, typically in the form of transactions with update capability. The second perspective should consider the operational reporting needs. These are the activities which could be supported by the operational data store. The third perspective should consider the strategic reporting needs. The data warehouse should be designed to address these.

The segregation of the activities has two impacts. The first is a feedback to the data model to ensure that the models for each of the three systems contains the information needed to support its activities. The second is, within the Activities dimension, to provide a basis for designing the transactions for the operational system and for designing the new standard reports and queries, if any, for the operational data store and data warehouse.

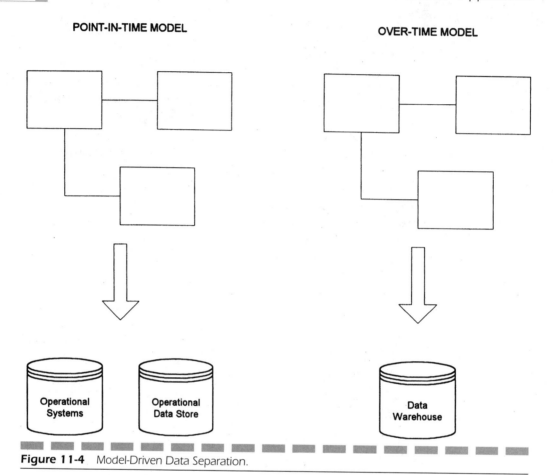

Figure 11-4   Model-Driven Data Separation.

Times   The separation of the activities has an impact on the Times dimension. The operating schedules for the various system components need to be set so that each meets its requirements with respect to timeliness and performance. The dependence among the activities also needs to be considered and hence among the system components supporting them. Analysis of this dependence will help determine the sequence in which legacy systems could be removed.

People   Since the users of the new system are likely to be the users of the existing system, the changes in this dimension should be minor or nonexistent, except as they may reflect changes in the organizational structure.

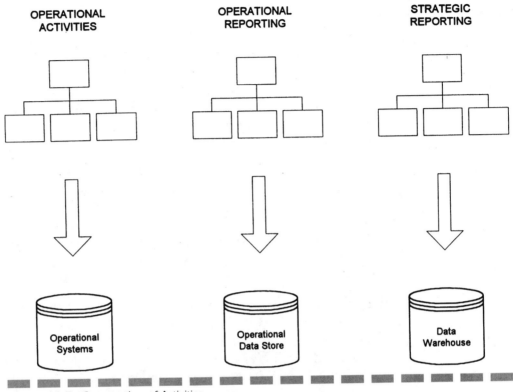

Figure 11-5 Segregation of Activities.

Technical Model Revisited

Once the system model has been updated, the technical model needs to be modified to reflect the changes. The physical design considerations for the technical model are beyond the scope of this book.

Out-of-Context Model

The out-of-context model is changed to reflect the updated technical model, and the various system components are built and assembled. An important aspect of effective out-of-context models is reuse. By definition, these models address components of a system. Hence, these components should be built to maximize their potential for serving needs beyond the system for which they are being built. Expansion of the model to maximize reuse may entail additional short-term costs and may require changes to the technical model.

Organizations which are serious about moving to a new environment should carefully consider the benefits of fully adopting the philosophies which are inherent in the separation of the technical model and the out-of-context model. This is a critical step in moving away from a *systems* perspective to a *transaction* philosophy.

Impact

Building on the artifacts of the Zachman Framework to gradually replace legacy systems has significant impacts. From a quality perspective, the integrity of the information should be significantly improved; from an operating perspective, the environment is simpler to maintain.

Data Integrity   During the development of the data warehouse and the operational data store, problems with the data quality of the source systems are often uncovered. Sometimes, the operational systems must be corrected for any progress to be made. Often, however, the cost to modify the operational system is prohibitive, and the transformation process deals with these errors and filters them to the extent possible prior to moving the data into the operational data store or data warehouse. At other times, particularly with the data warehouse, the errors can be accommodated, if their impact on the resultant strategic analysis is minimal. Both of the latter instances do not entail changes to the operational environment and therefore do not result in any improvements in the operational environment.

The list of data integrity problems should not go unnoticed. The items on this list are major factors in the assessment of the legacy system. It may even be possible to quantify some of the impacts of the data problems. It would certainly be foolish to migrate to the new environment without correcting the root causes of the data errors. The Zachman Framework architectural construct facilitates both the identification of the root cause and incorporation of changes in the appropriate places. If the errors are due to changes in the business rules, the artifacts in the business model must be changed (with a cascading effect into the other models). If the errors are due to implementation errors (e.g., system design or programming errors), then the system, technical, or out-of-context model artifacts must be changed.

Operating Environment   The replacement of the legacy systems can significantly simplify the operating environment. The legacy system environment typically consists of several operating systems, several database management systems, multiple databases with the same data, and a myriad of interfaces. In the new environment, the multiple databases are integrated, and the technology differences are resolved through the migration to the new environment. The environment changes over time, since the migration from the legacy systems to the new environment is evolutionary. (See Fig. 11-6.)

Summary of System Migration

Legacy systems can be removed or replaced in an evolutionary manner. The artifacts collected in the Zachman Framework during the development of the data warehouse and operational data store are a significant asset in the process of migrating away from the legacy systems. Upon completion of this process, artifacts exist for each and every cell of the Framework for the area within the scope of the new system. Stated another way, the enterprise will then have a complete set of explicitly stated models, vertically and horizontally integrated, at an excruciating level of detail. (See Fig. 11-7.)

Helping Companies Deal with a Dynamic Business Environment

In their book *Reengineering the Corporation: A Manifesto for Business Revolution*, Michael Hammer and James Champy define reengineering as "the fundamental rethinking and radical redesign of business processes to achieve dramatic improvements in critical, contemporary measures of performance, such as cost, quality, service, and speed."

They repeatedly emphasize that information technology is a critical enabler for effective reengineering. The advent of the computer terminal was an enabler in providing a new level of service to customers. The advent of the personal computer, combined with applications such as the early spreadsheets, was an enabler in personal productivity. The development of the local area network and wide area network was an enabler in improving communications and information sharing, partic-

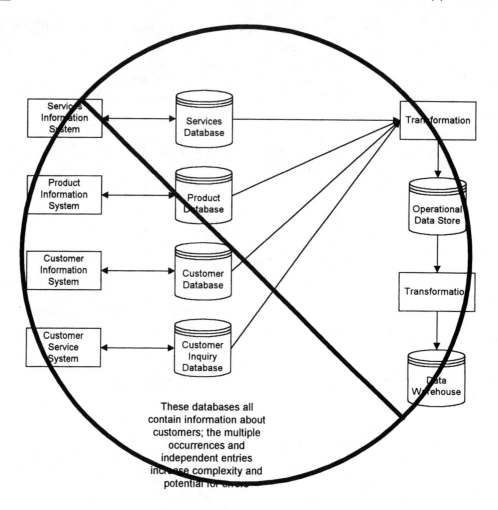

These databases all contain information about customers; the multiple occurrences and independent entries increase complexity and potential for errors

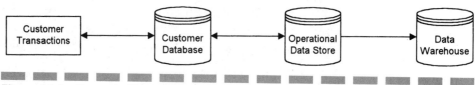

Figure 11-6 Removal of Legacy Systems.

	ENTITIES	ACTIVITIES	LOCATIONS	PEOPLE	TIMES	MOTIVATIONS
SCOPE DEFINITION	subject areas	major functions	major locations	major departments	major events	goals
BUSINESS MODEL	entity relationship model	business processes	network locations	departments	business events	objectives
SYSTEM MODEL	data model	application function	node functions	sections	system events	business rules
TECHNICAL MODEL	physical database schema	migration rules	node interaction	direct users	job schedules	operating characteristics
OUT-OF-CONTEXT MODEL	database definition	programs	operating network	access authorizations	interrupts	module operating characteristics

Explicitly defined

Implicitly defined

Figure 11-7   Completed Zachman Framework Cells.

ularly when combined with groupware which enables people at different locations to better interact with each other. The worldwide web is another enabler. Its potential is yet to be realized, but corporations throughout the world are rushing to identify ways in which the web can provide them a competitive advantage.

> **The Zachman Framework, data warehouse, and operational data store also need to be perceived as enablers for providing a means of building the needed flexibility into information systems to enable them to support existing needs and to evolve to meet future needs.**

Support from the Zachman Framework

The Framework is an enabler which provides an architectural construct for understanding the enterprise and its needs. The four frameworks described in Chap. 4 directly support the reengineering agenda.

- The Repository Framework helps to manage the knowledge of the enterprise,

- The Enterprise Engineering Framework provides knowledge about the enterprise architecture and facilitates change management.

- The Enterprise Framework provides knowledge about the enterprise itself.

- The Product Framework provides knowledge about the internal and external products of the enterprise.

Recognition of the four frameworks is the first step toward using them in the reengineering initiatives. The focus of the major portion of this book has been on the Enterprise Framework, specifically as it relates to computer systems. Artifacts from other frameworks have been implicitly absorbed through the meta-relationships among them. This is shown pictorially in Fig. 11-8 which is described in Chap. 4 as Fig. 4-22.

Application of the Zachman Framework as part of the reengineering process can help ensure that the ramifications of the decisions being made are appropriately addressed. In the early 1990s many companies initiated downsizing programs only to later realize that they either needed to increase their size or that they needed some of the personnel who had been discharged as part of the downsizing. These initiatives reflect a limited focus. They often responded to an objective related to cost reduction, with the identified source of the cost reduction being people. Some companies looked at the business model, adjusted business processes, and then made staffing decisions. Others made staffing decisions and let the business model evolve (implicitly).

The Framework architecture is such that lower-level rows are dependent on the rows above them. Also, a change in one cell in a row could have an impact on the other cells within that row. Even presuming that there are no changes in the top row of the Framework, Fig. 11-9 clearly demonstrates that changes may exist in many other cells. Without full consideration of the impact on the other cells, is it any wonder that so many of the downsizing initiatives did not smoothly achieve all their intended objectives?

Increasing the focus to the other dimensions could have helped companies make decisions which would have avoided a correction process of hiring discharged employees as contractors. Consideration of the cells of the Framework may not have changed the end decision concerning the personnel reductions, but it could have helped some companies better deal with the resultant changes.

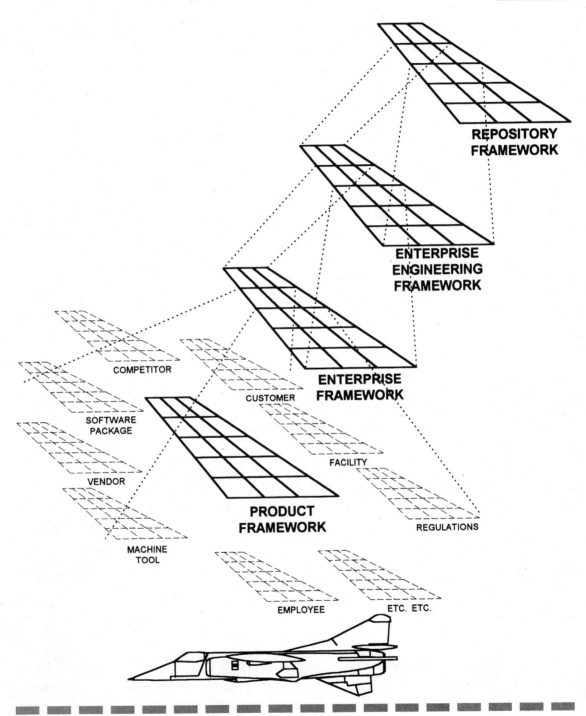

Figure 11-8 Comprehensive Knowledge Base of the Enterprise.

	ENTITIES	ACTIVITIES	LOCATIONS	PEOPLE	TIMES	MOTIVATIONS
SCOPE DEFINITION						
BUSINESS MODEL	Impact?	Modify activities	Impact?	Reorganize	Impact?	Reduce costs
SYSTEM MODEL	Impact?	Impact?	Impact?	Reduce people	Impact?	Impact?
TECHNICAL MODEL	Impact?	Impact?	Impact?	Impact?	Impact?	Impact?
OUT-OF-CONTEXT MODEL	Impact?	Impact?	Impact?	Impact?	Impact?	Impact?

Figure 11-9 Downsizing Focus.

Support from the Data Warehouse

The data warehouse is an enabler which provides companies with access to the untapped wealth contained in its information assets. It provides a means of using the operational systems which have been designed to meet the day-to-day requirements to also support the strategic needs. The benefits of the warehouse are well publicized, and it has been hailed in business (as well as information technology) publications as a valuable competitive weapon.

The value of this weapon is manifest in more than the data warehouse itself. The warehouse provides access to the information. Perhaps more important than the warehouse itself is the philosophy which accompanies it. The data warehouse architecture demands recognition of information as a corporate asset. This treatment of information underlies the methodology described in Chap. 6 and the four frameworks described in Chap. 4.

As the data gains in strategic importance, companies are recognizing the need to create data stewardship functions. The chief data steward can be compared to a chief financial officer. Both need to establish a means to classify the asset, and both need to establish rules for receipt, management, and disposition of the asset. In the case of the chief financial officer, the classification scheme is the chart of accounts. The chief data steward's classification scheme is the Repository Framework and its related frameworks. The chief financial officer sets the rules for how the company accounts for incoming funds and the rules for disbursement of funds, with the accounting department typically administering the activities. The chief data steward sets the rules for acceptance of data into the databases and for access to this data. The information technology department administers these rules through the validations and edits performed within the systems and through the security tools and procedures implemented to control access.

Support from the Operational Data Store

The operational data store is another enabler. It builds on the philosophies of the data warehouse and provides a bridge to meet a set of needs that neither the operational system nor the data warehouse address very well. It is operationally oriented in terms of its content and, as such, can support process management activities very well. With this support, enterprises are in a better position to apply principles of total quality management for the incremental improvement of their processes.

Support from New Operational Systems

The reengineering effort cannot be successful if the supporting computer systems cannot reflect the changes. The new information environment is much more responsive to change and hence can be modified much more rapidly to enable implementation of the reengineering directives.

Summary of Dealing with the Dynamic Business Environment

The processes described in this book provide for a reengineering of the information management environment as depicted in four frameworks. The streamlined operating environment and the wealth of artifacts gathered in the architectural construct of the Zachman Framework combine to support reengineering of not just the technical environment but reengineering of the enterprise as a whole.

Total Quality Management

Dr. W. Edwards Deming is commonly regarded as a leader in total quality management. In his work with various companies, he developed 14 points to which companies must subscribe to achieve total quality management.[1] Several of these points are directly supported by the construct of the Zachman Framework and by the data warehouse and operational data store. Deming's 14 points are

1. Create constancy of purpose for improvement of product and service
2. Adopt the new philosophy
3. Cease dependence on mass inspection
4. End the practice of awarding business on price tag alone
5. Improve constantly and forever the system of production and service
6. Institute training
7. Institute leadership
8. Drive out fear
9. Break down barriers between staff areas
10. Eliminate slogans, exhortations, and targets for the workplace
11. Eliminate numerical quotas
12. Remove barriers to pride of work quality
13. Institute a vigorous program of education and retraining
14. Take action to accomplish the transformation

A general theme throughout the 14 points is the importance of the top row of the Framework.

It is at this level that the company's role is defined and its philosophy and attitude toward quality and human resource management are determined. Several of Deming's points emphasize the importance of creating and communicating goals and objectives and following these through the various stages into their implementation. The dependency

---

[1]Mary Walton, *The Deming Management Method*, Dodd, Mead & Company, New York, 1986.

of everything else in the company on these goals and objectives is emphasized.

The Zachman Framework supports these points. (See Fig. 11-10.) From an architectural perspective, it recognizes that goals must be defined in the planner's view and that there is an interdependency between the goals and the other five dimensions in this view. The Framework further recognizes that the objectives represent transformed goals and that the dimensions in the owner's view are impacted both by the objectives and by the planner's view of each dimension.

Motivations is emphasized not as the most important dimension (which would violate one of the rules) but rather as the first dimension to be addressed, which is consistent with the Framework accommodating methodology-specific sequences of events.

A major tenant of total quality management is the use of data to identify opportunities, support analyses, and manage processes.

	ENTITIES	ACTIVITIES	LOCATIONS	PEOPLE	TIMES	MOTIVATIONS
SCOPE DEFINITION	subject areas	major functions	major locations	major departments	major events	goals
BUSINESS MODEL	entity relationship model	business processes	network locations	departments	business events	objectives
SYSTEM MODEL	data model	application function	node functions	sections	system events	business rules
TECHNICAL MODEL	physical database schema	migration rules	node interaction	direct users	job schedules	operating characteristics
OUT-OF-CONTEXT MODEL	database definition	programs	operating network	access authorizations	interrupts	module operating characteristics

Explicitly defined   Implicitly defined

Figure 11-10   Zachman Framework within TQM.

Companies vying for the Malcolm Baldrige Award are very familiar with the importance of data, as its use is inherent in addressing most of the award criteria. Because of the importance of data, a separate category, information and analysis, exists to examine the management and effectiveness with which data and information are used to support customer-driven performance excellence and marketplace success. The three sections of this category address the management of information and data, competitive comparisons and benchmarking, and analysis and use of company-level data.

Management of Information and Data

This area addresses the selection and management of the data and information which is used for management, strategic planning, and performance evaluation. Several items are examined as part of this area, and the Framework, data warehouse, and operational data store directly address these.

Companies need to demonstrate the relationship between the different types of data and information and the key business operations and business strategy. They need to document the performance measurement system and show the alignment of these measurements with the company priorities and business drivers. The derivation of requirements such as reliability, access, and update must be described along with their relationship to the user needs.

The architecture of the Zachman Framework mandates a linkage between the business strategy, its major activities, and the supporting data and information. It also relates the requirements (motivations system model) to the organization through a horizontal connection and to the priorities and business drivers through a vertical connection. These needs impact the system design within the Activities dimension, the database design within the Entities dimension, operating schedules within the Times dimension, and function distribution within the Locations dimension.

The use of the data warehouse to make strategic decisions and to examine their effectiveness also supports these examination criteria. The operational data store, on the other hand, supports the activity measurement system for managing continual process improvement.

A second major consideration within the management of information and data, which is the way in which companies evaluate and improve the selection, analysis, and integration of information and data, is aligning them with the company's key business drivers and operation. The process described in this chapter for migrating to the legacy environment addresses this area. The Framework is used in setting priorities, and the architecture of the resulting environment supports a means of addressing operational activities and reporting needs in an integrated manner.

Competitive Comparisons and Benchmarking

This area addresses the way companies use comparative information and data to support overall performance improvement and competitive position. Companies need to obtain appropriate external information, and this information can be fed into the data warehouse or the operational data store. Its application for benchmarking is apparent in that company information for similar metrics can be compared to the external data.

Benchmarking is a complex science, and its description is beyond the scope of this book. One of the early steps of the benchmarking process, however, is selecting the areas for which comparisons can be made and ensuring that data is available for the internal process. The architected environment facilitates obtaining, maintaining, and delivering this data.

Analysis and Use of Company-Level Data

This area addresses the way quality, customer, and operational performance data are used together with relevant financial information to support company-level review, action, and planning. The Entities dimension of the Framework provides a road map for integrating the information. The subject area model and logical data model of the first two levels portray the relationships among the data entities. Similarly, the function decomposition information provides information on the activities, and the relationship between the activities and entities describes the use of the information in support of the activities. The Framework architecture, which requires consideration of all six dimensions, supports the integration process. Its artifacts could be used to both ensure that the integration takes place and demonstrate that it has.

The data warehouse is designed to be a strategic competitive weapon. Its effective deployment should demonstrate the use of information to support the planning activities of the company which in turn dictate the company direction.

Summary of Total Quality Management Application

Information and an architected environment are at the heart of total quality management. The Zachman Framework provides the architecture, and the data warehouse, operational data store, and architected systems combine to provide the needed information. Together, data is available for companies to understand where they are and where they should head so that they can map a means of getting there.

Management by Fact

A common thread throughout the examination criteria related to information and analysis is the deployment of *management by fact*. Management by fact requires both a long-term and a short-term perspective. The long-term perspective, supported by the data warehouse is used to provide data for control charts and for trend analysis so that opportunities for improvement can be identified and specific performance criteria can be set. The short-term perspective, supported by the operational data store, provides timely detailed information which can be compared with control limits to help in the ongoing management of the process.

Root Cause Analysis

Total quality management emphasizes the need to address the root causes of problems, and not just the symptoms. The potential for identifying the root cause increases with the availability of well-organized historical information. The data warehouse provides this wealth of data, and the operational data store supports it by providing details for a short-term period.

The Framework can also support the root cause analysis. One of the tools used for root cause analysis is the cause and effect diagram which shows the relationship between a quality characteristic (or the effect) and contributing factors (or causes). The diagram, first used for this purpose by Professor Kaoru Ishikawa in the early 1950s looks like the skeleton of a fish, and is sometimes called a *fish-bone diagram*. The big bones are used to identify major contributing factors, with lower-level factors being shown as medium or small bones. A good starting point is to con-

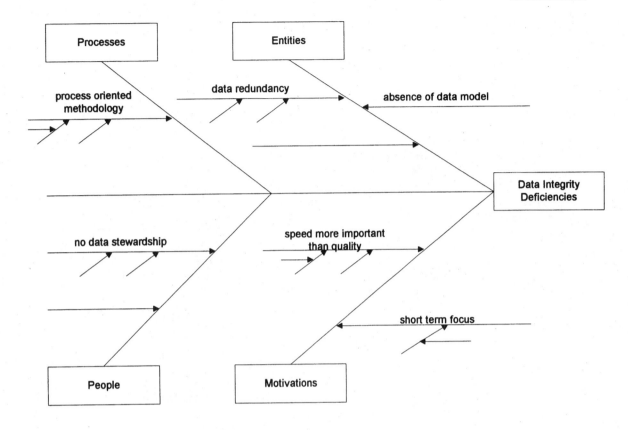

Figure 11-11 Start of a Fish-Bone Diagram.

sider the six Framework dimensions as a starting point for identifying the major factors. The perspective could be considered potential thought provokers for the medium-sized bones. Figure 11-11 shows the start of a fish-bone diagram which could be used to analyze the root cause for data integrity problems.

To apply the technique correctly requires information, including metrics, about the data integrity problems. One instantiation of a data integrity problem which could be represented as the head of the fish is, "Programs cannot effectively deal with the year 2000." This problem can be quantified. Applying the root cause analysis techniques to identify the reasons this situation exists is likely to uncover numerous facts. In the aggregate, analysis of the root causes is likely to point out the potential solutions, including construction of an architected environment. For this to be a valid solution, it needs to have a positive answer to the question, "If we build the architected environment, will this [repeat for each identified root cause] be eliminated or substantially reduced?"

Summary

The data warehouse is a useful tool, but its major value is derived through its application to improve the way in which information technology supports the corporation. The operational data store is a natural extension of the data warehouse, and the design considerations of both the data warehouse and the operational data store combine with the technological advances to help organizations gradually migrate their legacy systems to a new environment.

This migration is accomplished through the use of an architected approach. That approach employs a linkage between five successive views, each of which addresses the six interrogatories of what?, how?, where?, who?, when?, and why? The Zachman Framework, which is at the heart of this architecture can help companies attain knowledge so that they can be more responsive to change and hence are better poised to compete in a rapidly changing environment.

12

Knowledge

Knowledge reflects a useful collection of factual information which can be applied to further the goals of an
enterprise. The information aspect of the definition
requires that meaning is placed on raw data. A major role
of the traditional operational systems is to process data
and convert it into information.

The data warehouse is designed to create a useful subject-oriented, integrated, time-variant, and nonvolatile
collection of this information. The methodology for
building the data warehouse addresses the need for the
information to be factual—that is, accurate and complete. Achievement of this goal, however, is limited by
the quality of the data processed by the source systems
and the constraints of the systems themselves.

Knowledge can only be achieved if the entire process is addressed. The warehouse, as a means to an end, recognizes this requirement. The construction of the data warehouse begins with an architecture for the strategic reporting environment. Through the development of the operational data store, this architecture is extended to include the operational reporting environment, and to a limited extent, other operational activities. The next step in the evolution is to build upon the operational data store to gradually improve or replace the legacy systems. As part of this evolution, the related business processes are also improved.

Building knowledge is not inexpensive, and companies need to decide if the value of knowledge is worth the price. The approach outlined in this book is incremental. The Zachman Framework provides the backdrop. It is gradually applied to define strategies and methodologies, and then to capture artifacts as work is performed. This technique may not result in all the models being explicitly defined for all the work performed in a company. Over time, however, the models for the activities deemed to be important enough to warrant the associated expenses can be created and maintained. Once this is accomplished, knowledge, at least for that area of the company, becomes available. With this knowledge, the companies are better poised to thrive, and not just survive, in a dynamic business and technological environment.

GLOSSARY

access   The operation of seeking, reading, or writing data on a storage unit.

access method   A technique used to transfer a physical record from or to a mass storage device.

access mode   A technique in which a specific logical record is obtained from or placed onto a file assigned to a mass storage device.

access pattern   The general sequence in which the data structure is accessed (e.g., from tuple to tuple, from record to record, from segment to segment).

access plan   The control structure produced during program preparation and used by a database manager to process SQL statements during application execution.

access time   The time interval between the instant an instruction initiates a request for data and the instant the first of the data satisfying the request is delivered. Note that there is a difference—sometimes large—between the time data is first delivered and the time when *all* the data is delivered.

accuracy   A qualitative assessment of freedom from error or a quantitative measure of the magnitude of error, expressed as a function of relative error.

active data dictionary   A data dictionary that is the sole source for an application program insofar as metadata is concerned.

activity   (1) The lowest-level function on an activity chart (sometimes called the *atomic level*). (2) A logical description of a function performed by an enterprise. (3) A procedure (automated or not) designed for the fulfillment of an activity.

activity ratio   The fraction of records in a database which have activity or are otherwise accessed in a given period of time or in a given batch run.

ad hoc processing   One time only, casual access and manipulation of data on parameters never before used, usually done in a heuristic, iterative manner.

address   An identification (e.g., number, name, storage location, byte offset) for a location where data is stored.

addressing The means of assigning data to storage locations, and locating the data upon subsequent retrieval, on the basis of the key of the data.

afterimage The snapshot of data placed on a log upon the completion of a transaction.

agent of change A motivating force large enough to not be denied, usually aging of systems, changes in technology, radical changes in requirements, etc.

AIX Advanced Interactive eXecutive—IBM's version of the UNIX operating system.

algorithm A set of statements organized to solve a problem in a finite number of steps.

alias An alternative label used to refer to a data element.

alphabetic A representation of data using only uppercase and/or lowercase letters.

alphanumeric A representation of data using numbers and/or letters and punctuation.

analytical processing The usage of the computer to produce an analysis for management decision, usually involving trend analysis, drill-down analysis, demographic analysis, profiling, etc.

anticipatory staging The technique of moving blocks of data from one storage device to another with a shorter access time, in anticipation of their being needed by a program in execution or a program soon to go into execution.

application A group of algorithms and data interlinked to support an organizational requirement.

application blocking of data The grouping into the same physical unit of storage of multiple occurrences of data controlled at the application level.

application database A collection of data organized to support a specific application.

archival database A collection of data containing data of a historical nature. As a rule, archival data cannot be updated. Each unit of archival data is relevant to a moment in time, now passed.

area In network databases, a named collection of records that can contain occurrences of one or more record types. A record type can occur in more than one area.

artifact   (1) A design technique used to represent referential integrity in a decision support environment. (2) Information pertaining to the scope, analysis, design or construction of a system, or any other product.

artificial intelligence   The capability of a system to perform functions typically associated with human intelligence and reasoning.

association   A relationship between two entities that is represented in a data model.

associative storage   (1) A storage device whose records are identified by a specific part of their contents rather than by their name or physical position in the database. (2) Content addressable memory. See also **parallel search storage.**

atomic   Describes the lowest level of process analysis.

atomic database   (1) A database made up of primarily atomic data. (2) A data warehouse. (3) A decision-support-system foundation database.

atomic-level data   Data with the lowest level of granularity. Atomic-level data sits in a data warehouse and is time-variant (i.e., accurate as of some moment in time now passed).

attribute   A property that can assume values for entities or relationships. Entities can be assigned several attributes (e.g., a tuple in a relationship consists of values). Some systems also allow relationships to have attributes as well.

audit trail   Data that is available to trace activity, usually update activity.

authorization identifier   A character string that designates a set of privilege descriptors.

availability   A measure of the reliability of a system, indicating the amount of time when the system is up and available divided by the amount of time the system should be up and available. Note there is a difference between a piece of hardware being available and the systems running on the hardware also being available.

back-end processor   A database machine or an intelligent disk controller.

backup   (1) To restore the database to its state as of some previous moment in time. (2) A file serving as a basis for the activity of backing up a database. Usually a snapshot of a database as of some previous moment in time.

backward recovery   A recovery technique that restores a database to an earlier state by applying before-images.

base relation   A relation that is not derivable from other relations in the database.

batch   Computer environment in which programs (usually long-running, sequentially oriented) access data exclusively, and user interaction is not allowed while the activity is occurring.

batch environment   A sequentially dominated mode of processing; in batch, input is collected and stored for future processing. Once collected, the batch input is transacted sequentially against one or more databases.

batch window   The time at which the on-line system is available for batch or sequential processing. The batch window occurs during non-peak processing hours.

before-image   A snapshot of a record prior to update, usually placed on an activity log.

bill of materials   A listing of the parts used in a manufacturing process along with the relation of one product to another insofar as assembly of the final product is concerned. The bill of materials is a classical recursive structure.

binary element   A constituent element of data that has either of two values or states—true or false, one or zero.

binary search   A dichotomizing search with steps in which the sets of remaining items are partitioned into two equal parts.

bind   (1) To assign a value to a data element, variable, or parameter. (2) The attachment of a data definition to a program prior to the execution of the program.

binding time   The moment in time when the data description known to the dictionary is assigned to or bound to the procedural code.

bit   *b*inary digi*t*—The lowest level of storage. A bit can be in a 1 state or a 0 state.

bit map   A specialized form of an index indicating the existence or nonexistence of a condition for a group of blocks or records. Bit maps are expensive to build and maintain but provide very fast comparison and access facilities.

block   (1) A basic unit of structuring storage. (2) The physical unit of transport and storage. A block usually contains one or more records (or contains the space for one or more records). In some database management systems, a block is called a *page*.

block splitting   The data management activity in which a filled block is written into two unfilled blocks, leaving space for future insertions and updates in the two partially filled blocks.

blocking   The combining of two or more physical records so that they are physically collocated together. The result of their physical collocation is that they can be accessed and fetched by a single execution of a machine instruction.

B tree   A binary storage structure and access method that maintains order in a database by continually dividing possible choices into two equal parts and reestablishing pointers to the respective sets but not allowing more than two levels of difference to exist concurrently.

buffer   An area of storage that holds data temporarily in main memory while data is being transmitted, received, read, or written. A buffer is often used to compensate for the differences in the timing of transmission and execution of devices. Buffers are used in terminals, peripheral devices, storage units, and central processing units.

bus   The hardware connection that allows data to flow from one component to another (e.g., from the central processing unit to the line printer).

byte   A basic unit of storage made up of 8 bits.

C   A programming language.

cache   A buffer usually built and maintained at the device level. Retrieving data out of a cache is much quicker than retrieving data out of a cylinder.

call   To invoke the execution of a module.

canonical model   A data model that represents the inherent structure of data without regard to either individual use or hardware or software implementation.

cardinality (of a relation)   The number of tuples (i.e., rows) in a relation. See also **degree (of a relation).**

CASE   Computer-Aided Software Engineering.

catalog   A directory of all files available to the computer.

chain list   A list in which the items cannot be located in sequence but in which each item contains an identifier (i.e., pointer) for the finding of the next item.

character   A member of the standard set of elements used to represent data in the database.

character type   The characters that can represent the value of an attribute.

checkpoint   An identified snapshot of the database or a point at which the transactions against the database have been frozen.

checkpoint/restart   A means of restarting a program at some point other than the beginning, for example, when a failure or interruption has occurred. N checkpoints may be used at intervals throughout an application program. At each of those points sufficient information is stored to permit the program to be restored to the moment in time the checkpoint has been taken.

child   A unit of data existing in a 1:n relationship with another unit of data called a parent where the parent must exist before the child can exist, but the parent can exist even if no child unit of data exists.

CICS   Customer Information Control System   An IBM teleprocessing monitor.

CIO   Chief information officer   An organizational position managing all the information-processing functions.

claimed block   A second or subsequent physical block of data designated to store table data when the originally allocated block has run out of space.

class (of entities)   All possible entities held by a given proposition.

"CLDS"   The facetiously named system development life cycle for analytical decision support systems. CLDS is so named because it is, in fact, the reverse of the classical systems development life cycle (SDLC).

cluster   (1) In Teradata, a group of physical devices controlled by the same AMP. (2) In DB2 and Oracle, the practice of physically collocating data in the same block based on the content of data.

cluster key   The key around which data is clustered in a block (DB2/Oracle).

coalesce   To combine two or more sets of items into any single set.

COBOL   COmmon Business Oriented Language. A very common computer language for the business world.

CODASYL model   A network database model that was originally defined by the Database Task Group (DBTG) of the COnference on DAta SYstem Language (CODASYL) organization.

code   (1) To represent data or a computer program in a form that can be accepted by a data processor. (2) To transform data so that it cannot be understood by anyone who does not have the algorithm used to decode the data prior to presentation (sometimes called *encode*).

collision The event that occurs when two or more records of data are assigned the same physical location. Collisions are associated with randomizers or hashers.

column A vertical table in which values are selected from the same domain. A row is made up of one or more columns.

command (1) The specification of an activity by the programmer. (2) The actual execution of the specification.

commit A condition raised by the programmer signaling to the database management system that all update activity done by the program be executed against a database. Prior to the commit, all update activity can be rolled back or canceled with no ill effects on the contents of the database.

commit protocol An algorithm to ensure that a transaction is successfully completed.

commonality of data Similar or identical data that occurs in different applications or systems. The recognition and management of commonality of data is one of the foundations of conceptual and physical database design.

communication network The collection of transmission facilities, network processors, and so on, which provides for data movement among terminals and information processors.

compaction A technique for reducing the number of bits required to represent data without losing the content of the data. With compaction, repetitive data is represented very concisely.

component A data item or array of data items whose component type defines a collection of occurrences with the same data type.

compound index An index over multiple columns.

concatenate To link or connect two strings of characters, generally for the purpose of using them as a single value.

conceptual schema A consistent collection of data structures expressing the data needs of the organization. This schema is a comprehensive, base level, and logical description of the environment in which an organization exists, free of physical structure and application system considerations.

concurrent operations Activities executed simultaneously or during the same time interval.

condensation The process of reducing the volume of data managed without reducing the logical consistency of the data. Condensation is essentially different than compaction.

connect To forge a relationship between two entities, particularly in a network system.

connector A symbol used to indicate that one occurrence of data has a relationship with another occurrence of data. Connectors are used in conceptual database design and can be implemented hierarchically, relationally, in an inverted fashion, or by a network.

content addressable memory Main storage that can be addressed by the contents of the data in the memory, as opposed to conventional location addressable memory.

contention The condition that occurs when two or more programs try to access the same data at the same time.

continuous time-span data Data organized so that a continuous definition of data over a span of time is represented by one or more records.

control character A character whose occurrence in a particular context initiates, modifies, or stops an operation.

control database A utilitarian database containing data not directly related to the application being built. Typical control databases are audit databases, terminal databases, and security databases.

cooperative processing The ability to distribute resources (programs, files, and databases) across the network.

coordinator The two-phase commit protocol defines one database management system as coordinator for the commit process. The coordinator is responsible for communicating with the other database manager involved in a unit of work.

CPU Central processing unit.

CPU-bound The state of processing in which the computer can produce no more output because the CPU portion of the processor is being used at 100 percent capacity. When the computer is CPU-bound, typically the memory and storage processing units are utilized less than 100 percent. With modern database management systems, it is much more likely that the computer be input-output—bound, rather than CPU-bound.

CUA Common user access. Specifies the ways in which the user interface to systems is to be constructed.

cube   A dimensional database.

current-value data   Data whose accuracy is valid as of the moment of execution. See **time-variant data.**

cursor   (1) An indicator that designates a current position on a screen. (2) A system facility that allows the programmer to thumb from one record to the next when the system has retrieved a set of records.

cursor stability   An option that allows data to move under the cursor. Once the program is through using the data examined by the cursor, it is released, as opposed to a repeatable read.

cylinder   The area of storage of a direct-access storage device that can be read without the movement of the arm. The term originated with disk files, in which a cylinder consisted of one track on each disk surface so that each of these tracks could have a read/write head positioned over it simultaneously.

DASD   See **direct-access storage device.**

data   A recording of facts, concepts, or instructions on a storage medium for communication, retrieval, and processing by automatic means and presentation as information that is understandable by human beings.

data administrator (DA)   The individual or organization responsible for the specification, acquisition, and maintenance of data management software and the design, validation, and security of files or databases. The data model and the data dictionary are classically the charge of the DA.

data aggregate   A collection of data items.

database   A collection of interrelated data stored (often with controlled, limited redundancy) according to a schema. A database can serve single or multiple applications.

database administrator (DBA)   The organizational function charged with the day-to-day monitoring and care of the databases. The DBA function is more closely associated with physical database design than that of the DA.

database key   A unique value that exists for each record in a database. The value is often indexed, although it can be randomized or hashed.

database machine   A dedicated-purpose computer that provides data access and management through total control of the access method, physical storage, and data organization. Often called a *back-end processor.* Data is usually managed in parallel by a database machine.

database management system (DBMS) A computer-based software system used to establish and manage data.

database record A physical root and all its dependents (in IMS).

data definition The specification of the data entities, their attributes, and their relationships in a coherent database structure to create a schema.

data definition language (DDL) The language used to define the database schema and additional data features that allow the database management system to generate and manage the internal tables, indexes, buffers, and storage necessary for database processing. Also called *data description language*.

data description language See **data definition language.**

data dictionary A software tool for recording the definition of data, the relationship of one category of data to another, the attributes and keys of groups of data, and so forth.

data division (COBOL) The section of a COBOL program that consists of entries used to define the nature and characteristics of the data to be processed by the program.

data-driven development The approach to development that centers around identifying the commonality of data through a data model and building programs that have a broader scope than the immediate application. Data-driven development differs from classical application-oriented development.

data-driven process A process whose resource consumption depends on the data on which it operates. For example, a hierarchical root has a dependent. For one occurrence there are two dependents for the root. For another occurrence of the root there are 1000 occurrences of the dependent. The same program that accesses the root and all its dependents will use very different amounts of resources when operating against the two roots although the code will be exactly the same.

data element (1) An attribute of an entity. (2) A uniquely named and well-defined category of data that consists of data items and that is included in a record of an activity.

data engineering The planning and building of data structures according to accepted mathematical models, on the basis of the inherent characteristics of the data itself, and independent of hardware and software systems. See **information engineering.**

data independence The property of being able to modify the overall logical and physical structure of data without changing any of the application code supporting the data.

data item   A discrete representation having the properties that define the data element to which it belongs. See **data element.**

data item set (DIS)   A grouping of data items, each of which directly relates to the key of the grouping of data in which the data items reside. The data item set is found in the midlevel model.

data manipulation language (DML)   (1) A programming language that is supported by a database management system and used to access a database. (2) Language constructs added to a higher-order language (e.g., COBOL) for the purpose of database manipulation.

data model   (1) The logical data structures, including operations and constraints provided by a database management system for effective database processing. (2) The system used for the representation of data (e.g., the entity-relationship diagram or relational model).

data record   (1) An identifiable set of data values treated as a unit. (2) An occurrence of a schema in a database. (3) A collection of atomic data items describing a specific object, event, or tuple.

data security   The protection of the data in a database against unauthorized disclosure, alteration, or destruction. There are different levels of security.

data set   A named collection of logically related data items, arranged in a prescribed manner, and described by control information to which the programming systems have access.

data steward   A person or group of people responsible for defining, setting, and enforcing policy for data.

data storage description language (DSDL)   A language to define the organization of stored data in terms of an operating system and device-independent storage environment. See also **device media control language.**

data structure   A logical relationship among data elements that is designed to support specific data manipulation functions (e.g., trees, lists, and tables.)

data type   The definition of a set of representable values that is primitive and without meaningful logical subdivision.

data volatility   The rate of change of the content of data.

data warehouse   A collection of integrated subject-oriented databases designed to support the decision-support-system function, where each unit of data is relevant to some moment in time. The data warehouse contains atomic data and lightly summarized data.

DatacomDB   A database management system by CA.

datamart   Departmental or personal-level data warehouse derivatives constrained to that information which is of value to a specific group of people.

DB2   A database management system by IBM.

DB/DC   Database/data communications.

DBMS language interface (DB input-output module)   Software that applications invoke in order to access a database. The module in turn has direct access with the database. Standards enforcement and standard error checking are often features of an input-output module.

deadlock   See **deadly embrace.**

deadly embrace   The event that occurs when transaction *A* desires to access data currently protected by transaction *B*, while at the same time transaction *B* desires to access data that is currently being protected by transaction *A*. The deadly embrace condition is a serious impediment to performance.

decision support system (DSS)   A system used to support managerial decisions. Usually DSS involves the analysis of many units of data in a heuristic fashion. As a rule, DSS processing does not involve the update of data.

decompaction   The opposite of compaction; once data is stored in a compacted form, it must be decompacted to be used.

decryption   The opposite of encryption. Once data is stored in an encrypted fashion, it must be decrypted in order that it can be used.

degree (of a relation)   The number of attributes or columns of a relation. See **cardinality (of a relation).**

delimiter   A flag, symbol, or convention used to mark the boundaries of a record, field, or other unit of storage.

demand staging   The movement of blocks of data from one storage device to another device with a shorter access time when programs request the blocks and the blocks are not already in the faster access storage.

Deming Prize   Annual prize awarded by the Union of Japanese Scientists and Engineers to companies which exhibit an all-encompassing approach to quality consistent with Dr. Deming's 14 points.

denormalization   The technique of placing normalized data in a physical location that optimizes the performance of the system.

derived data   Data whose existence depends on two or more occurrences of a major subject of the enterprise.

derived data element   A data element that is not necessarily stored but that can be generated when needed (e.g., age can be generated when current date and date of birth are given.)

derived relation   A relation that can be obtained from previously defined relations by applying some sequence of retrieval and derivation operator (e.g., a table that results from the join of others plus some projections.)

design review   The quality-assurance process in which all aspects of a system are reviewed publicly prior to the striking of code.

device media control language (DMCL)   A language used to define the mapping of the data onto the physical storage media. See **data storage description language.**

dimension   An independent entity in the model of an organization which serves as an entry point for slicing the additive measures, or facts, of the organization.

dimension table   A table in a star schema with a single-part primary key.

dimensional data warehouse   A data warehouse designed using star schemas.

dimensional model   A model, developed top-down, for depicting a business process through its relevant dimensions and facts.

direct access   Retrieval or storage of data by reference to its location on a volume. The access mechanism goes directly to the data in question, as is generally required with on-line use of data. Also called *random access* or *hashed access.*

direct-access storage device (DASD)   A data storage unit on which data can be accessed directly without having to progress through a serial file such as a magnetic tape file. A disk unit is a direct-access storage device.

directory   A table specifying the relationships between items of data. Sometimes the table or index gives the addresses of data.

distributed catalog   A distributed catalog is needed to achieve site autonomy. The catalog at each site maintains information about objects in the local databases. The distributed catalog keeps information on replicated and distributed tables stored at that site and information on remote tables located at another site that cannot be accessed locally.

distributed database   A database controlled by a central database management system but in which the storage devices are geographically dispersed or not attached to the same processor. See **parallel I/O.**

distributed environment   A set of related data-processing systems, in which each system has its own capacity to operate autonomously but with some applications which execute at multiple sites. Some of the systems may be connected with teleprocessing links into a network in which each system is a node.

distributed free space   Space left empty at intervals in a data layout to permit insertion of new data.

distributed request   A transaction across multiple nodes.

distributed unit of work   The work done by a transaction that operates against multiple nodes.

division   An operation that partitions a relation on the basis of the contents of data found in the relation.

DL/1   IBM's Data Language One, for describing logical and physical data structures.

domain   The set of legal values from which actual values are derived for an attribute or a data element.

download   The stripping of data from one database to another based on the content of data found in the first database.

drill-down analysis   The type of analysis where examination of a summary number leads to the exploration of the components of the sum.

dual database   The practice of separating high-performance, transaction-oriented data from decision support data.

dual database management systems   The practice of using multiple database management systems to control different aspects of the database environment.

dumb terminal   A device used to interact directly with the end user where all processing is done on a remote computer. A dumb terminal acts as a device that gathers data and displays data only.

dynamic SQL   SQL statements that are prepared and executed within a program while the program is executing. In dynamic SQL the SQL source is contained in host language variables rather than being coded into the application program.

dynamic storage allocation   A technique in which the storage areas assigned to computer programs are determined during processing.

dynamic subset of data   A subset of data selected by a program and operated on only by the program and released by the program once the program ceases execution.

EDI   Electronic data interchange.

EIS Executive information systems   Systems designed for the top executive, featuring drill-down analysis and trend analysis.

embedded pointer   A record pointer (i.e., a means of internally linking related records) that is not available to an external index or directory. Embedded pointers are used to reduce search time but require maintenance overhead.

encoding   A shortening or abbreviation of the physical representation of a data value (e.g., male = "M", female = "F").

encryption   The transformation of data from a recognizable form to a form unrecognizable without the algorithm used for the encryption. Encryption is usually done for the purposes of security.

enterprise   The generic term for the company, corporation, agency, or business unit. It is often associated with data modeling.

Enterprise Framework   A framework that embodies the process of designing, building, distributing, etc., the product or service of the enterprise.

Enterprise Engineering Framework   A framework that embodies the process of designing, building, distributing, etc., the enterprise itself, as differentiated from the product or service.

entity   A person, place, or thing of interest to the data modeler at the highest level of abstraction.

entity-relationship-attribute (ERA) model   A data model that defines entities, the relationship between the entities, and the attributes that have values to describe the properties of entities and/or relationships.

entity-relationship diagram (ERD)   A high-level data model. The schematic shows all the entities within the scope of integration and the direct relationship between those entities.

event   A signal that an activity of significance has occurred. An event is noted by the information system.

event discrete data   Data relating to the measurement or description of an event.

expert system   A system that captures and automates the usage of human experience and intelligence.

extent   (1) A list of unsigned integers that specifies an array. (2) A physical unit of disk storage attached to a data set after the initial allocation of data has been made.

external data   (1) Data originating from other than the operational systems of a corporation. (2) Data residing outside the central processing complex.

external schema   A logical description of a user's method of organizing and structuring data. Some attributes or relationships can be omitted from the corresponding conceptual schema or can be renamed or otherwise transformed.

extract   The process of selecting data from one environment and transporting it to another environment.

fact   A measurement, typically numeric and additive, that is stored in a fact table.

fact table   The central table of a star join schema. It is characterized by a composite key whose elements are foreign keys drawn from the dimension tables.

factless fact table   A fact table which has no facts.

field   See **data item.**

file   A set of related records treated as a unit and stored under a single logical file name.

first-in first-out (FIFO)   A fundamental ordering of processing in a queue.

first-in last-out (FILO)   A standard order of processing in a stack.

flag   An indicator or character that signals the occurrence of some condition.

flat file   A collection of records containing no data aggregates, nested repeated data items, or groups of data items.

floppy disk   A device for storing data on a personal computer.

foreign key   An attribute that is not a primary key in a relational system but whose values are the values of the primary key of another relation.

format   The arrangement or layout of data in or on a data medium or in a program definition.

forward recovery   A recovery technique that restores a database by reapplying all transactions using a before-image from a specified point in time to a copy of the database taken at that moment in time.

fourth-generation language (4gl)   Language or technology designed to allow the end user unfettered access to data.

functional decomposition   The division of operations into hierarchical functions (i.e., activities) that form the basis for procedures.

granularity   The level of detail contained in a unit of data. The more detail there is, the lower the level of granularity. The less detail there is, the higher the level of granularity.

graphic   A symbol produced on a screen representing an object or a process in the real world.

guiding principle   A statement for guiding actions which reflects the philosophy and beliefs of an organization.

hash   To convert the value of the key of a record into a location on a direct-access storage device.

hash total   A total of the values of one or more fields, used for the purposes of audibility and control.

header record or **header table**   A record containing common, constant, or identifying information for a group of records that follow.

heuristic   The mode of analysis in which the next step is determined by the results of the current step of analysis. Used for decision support processing.

hierarchical model   A data model providing a tree structure for relating data elements or groups of data elements. Each node in the structure represents a group of data elements or a record type. There can be only one root node at the start of the hierarchical structure.

hit   An occurrence of data that satisfies some search criteria.

hit ratio   A measure of the number of records in a file expected to be accessed in a given run. Usually expressed as a percentage: number of input transactions per number of records in the file × 100 = hit ratio.

homonyms   Identical names that refer to different attributes.

horizontal distribution   The splitting of a table across different sites by rows. With horizontal distribution, rows of a single table reside at different sites in a distributed database network.

host   The processor receiving and processing a transaction.

Huffman code   A code for data compaction in which frequently used characters are encoded with fewer bits than infrequently used characters.

IDMS   A network database management system from CA.

IEEE   Institute of Electrical and Electronics Engineers.

image copy   A procedure in which a database is physically copied to another medium for the purposes of backup.

IMS   Information Management System. An operational database management system by IBM.

index   The portion of the storage structure maintained to provide efficient access to a record when its index key item is known.

index chains   Chains of data within an index.

index point   A hardware reference mark on a disk or drum; used for timing purposes.

index sequential access method (ISAM)   A file structure and access method in which records can be processed sequentially (e.g., in order, by key) or by directly looking up their locations on a table, thus making it unnecessary to process previously inserted records.

indirect addressing   Any method of specifying or locating a record through calculation (e.g., locating a record through the scan of an index).

information   Data that human beings assimilate and evaluate to solve a problem or make a decision.

information center   The organizational unit charged with identifying and accessing information needed in decision-support-system processing.

information engineering (IE)   The discipline of creating a data-driven development environment.

Informix   A UNIX-based database management system.

input-output (I/O)   The means by which data is stored and/or retrieved on direct-access storage devices. It is measured in milliseconds (i.e., mechanical speeds), whereas computer processing is measured in nanoseconds (i.e., electronic speeds).

instance   A set of values representing a specific entity belonging to a particular entity type. A single value is also the instance of a data item.

integrity The property of a database that ensures that the data contained in the database is as accurate and consistent as possible.

intelligent database A database that contains shared logic as well as shared data and which automatically invokes that logic when the data is accessed. Logic, constraints, and controls relating to the use of the data are represented in an intelligent data model.

interactive A mode of processing that combines some of the characteristics of on-line transaction processing and batch processing. In interactive processing the end user interacts with data over which he or she has exclusive control. In addition, the end user can initiate background activity to be run against the data.

interleaved data Data from different tables mixed into a simple table space where there is commonality of physical collocation based on a common key value.

internal schema The schema that describes logical structures of the data and the physical media over which physical storage is mapped.

interpretive A mode of data manipulation in which the commands to the database management system are translated as the user enters them (as opposed to the programmed mode of process manipulation).

intersection data Data that is associated with the junction of two or more record types or entities but which has no meaning when disassociated with any records or entities forming the junction.

inverted file A file structure that uses an inverted index, where entries are grouped according to the content of the key being referenced. Inverted files provide for the fast spontaneous searching of files.

inverted index An index structure organized by means of a nonunique key to speed the search for data by content.

inverted list A list organized around a secondary index instead of around a primary key.

I/O See **input-output.**

I/O bound The point after which no more processing can be done because the I/O subsystem is saturated.

ISAM See **index sequential access method.**

is a type of An analytical tool used in abstracting data during the process of conceptual database design (e.g., a cocker spaniel is a type of dog.)

ISDN Integrated Services Digital Network. Telecommunications technology that enables companies to transfer data and voice through the same phone lines.

ISO International Standards Organization.

item See **data item.**

item type A classification of an item according to its domain, generally in a gross sense.

iterative analysis The mode of processing in which the next step of processing depends on the results obtained by the existing step in execution; heuristic processing.

JAD Joint application design. An analysis and design approach which involves an organization of people, usually end users, who create and refine application system requirements.

join An operation that takes two relations as operands and produces a new relation by concatenating the tuples and matching the corresponding columns when a stated condition holds between the two.

judgment sample A sample of data where data is accepted or rejected for the sample based on one or more parameters.

junction From the network environment, an occurrence of data that has two or more parent segments. For example, an order for supplies must have a supplier parent and a part parent.

justify To adjust the value representation in a character field to the right or to the left, ignoring blanks encountered.

keep list A sequence of database keys maintained by the database management system for the duration of the session.

key A data item or combination of data items used to identify or locate a record instance (or other similar data groupings).

key compression A technique for reducing the number of bits in keys; used in making indexes occupy less space.

key, primary A unique attribute used to identify a single record in a database.

key, secondary A nonunique attribute used to identify a class of records in a database.

knowledge Factual information which is retained with an understanding about the significance of that information.

label A set of symbols used to identify or describe an item, record, message, or file. Occasionally a label may be the same as the address of the record in storage.

language   A set of characters, conventions, and rules used to convey information and consisting of syntax and semantics.

latency   The time taken by a direct-access storage device to position the read arm over the physical storage medium. For general purposes, average latency time is used.

least frequently used (LFU)   A replacement strategy in which new data must replace existing data in an area of storage; the least frequently used items are replaced.

least recently used (LRU)   A replacement strategy in which new data must replace existing data in an area of storage; the least recently used items are replaced.

legacy system   An operational system which is used to support day-to-day activities. It typically resides on the mainframe computer. It is often used with a negative connotation.

line   The hardware by which data flows to or from the processor. Lines typically go to terminals, printers, and other processors.

line polling   The activity of the teleprocessing monitor in which different lines are queried to determine whether they have data and/or transactions that need to be transmitted.

line time   The length of time required for a transaction to go from either the terminal to the processor or the processor to the terminal. Typically line time is the single largest component of on-line response time.

linkage   The ability to relate one unit of data to another.

linked list   Set of records in which each record contains a pointer to the next record on the list. See **chain list.**

list   An ordered set of data items.

living sample   A representative database typically used for heuristic statistical analytical processing in place of a large database. Periodically the very large database is selectively stripped of data so that the resulting living sample database represents a cross section of the very large database as of some moment in time.

load   To insert data values into a database that was previously empty.

local site support   Within a distributed unit of work, a local site update allows a process to perform SQL update statements referring to the local site.

local transaction   In a distributed database management system, a transaction that requires reference only to data that is stored at the site where the transaction originated.

locality of processing   In a distributed database, the design of processing so that remote access of data is eliminated or reduced substantively.

lockup   The event that occurs when an update is done against a database record and the transaction has not yet reached a commit point. The on-line transaction needs to prevent other transactions from accessing the data while update is occurring.

log   A journal of activity.

logging   The automatic recording of data with regard to the access of the data, the updates to the data, etc.

logical representation   A data view or description that does not depend on a physical storage device or a computer program.

loss of identity   When data is brought in from an external source and the identity of the external source is discarded, loss of identity occurs. This is a common practice with microprocessor data.

LU6.2   Logical Unit Type 6.2. Peer-to-peer data stream with network operating system for program-to-program communication. LU6.2 allows midrange machines to talk to one another without the involvement of the mainframe.

machine learning   The ability of a machine to improve its performance automatically based on past performance.

magnetic tape   (1) The storage medium most closely associated with sequential processing. (2) A large ribbon on which magnetic images are stored and retrieved.

main storage database (MSDB)   A database that resides entirely in main storage. Such databases are very fast to access but require special handling at the time of update. Another limitation of MSDBs is that they can only manage small amounts of data.

Malcolm Baldrige National Quality Award   An annual award to recognize U.S. companies for business excellence.

master file   A file that holds the system of record for a given set of data (usually bound by an application).

maximum transaction arrival rate (MTAR) The rate of arrival of transactions at the moment of peak period processing.

message (1) The data input by the user in the on-line environment that is used to drive a transaction. (2) The output of a transaction.

metadata (1) Data about data. (2) The description of the structure, content, keys, indexes, etc., of data.

metalanguage A language used to specify other languages.

microprocessor A small processor serving the needs of a single user.

migration The process by which frequently used items of data are moved to more readily accessible areas of storage and infrequently used items of data are moved to less readily accessible areas of storage.

MIPS Million instructions per second. The standard measurement of processor speed for minicomputers and mainframe computers.

mode of operation A classification for systems that execute in a similar fashion and share distinctive operational characteristics. Some modes of operation are operational, direct support system, on-line, and interactive.

modulo An arithmetic term describing the remainder of a division process. For example, 10 modulo 7 is 3. Modulo is usually associated with the randomization process.

multilist organization A chained file organization in which the chains are divided into fragments and each fragment is indexed. This organization of data permits faster access to the data.

multiple key retrieval Searches of data on the basis of the values of several key fields (some or all of which are secondary keys).

MVS Multiple virtual storage. IBM's mainline operating system for mainframe processors. There are several extensions of MVS.

Named Pipes Program-to-program protocol with Microsoft's LAN manager. The Named Pipes API supports intramachine and intermachine process-to-process communications.

natural join A join in which the redundant logic components generated by the join are removed.

natural language A language generally spoken whose rules are based on current usage and not explicitly defined by a grammar.

navigate To steer a course through a database, from record to record, by means of an algorithm which examines the content of data.

network A computer network consists of a collection of circuits, data switching elements, and computing systems. The switching devices in the network are called *communication processors*. A network provides a configuration for computer systems and communication facilities within which data can be stored and accessed and within which database management systems can operate.

network model A data model that provides data relationships on the basis of records, and groups of records (i.e., sets) in which one record is designated as the set owner and a single member record can belong to one or more sets.

nine's complement Transformation of a numeric field calculated by subtracting the initial value from a file consisting of all nines.

node A point in the network at which data is switched.

nonadditive fact A fact that cannot be logically added across records. If it is numeric, it must usually be combined in a computation with other facts before being added across records. If it is nonnumeric, it can only be used in constraints, counts, or groupings.

nonprocedural language Syntax that directs the computer as to what to do, not how to do it. Typical nonprocedural languages include RAMIS, FOCUS, NOMAD, and SQL.

normalize To decompose complex data structures into natural structures. The common normal forms are:

first normal form Data that has been organized into two-dimensional flat files without repeating groups.

second normal form Data that functionally depends on the entire candidate key.

third normal form Data that has had all transitive dependencies on data items other than the candidate key removed.

fourth normal form Data whose candidate key is related to all data items in the record and that contains no more than one nontrivial multivalued dependency on the candidate key.

null An item or record for which no value currently exists or possibly may ever exist.

numeric A representation using only numbers and the decimal point.

occurrence See **instance.**

offset pointer An indirect pointer. An offset pointer exists inside a block, and the index points to the offset. If data must be moved, only the offset pointer in the block must be altered; the index entry remains untouched.

on-line analytic processing (OLAP) A set of principles that provides a dimensional framework for decision support.

on-line storage Storage devices and storage media where data can be accessed in a direct fashion.

on-line transaction processing (OLTP) A system which supports entering data reliably into a database.

operating system Software that enables a computer to supervise its own operations and automatically call in programs, routines, languages, and data as needed for continuous operation throughout the execution of different types of jobs.

operational data Data used to support the daily processing a company does.

operational data store (ODS) The architectural construct where collective integrated operational data is stored.

operations The department charged with the running of the computer.

optical disk A storage medium using lasers as opposed to magnetic devices. Optical disk is typically write-only, is much less expensive per byte than magnetic storage, and is highly reliable.

ORACLE A database management system by ORACLE Corporation.

order To place items in an arrangement specified by such rules as numeric or alphabetic order.

OS/2 The operating system for IBM's Personal System/2.

OSF Open Software Foundation.

OSI Open Systems Interconnection.

overflow (1) The condition in which a record or a segment cannot be stored in its home address because the address is already occupied. In this case the data is placed in another location referred to as overflow. (2) The area of direct-access storage device where data is sent when the overflow condition is triggered.

ownership The responsibility for updating operational data.

padding A technique used to fill a field, record, or block with default data (e.g., blanks or zeros).

page (1) A basic unit of data on a direct-access storage device. (2) A basic unit of storage in main memory.

page fault A program interruption that occurs when a page that is referred to is not in main memory and must be read in from external storage.

page fixed   The state in which programs or data cannot be removed from main storage. Only a limited amount of storage can be page fixed.

paging   In virtual storage systems, the technique of making memory appear to be larger than it really is by transferring blocks (pages) of data or programs into external memory.

parallel data organization   An arrangement of data in which the data is spread over independent storage devices and is managed independently.

parallel I/O   The process of accessing or storing data on multiple physical data devices.

parallel search storage   A storage device in which one or more parts of all storage locations are queried simultaneously for a certain condition or under certain parameters. See **associative storage.**

parameter   An elementary data value used as a criteria for qualification, usually of searches of data or in the control of modules.

parent   A unit of data in a 1:n relationship with another unit of data called a child, where the parent can exist independently, but the child cannot exist unless there is a parent.

parsing   The algorithm that translates syntax into meaningful machine instructions. Parsing determines the meaning of statements issued in the data manipulation language.

partition   A segmentation technique in which data is divided into physically different units. Partitioning can be done at the application or the system level.

path length   The number of instructions executed for a given program or instruction.

peak period   The time when the most transactions arrive at the computer with the expectation of execution.

performance   The length of time from the moment a request is issued until the first of the results of the request are received.

periodic discrete data   A measurement or description of data taken at a regular time interval.

physical representation   (1) The representation and storage of data on a medium such as magnetic storage. (2) The description of data that depends on such physical factors as length of elements, records, and pointers.

pipes Vehicles for passing data from one application to another.

plex or network structure A relationship between records or other groupings of data in which a child record can have more than one parent record.

plug compatible manufacturer (PCM) A manufacturer of equipment that functionally is identical to that of another manufacturer (usually IBM).

pointer The address of a record or other grouping of data contained in another record so that a program may access the former record when it has retrieved the latter record. The address can be absolute, relative, or symbolic, and hence the pointer is referred to as absolute, relative, or symbolic.

pools The buffers made available to the on-line controller.

populate To place occurrences of data values in a previously empty database. See **load.**

precision The degree of discrimination with which a quantity is stated. For example, a three-digit numeral discriminates among 1000 possibilities, from 000 to 999.

precompilation The processing of source text prior to compilation. In an SQL environment, SQL statements are replaced with statements that will be recognized by the host language compiler.

prefix data Data in a segment or a record used exclusively for system control, usually unavailable to the user.

primary key An attribute that contains values that uniquely identify the record in which the key exists.

primitive data Data whose existence depends on only a single occurrence of a major subject area of the enterprise.

privacy The prevention of unauthorized access and manipulation of data.

privilege descriptor A persistent object used by a database management system to enforce constraints on operations.

problems database The component of a decision-support-system application where previously defined decision parameters are stored. A problems database is consulted to review characteristics of past decisions and to determine ways to meet current decision making needs.

processor The hardware at the center of execution of computer programs. Generally speaking, processors are divided into three categories—mainframes, minicomputers, and microcomputers.

processor cycles The hardware's internal cycles that drive the computer (e.g., initiate input-output, perform logic, move data, perform arithmetic functions)

production environment The environment where operational, high-performance processing is run.

program area The portion of main memory in which application programs are executed.

progressive overflow A method of handling overflow in a randomly organized file that does not require the use of pointers. An overflow record is stored in the first available space and is retrieved by a forward serial search from the home address.

projection An operation that takes one relation as an operand and returns a second relation that consists of only the selected attributes or columns, with duplicate rows eliminated.

proposition A statement about entities that asserts or denies that some condition holds for those entities.

protocol The call format used by a teleprocessing monitor.

punched cards An early storage medium on which data and input were stored. Today punched cards are rare.

purge data The data on or after which a storage area may be overwritten. Used in conjunction with a file label, it is a means of protecting file data until an agreed-upon release date is reached.

quality Conformance with valid customer requirements.

query language A language that enables an end user to interact directly with a database management system to retrieve and possibly modify data held under the database management system.

record An aggregation of values of data organized by their relationship to a common key.

record-at-a-time processing The access of data one record at a time, a tuple at a time, etc.

recovery The restoration of the database to an original position or condition, often after major damage to the physical medium.

redundancy The practice of storing more than one occurrence of data. In the case where data can be updated, redundancy poses serious problems. In the case where data is not updated, redundancy is often a valuable and necessary design technique.

referential integrity   The facility of a database management system to ensure the validity of predefined relationships.

reorganization   The process of unloading data in a poorly organized state and reloading the data in a well-organized state. Reorganization in some database management systems is used to restructure data. Reorganization is often called *reorg* or an *unload/reload* process.

repeating groups   A collection of data that can occur several times within a given record.

rolling summary   A form of storing archival data where the most recent data has the most details stored and data that is older has fewer details stored.

scope of integration   The formal definition of the boundaries of the system being modeled.

SDLC   See **systems development life cycle.**

sequential file   A file in which records are ordered according to the values of one or more key fields. The records can be processed in this sequence starting from the first record in the file and continuing to the last record in the file.

serial file   A sequential file in which the records are physically adjacent, in sequential order.

set-at-a-time processing   Access of data by groups, each member of which satisfies a selection criterion.

slice and dice   The ability to access a data warehouse equally through any of its dimensions.

snapshot   A database dump or the archiving of data out of a database as of some moment in time.

snowflake   In a star schema, a normalized dimension which entails a flat single table dimension which is decomposed into a tree structure with potentially many nesting levels. Snowflakes generally compromise user understandability and browsing performance.

solutions database   The component of a decision-support-systems environment in which the results of previous decisions are stored. Solutions databases are consulted to help determine the proper course of action in a current decision making situation.

SQL   Sequential Query Language. A commonly used programming language for working with relational database management systems.

star schema   An organization of a database in which a fact table is joined to a number of single-level dimension tables. Sometimes called *star join schema.*

storage hierarchy   Storage units linked to form a storage subsystem in which some units are fast but small and expensive and other units are large but slower and less expensive.

subject database   A database organized around a major subject of the corporation. Classical subject databases are for customer, product, transaction, supplier, etc.

system log   An audit trail of relevant system events (for example, transaction entries, database changes)

system of record   The definitive and singular source of operational data. If a data element has a value of 25 in a database record but a value of 50 in the system of record, by definition the first value is incorrect and must be reconciled. The system of record is useful for managing data redundancy.

systems development life cycle   The classical approach for developing operational systems typically consisting of the sequential activities of requirements gathering, analysis, design, programming, testing, integration, and implementation.

table   A relation that consists of a set of columns with a heading and a set of rows (e.g., tuples).

time stamping   The practice of tagging each record with some moment in time, usually when the record was created or when the record was passed from one environment to another.

time-variant data   Data whose accuracy is relevant to some moment in time. The three forms of time-variant data are continuous time span, event discrete, and periodic discrete data.

total quality management (TQM)   An all-encompassing approach to quality consistent with Dr. Deming's 14 points.

transition data   Data possessing both primitive and derived characteristics, usually very sensitive to the running of the business. Typical transition data are interest rates for a bank and policy rates for an insurance company.

trend analysis   The process of looking at homogeneous data over a period of time. See **EIS.**

true archival data   Data at the lowest level in the atomic database, usually stored on bulk storage media.

update   To change, add, delete, or replace values in all or selected entries, groups, or attributes stored in a database.

user   A person or process issuing commands and messages to the information system.

Windows NT   An operating system from Microsoft, commonly used on servers.

Zachman Framework   A model which major organizations can use to view and communicate their enterprise information infrastructure. The Zachman Framework draws upon the discipline of classical architecture to establish a common vocabulary and set of perspectives, or framework, for defining and describing today's complex enterprise systems. Sometimes called the Zachman Framework for Information Systems Architecture or Framework for Information Systems Architecture.

Zachman Institute for Framework Advancement (ZIFA)   An organization with the mission of exercising the Zachman Framework for the purpose of advancing the conceptual and implementation understanding of the enterprise architecture.

BIBLIOGRAPHY

Zachman Framework—Related Articles

Babichuk and Eulenberg, "An Information Architecture Framework," GUIDE Project 1234, October 30, 1989.

Brown, Robert G., "An Objective Framework for Information Systems Architecture," The Database Design Group, Inc., (714) 675-3298.

Bruce, Thomas A., "Simplicity and Complexity in the Zachman Framework," Database Newsletter, vol. 20, no. 3, May/June 1992.

English, Larry P., "Extending the Benefits of Data Resource Management Through Object-Oriented Modeling," *Data Resource Management,* Winter 1992.

Geiger, Jonathan G., "Information Management for Competitive Advantage," *Strategic Systems Journal,* ACR, June 1993.

Gjerding, Kristian, "Architectures for Enterprise Information Systems," re: VITAL. Gjerding and Gunther Consulting, Copenhagen.

"The IDEF Framework," IDEF Users Group, IDEF-UG-0001, September 1993.

Katz, R. L., "Business/Enterprise Modeling," *IBM Systems Journal,* vol. 29, no. 4, 1990.

Kieman, Casey, "Client Server: Learning from History," *Database Programming & Design,* September 1993.

Koenig, Michael E. D., "The Productivity Paradox: Real or Apparent," Rosary College, (708) 366-2490.

Loosley, Chris, "Separation and Integration in the Zachman Framework," *Database Newsletter,* vol. 20, no. 1, January/February 1992.

McKee, Richard L., and Jeffery Rodgers, "N-Ary Versus Binary Data Modeling: A Matter of Perspective," *Data Resource Management,* Fall 1992.

Ross, Ronald G., "An Interview with John A. Zachman," *Database Newsletter,* vol. 17, no. 5, November/December 1989.

———, "Zachman Framework Extensions: An Update," *Database Newsletter,* vol. 19, no. 4, July/August 1991.

———, "Rules for the Zachman Framework Architecture," *Database Newsletter,* vol. 19, no. 4, July/August 1991.

Seer, Kristen, and Mark Wise, "A Framework for Managing Model Objects," *Database Programming & Design,* August 1994.

Sowa, J. F., and John A. Zachman, "Extending and Formalizing the Framework for Information Systems Architecture," *IBM Systems Journal,* vol. 31, no. 3, 1992, IBM Publication G321-5488.

Staples, Geoffrey, "A Conversation with John Zachman," *Strategic Systems Newsletter,* vol. 4, no. 10, May 1992.

Sweet, Frank, "The Winchester House Syndrome," *Datamation,* April 15, 1984.

von Halle, Barbara, *Database Programming & Design,* (regular Data Architect column).

Winter, Paul K., "The Zachman Architecture Framework: Reflections from the Trenches," *Database Newsletter,* vol. 21, no. 1, January/February 1993.

Wong, Chee-Pun, "Fried Rice: A Recipe for Data Modeling and Design," *Database Programming & Design,* April 1995.

Zachman, John A., "A Framework for Information Systems Architecture," *IBM Systems Journal,* vol. 26, no. 3, 1987, IBM Publication G321-5298.

Zachman, John A., et al., "Integration of Systems Planning, Development, and Maintenance Tools and Methods," *Information Management Directions: The Integration Challenge,* NIST Special Publication 500-167.

Data Warehouse—Related Articles

Adelman, Sid, "Exploring the Data Warehouse's Organizational and Cultural Issues," *Database Programming & Design,* June 1995. (Article emphasizes the need for cultural adjustments to be successful with data warehouse efforts.)

Ashbrook, Jim, "Information Preservation," *CIO Magazine,* July 1993. (Article provides an executive's view of the data warehouse.)

Desio, Vince, "Impact of Data Warehouse on MIS," *Data Management Review,* April 1995. (Article emphasizes the need for a program versus a project mentality for successful development and implementation of a data warehouse.)

Edelstein, Herb, "Mining Data Warehouses," *Information Week,* January 8, 1996. (Article describes major types of information which data mining yields.)

Egan, Nancy T., "The Customer-Oriented Data Warehouse," *Data Management Review,* October 1995. (Article describes characteristics and operation of a data warehouse which addresses customer relationships.)

Goldberg, Paula, Robert Lambert, and Katherine Powell, "Guidelines for Defining Requirements for Decision Support Systems," *Data Resource Management Journal,* Spring 1991. (Article describes how to define end-user requirements before building the data warehouse.)

Griffin, Jane, "Aligning Data Warehouses with Business Strategies," *Relational Database Journal,* July-August 1995. (Article emphasizes the need for a data warehouse strategy which recognizes the company's business objectives and critical success factors.)

———, "Customer Information Architecture," *DBMS,* July 1995. (Article describes how a customer information architecture helps companies better understand, manage, and nurture customer relationships.)

Hackney, Douglas, "Metadata Maturity," *Data Management Review,* April 1996. (Article presents important facts about metadata.)

Hildebrand, Carol, "Form Follows Function," *CIO,* November 1, 1995. (Article describes how the data warehouse can provide valuable insights with direct bottom-line results.)

Hufford, Duane, "Data Administration Support for Business Process Improvement," *AMS,* Washington, DC. (Article describes data warehousing and data administration.)

Hufford, Duane, "A Conceptual Model for Documenting Data Synchronization Requirements," *AMS,* Washington, DC. (Article addresses data synchronization and the data warehouse.)

Imhoff, Claudia, and Jonathan G. Geiger, "Data Quality in the Data Warehouse," *Data Management Review,* April 1996. (Article describes quality issues related to the data warehouse and the importance of correctly setting related expectations.)

Inmon, W. H., "At the Heart of the Matter," *Data Base Programming & Design,* July 1988. (Article defines primitive and derived data and describes their differences.)

———, "Going Against the Grain," *Data Base Programming & Design,* July

1990. (Article describes the relationship of data granularity to the data warehouse.)

———, "The Cabinet Effect," *Data Base Programming & Design,* May 1991. (Article emphasizes the importance of a data warehouse architecture in avoiding a degeneration into the spider web environment.)

———, "Data Structures in the Information Warehouse," *Enterprise Systems Journal,* January 1992. (Article describes common data warehouse data structures.)

———, "Winds of Change," *Data Base Programming & Design,* January 1992. (Article describes the evolution of data administration and its role in the data warehouse.)

———, "Data Warehouse—A Perspective of Data Over Time," *370/390 Data Base Management,* February 1992. (Article describes the role of the data warehouse in managing data over time.)

———, "Building the Data Bridge," *Data Base Programming & Design,* April 1992. (Article delineates ten critical success factors in building the data warehouse.)

———, "Metadata: A Checkered Past, A Bright Future," *370/390 Data Management Review,* July 1992. (Article describes metadata and its relationship to the data warehouse.)

———, "The Need for Reporting," *Data Base Programming & Design,* July 1992. (Article defines the different types of reports found in the different parts of the architecture.)

———, "Neat Little Packages," *Data Base Programming & Design,* August 1992. (Article describes the treatment of data relationships in the data warehouse.)

———, "EIS and the Data Warehouse," *Data Base Programming & Design,* November 1992. (Article presents the relationship between executive information systems and data warehouse.)

———, "Untangling the Web," *Data Base Programming & Design,* May 1993. (Article explores the factors that turn data into useful information.)

———, "The Structure of the Information Warehouse," *Data Management Review,* August 1993. (Article describes the different levels of data found within the data warehouse.)

———, "Data Warehouse Lays Foundation for Bringing Data Investment Forward," *Application Development Trends,* January 1994. (Article describes the relationship of the data warehouse to legacy systems.)

————, "The Data Warehouse—All Your Data at Your Fingertips," *Communications Week,* August 29, 1994. (Article provides an overview of the data warehouse.)

————, "The Data Warehouse: Managing the Infrastructure," *Data Management Review,* December 1994. (Article describes the data warehouse infrastructure and the budget associated with it.)

————, "EIS and Detail," *Data Management Review,* January 1995. (Article describes the amount of detail needed to support executive information systems and the role of summarization in the data warehouse environment.)

————, "Multidimensional Data Bases and Data Warehousing," *Data Management Review,* February 1995. (Article describes how current detailed data in the data warehouse fits with multidimensional database management systems.)

————, "Profiling the DSS Analyst," *Data Management Review,* March 1995. (Article describes two types of decision-support-system analysts— farmers and explorers.)

————, "Data Warehouse Success Requires Development Automation," *Application Development Trends,* March 1995. (Article identifies major reasons for automating data warehouse development.)

————, "Different Degrees of Data Warehouse," *Data Management Review,* May 1995. (Article notes the importance of the data warehouse as a competitive weapon.)

————, "Multidimensional DBMS's and the Data Warehouse," *Data Management Review,* June 1995. (Article emphasizes the importance of a data warehouse for effective multidimensional database-management-system application.)

————, "Data Warehouse and Contextual Data: Pioneering a New Dimension," *Database Newsletter,* vol. 23, no. 4, July/August 1995. (Article describes three types of metadata and their importance in the effective use and interpretation of historical data.)

————, "Anatomy of a Data Warehouse Record," *Data Management Review,* July 1995. (Article describes the four primary components of the data warehouse record.)

————, "Transformation Complexity," *Data Management Review,* September 1995. (Article describes the complexities of moving data from the legacy environment.)

————, "Data Warehouse in the Operational Environment: The Operational Data Store," *Data Management Review,* October 1995. (Article provides an overview of the operational data store and describes its three classes.)

————, "The Ladder of Success," *Data Management Review,* November 1995. (Article describes the components for data warehouse success.)

————, "Growth in the Data Warehouse," *Data Management Review,* December 1995. (Article describes the growth of data in the warehouse and ways of managing it.)

————, "Monitoring the Data Warehouse Environment," *Data Management Review,* January 1996. (Article describes two types of monitors—activity monitors and database monitors—needed to manage the data warehouse.)

————, "Managing the Data Warehouse Environment," *Data Management Review,* February 1996. (Article describes the role of the data warehouse administration group.)

————, "Choosing the Correct Approach to Data Warehousing," *Data Management Review,* April 1996. (Article describes the iterative approach for data warehouse development and the importance of the data model for ensuring that the iterations fit together.)

————, "Virtual Data Warehouse: The Snake Oil of the '90's," *Data Management Review,* April 1996. (Article describes forms of virtual data warehouses which should be avoided.)

Inmon, W. H., and Chuck Kelley, "The 12 Rules of Data Warehouse for a Client/Server World," *Data Management Review,* May 1994. (Article delineates 12 defining characteristics of a data warehouse.)

Inmon, W. H., and Michael Loper, The Unified Data Architecture: A Systems Integration Solution, *Data Resource Management,* Auerbach Publications, 1992. [The original paper (republished in a revised state) suggests that a data architecture was in order for future systems development.]

Inmon, W. H., and Sue Osterfelt, "Data Patterns Say the Darndest Things," *Computerworld,* February 3, 1992. (Article describes the use of the data warehouse in the decision-support-system community and how informational processing can be derived from a warehouse.)

Inmon, W. H., and Phyliss Koslow, "Commandeering Mainframe Database for Data Warehouse Use," *Application Development Trends,* August 1994. (This article discusses optimal data warehouse use inside the mainframe.)

Kimball, Ralph S., "The Doctor of DSS," *DBMS*, July 1994. (This article provides an interview with Ralph Kimball.)

Kimball, Ralph S., and Kevin Strehlo, "Why Decision Support Fails and How to Fix It," *Datamation*, June 1994. (This article provides a good description of fact tables and star joins, with a lengthy discussion about Ralph Kimball's approach to the data warehouse and decision support.)

Konrad, Walecia, "Smoking Out the Elusive Smoker," *Business Week*, March 16, 1992. (This article describes database marketing in the advertising restricted marketing environments.)

Moseley, Martin, "Taming the Warehouse Beast," *Computerworld Client/Server Journal*, April 1996. (Article describes the desired characteristics of the data warehouse manager.)

Novack, Janet, "The Data Miners," *Forbes*, February 12, 1996. (Article provides examples of data mining and explains why it is important for managing customer relationships.)

Radding, Alan, "Support DECISION Makers with a DATA Warehouse," *Datamation*, March 15, 1996. (Article provides information on the value of a data warehouse, particularly as a vehicle generating questions and getting answers. The importance of the difficult task of building the data model is emphasized.)

Raden, Neil, "Modeling a Data Warehouse," *Information Week*, January 29, 1996. (Article describes the steps for developing a multidimensional model.)

Richman, Dan, "Firms Follow Less Costly Datamart Route," *Computerworld*, April 29, 1996. (Article discusses why datamarts are attractive and describes their drawbacks in the areas of scalability and integration.)

Santosus, Megan, "Distributing the Data Wealth," *CIO*, September 15, 1995. (Article emphasizes the need to avoid traditional cost justification for building the data warehouse.)

Sloan, Robert, and Hal Green, "An Information Architecture for the Global Manufacturing Enterprise," *Data Resource Management*, Auerbach Publications, 1993. (This article describes an information architecture in the large-scale manufacturing environment.)

Thiessen, Mark, "Proving the Data Warehouse to Management and Customers: Where Are the Savings?," A presentation by Mark Thiessen, Hughes Aircraft, 1994 Data Warehouse Conference, foils and handouts, (714) 732-9039.

Verity, John, "A Trillion Byte Weapon," *Business Week,* July 31, 1995. (Article describes the importance of the data warehouse as a competitive weapon for understanding and retaining customers.)

Wahl, Dan, and Duane Hufford, "A Case Study: Implementing and Operating an Atomic Data Base," *Data Resource Management Journal,* Auerbach Publications, April 1992. (Article describes the U.S. Army's decision-support-system architecture.)

Wallace, Peggy, "Building a Data Warehouse," *Infoworld,* February 21, 1994. (This article describes the data warehouse marketplace.)

Watson, Hugh J., and John Satzinger, "Guidelines for Designing EIS Interfaces," *Information Systems Today,* October 1994. (Article describes criteria for designing the interface for executives' access.)

Welch, J. D., "Providing Customized Decision Support Capabilities: Defining Architectures," *Data Resource Management,* Auerbach Publications, 1990. (Article describes decision support systems and architecture based on the PacTel Cellular decision-support-system architecture.)

Other Articles of Interest

Adamczyk, James P., "Strategy First, Reuse Benefits Later," *Client/Server Computing,* June 1995.

Adelman, Sid, and Dusan Ecimovic, "Assessing New Technologies" [i.e., Client/Server], *Internal Auditor Magazine,* June 1994.

Appleton, Daniel S., "Principles of Information Asset Management," a collection of articles, D. Appleton Co., (310) 374-3939.

Brown, Robert G., "Business Rule Modeling," The Database Design Group, (714) 675-3298.

English, Larry P., "Accountability to the Rescue," *Database Programming & Design,* April 1993.

———, "From Data Modeling to Object Modeling," The Database Design Group, (714) 675-3298.

Hammer, Michael, "Reengineering Work: Don't Automate, Obliterate," *Harvard Business Review,* July-August 1990.

Ives, B., S. L. Jarvenpaa, and R. O. Mason, "Global Business Drivers: Aligning Information Technology to Global Business Strategy," *IBM Systems Journal,* vol. 32, no. 1, 1993, IBM Publication G321-5507.

Jenkins, Avery, "One Bit at a Time," *Computerworld Client/Server Journal,* February 1995.

Keen, P. G. W., "Information Technology and the Management Difference: A Fusion Map," *IBM Systems Journal,* vol. 32, no. 1, 1993, IBM Publication G321-5501.

Loosley, Chris, and Chris Gane, "Information Systems Modeling," *InfoDB,* 1991.

McDougall, Peter, "Entity Definitions: A Crucial Component," *Data Management Review,* January 1996.

Nadeau, Linda, and Jeff Rodgers, "Evaluating Tools: CASE Studies," *Computer Decisions,* March 1988.

Nolan, Richard, "Managing the Crisis in Data Processing," *Harvard Business Review,* March/April 1979.

Quinlan, Tim, "Building for Strength," *Database Programming & Design,* September 1995.

Zachman, John A. "Business Systems Planning and Business Information Control Study: A Comparison," *IBM Systems Journal,* vol. 21, no. 1, 1982, IBM Publication G321-5160.

Technical Books with Direct References to the Zachman Framework

Bruce, Thomas A., *Designing Quality Databases with IDEF1X Information Models,* New York, Dorset House, 1992.

Burgess, Bruce, and Tom Hokel, *A Brief Introduction to the Zachman Framework,* Framework Software, Redondo Beach, Calif., (310) 374-8076, 1994.

Inmon, W. H., *Advanced Topics in Information Engineering,* QED, Wellesley, MA, 1989.

Spewak, Steven H., *Enterprise Architecture Planning,* QED, Wellesley, MA, 1992.

Tasker, Dan, *The Problem Space,* Published electronically by Dan Tasker, Sydney Australia.

Technical Books of Interest

Appleton, Daniel S., *PROBE: Principles of Business Engineering,* Talon Press, Manhattan Beach, CA, 1994.

Brackett, Michael H., *Data Sharing: Using a Common Data Architecture,* Wiley, New York, 1994.

————, *The Data Warehouse Challenge,* Wiley, New York, 1996.

Cook, Melissa A., *Building Enterprise Information Architectures,* Prentice-Hall, Upper Saddle River, N.J., 1996.

Finkelstein, Clive, *An Introduction to Information Engineering,* Addison-Wesley, Reading, Mass., 1989.

————, *Strategic Systems Development,* Addison-Wesley, Reading, Mass., 1992.

Hudson, Debra L., *Practical Model Management Using CASE Tools,* QED, Wellesley, MA, 1993.

Humphrey, Watts S., *Managing the Software Process,* Addison-Wesley, 1990.

Inmon, W. H., *Data Architecture: The Information Paradigm,* John Wiley/QED, New York, 1989.

————, *Information Systems Architecture: Development in the 90's,* John Wiley/QED, New York, 1993.

————, *Rdb/VMS: Developing the Data Warehouse,* John Wiley/QED, New York, 1993.

————, *Third Wave Processing: Database Machines and Decision Support Systems,* John Wiley/QED, New York, 1991.

————, *Building the Data Warehouse,* 2d ed., John Wiley, New York, 1996.

Inmon, W. H., and Richard D. Hackathorn, *Using the Data Warehouse,* John Wiley, New York, 1994.

Inmon, W. H., Claudia Imhoff, and Greg Battas, *Building the Operational Data Store,* John Wiley, New York, 1995.

Kelly, Sean, *Data Warehousing: The Route to Mass Customization,* John Wiley, New York, 1994.

Kimball, Ralph S., *The Data Warehouse Toolkit,* John Wiley, New York, 1996.

Love, Bruce, *Enterprise Information Technologies,* Van Nostrand Reinhold, New York.

Moore, Geoffrey A., *Crossing the Chasm,* HarperCollins, New York, 1991.

Nolan, Richard L., *Managing the Data Resource Function,* West Publishing Co., St. Paul, Minn., 1974.

Ross, Ronald G., *The Business Rule Book: Classifying, Defining and Modeling Rules,* Database Research Group, Inc., Boston, 1994.

Tasker, Dan, *Fourth Generation Data: A Guide to Data Analysis for New and Old Systems,* Prentice-Hall, New York, 1989.

Business Books of Interest

Anthony, Robert N., *Planning and Control Systems: A Framework for Analysis,* Harvard Press, Boston, 1965.

Blumenthal, Sherman C., *Management Information Systems: A Framework for Planning and Development,* Prentice-Hall, Englewood Cliffs, N.J., 1969.

Boulding, Kenneth E., *The Image,* Ann Arbor Paperback, University of Michigan, 1956.

Champy, James, *Reengineering Management,* Harper, New York, 1995.

Crosby, Philip B., *Quality is Free,* Penguin Group, New York, 1980.

———, *The Eternally Successful Organization,* McGraw-Hill, New York, 1988.

Drucker, Peter F., *Managing in Turbulent Times,* Harper & Row, New York, 1980.

———, *The New Realities,* Harper & Row, New York, 1989.

———, *Managing for the Future: The 1990's and Beyond,* Dutton, New York, 1992.

———, *The Post Capitalist Society,* Harper Business, New York, 1994.

Forrester, Jay, *Industrial Dynamics,* M.I.T. Press, Cambridge, Mass., 1965.

Goldman, Steven L., Rober N. Nagel, and Kenneth Preiss, *Agile Competitors and Virtual Corporations: Strategies for Enriching the Customer,* Van Nostrand Reinhold, New York, 1995.

Hammer, Michael, *Beyond Reengineering,* Harper, New York, 1996.

Hammer, Michael, and James Champy, *Reengineering the Corporation,* Harper, New York, 1993.

Imai, Masaaki, *Kaizen,* Random House, New York, 1986.

Kantor, Rosabeth Moss, *The Change Masters,* Simon & Schuster, New York, 1984.

———, *When Giants Learn to Dance,* Simon and Schuster, New York, 1989.

Kume, Hitoshi, *Statistical Methods for Quality Improvement,* The Association for Overseas Technical Scholarship, Tokyo, 1985.

Naisbitt, John, *Megatrends,* Warner Books, New York, 1982.

Naisbitt, John, and Patricia Aburdene, *Reinventing the Corporation,* Warner Books, New York, 1985.

——, *Megatrends 2000,* Morrow, New York, 1990.

Peters, Thomas J., *Thriving on Chaos,* Knopf, New York, 1988.

——, *Liberation Management,* Knopf, New York, 1992.

——, *The Tom Peters Seminar,* Vintage Books, New York, 1994.

Peters, Thomas J., and Nancy Austin, *A Passion for Excellence,* Random House, New York, 1985.

Peters, Thomas J., and Robert H. Waterman, Jr., *In Search of Excellence,* Harper & Row, New York, 1982.

Porter, Michael, *Competitive Advantage,* Macmillan, London, 1985.

Senge, Peter M., *The Fifth Discipline,* Doubleday, New York, 1990.

Stalk, Jr., George, and Thomas M. Hout, *Competing Against Time,* The Free Press, New York, 1990.

Tannenbaum, Adrienne, *Implementing a Corporate Repository: The Models Meet Reality,* John Wiley, New York, 1994.

Toffler, Alvin, *Future Shock,* Bantam Books, New York, 1970.

——, *The Third Wave,* Morrow, New York, 1980.

——, *Powershift,* Bantam Books, New York, 1990.

Walton, Mary, *The Deming Management Method,* Dodd, Mead & Company, New York, 1986.

Womack, James P., Daniel T. Jones, and Daniel Roos, *The Machine that Changed the World,* Harper Perennial, New York, 1991.

Prism Solutions Tech Topics

1. *What Is a Data Warehouse?* This Tech Topic defines a data warehouse and its structure. It provides a basic description which is appropriate to anyone investigating data warehouses.*

---

*Tech Topics and Executive Briefings can be obtained at PRISM Solutions, 1000 Hamlin Court, Sunnyvale, CA 94089, 1-800-995-2928, or 408-481-0240.

2. *Creating the Data Warehouse Data Model from the Corporate Data Model.* This Tech Topic delineates the steps for transforming the corporate data model into a data warehouse model.

3. *Defining the System of Record.* This Tech Topic provides design considerations for identifying and defining the system of record.

4. *Snapshots of Data in the Warehouse.* This Tech Topic describes the advantages and disadvantages of each type of snapshot.

5. *Representing Data Relationships in the Data Warehouse: Artifacts Of Data.* This Tech Topic presents the design issues for the building of data relationships in the data warehouse.

6. *Metadata in the Data Warehouse.* This Tech Topic emphasizes the importance of metadata in the data warehouse. It presents the different components of metadata and discusses why they are important.

7. *Parallel Processing in the Data Warehouse.* The management of volumes of data is the first and major challenge facing the data architect. Parallel technology offers the possibility of managing much data. This Tech Topic is on the issues of parallel technology in the data warehouse environment.

8. *Operational and DSS Processing from a Single Data Base: Separating Fact and Fiction.* An early notion was that a single database should serve as the basis for both operational processing and decision-support-system analytical processing. This Tech Topic explores the issues and describes why the data warehouse is the appropriate foundation for decision-support-system informational processing.

9. *Time Dependent Data Structures.* A discussion of the different types of data structures and their advantages and disadvantages.

10. *Capacity Planning for the Data Warehouse.* This Tech Topic discusses the issue of capacity planning and projection for both disk storage and processor resources for the data warehouse environment.

11. *Loading the Data Warehouse.* At first glance loading data into the data warehouse seems to be an easy task. It is not. This discussion is on the many different considerations of loading data from the operational environment into the data warehouse.

12. *Accessing Data Warehouse Data from the Operational Environment.* Most flow of data is from the operational environment to the data warehouse environment, but not all. This Tech Topic discusses the backward flow of data.

13. *Information Architecture for the 90's: Legacy Systems, Operational Data Stores, Data Warehouses.* This Tech Topic describes the role of operational data stores and gives a description of them, along with a description of the architecture that results when you mix an operational data store and a data warehouse.

14. *Client/Server and Data Warehouse.* Client/server processing is quite able to support data warehouse processing. This Tech Topic addresses the issues of architecture and design.

15. *Information Engineering and the Data Warehouse.* The data warehouse architecture is extremely compatible with the design and modeling practices of information engineering. This Tech Topic describes that relationship.

16. *Reengineering and the Data Warehouse.* Many organizations are not aware of the very strong and very positive relationship between reengineering and the data warehouse. This topic identifies the relationship and discusses the ramifications.

17. *The Operational Data Store.* The operational counterpoint of the data warehouse is the operational data store (the ODS). The ODS is defined and described in detail in this Tech Topic.

18. *Security in the Data Warehouse.* Security takes on a very different dimension in the data warehouse than in other data-processing environments. This Tech Topic describes the issues.

19. *Using the Generic Data Model.* Some corporations have a data model as a point of departure for the design of their data warehouse; others do not. The generic data model "jump starts" the data warehouse design and development effort.

20. *Service Level Agreements in the Data Warehouse Environment.* One of the cornerstones of on-line operations is the service-level agreement. Service-level agreements are applicable to the data warehouse but are implemented quite differently.

21. *Getting Started.* The data warehouse is built iteratively. This Tech Topic describes in a detailed manner the first steps you need to take.

22. *Telling the Difference Between Operational and DSS.* In every shop the issue arises—what is operational and what is decision support system? This Tech Topic tells you how to tell the difference between the two environments.

23. *Managing Multiple Data Warehouse Development Efforts.* When the organization starts to build multiple data warehouse efforts simul-

taneously, a new set of design and development issues arise. This Tech Topic identifies and addresses those issues.

24. *Summary Data in the Data Warehouse/Operational Data Store.* Summary data has its own set of unique considerations. For example, there is dynamic summary data and static summary data. Both types of summary data require very different treatments. This Tech Topic goes into a taxonomy of summary data and how it relates to both the data warehouse and the ODS.

25. *Explaining Metadata to the End User.* When the layperson first encounters metadata, the reaction usually is, "What in the world is metadata and why would I ever need it?" This Tech Topic addresses this issue in very plain, straightforward terms.

26. *The Data Warehouse Budget.* This Tech Topic addresses the different patterns of spending and the rate at which they are spent. In addition, some suggestions for minimizing expenses are discussed.

27. *DSS and Data Warehouse Hardware: Changing the Amdahl Ratios.* Dr Amdahl suggested that there was a constant ratio of memory to CPU to I/O rates. Dr Amdahl's ratios held true as long as people were doing operational processing. This Tech Topic discusses how the ratios change in a world of decision support systems.

28. *Data Warehouse and Software Development.* The data warehouse has had a profound effect on software development. This Tech Topic outlines what that effect has been.

Prism Solutions Executive Topics of Interest

1. *EIS and Data Warehouse.* EIS under a foundation of legacy systems is very shaky, but EIS under a data warehouse foundation is very solid, as detailed in this Executive Topic.

2. *Data Warehouse and Cost Justification.* A priori cost justification is a difficult thing to do for a data warehouse. This Executive Topic discusses the issues.

3. *Changed Data Capture.* The resources required for repeatedly scanning the operational environment for the purpose of refreshing the data warehouse can be enormous. This Executive Topic addresses an alternative way to accomplish the same thing through changed data capture.

INDEX

345

Q

About the Authors

W. H. Inmon (Castle Rock, Colorado) is the father of the data warehouse concept and the author of more than 30 books on data management.

John A. Zachman (Glendale, California) is the creator of the Zachman Framework and is a highly sought-after speaker and consultant on the subject.

Jonathan G. Geiger (Jupiter, Florida) is an independent consultant specializing in data warehouse development.